W9-BKX-473

"Dr. Beck has written a new book that will be of value and interest to those both in and beyond the Christian counseling community. It was clearly written by a man with a love for the Word and a love for his Lord. You may not agree with all of his conclusions. But after reading this book you will have a better understanding of Christ and of yourself—and a new appreciation for the practicality and relevance of God's authoritative Word."

GARY J. OLIVER
Executive Director, *The Center for Marriage and Family Studies*

"For long years the relationship between psychotherapy and biblical faith has been a hotly debated issue, especially among evangelicals. In this wide-ranging discussion, informed by an impressive command of both theological sources and therapeutic theories, James Beck gives a definitive reply to that question. This is the best example I have come across thus far of how much-mooted integration is to be achieved. It demonstrates that the truths and teachings of Scripture dovetail with the soundest of contemporary counseling approaches. But this book is not for counselors and psychologists only. By no means! Beck's treatment of biblical materials is illuminating and yet down-to-earth. I hope that this lucid work of scholarship will win the appreciative readership it deserves."

VERNON GROUNDS
Chancellor, *Denver Seminary*

"Beck approaches the task of unpacking the implications of Christ's life and teachings for counselors with a solid grasp of contemporary personality and psychotherapeutic theory—and an obviously deep understanding of and appreciation for the richness of grace that is presented in Christ. The result is a book that should be required reading for all clergy and Christian counselors!"

DAVID G. BENNER
Professor of Psychology, *Redeemer College, Ancaster, Ontario*;
Director, *Institute for Psychospiritual Health*

"Applied integration of psychology and Christian teachings at its best. By examining the highly reputed and empirically established five-factor model of personality in light of equally tested teachings of Christ, Beck has done the Christian community a great service. Whether acknowledged or not, he has done the same for psychology."

PETER C. HILL
Editor, *Journal of Psychology and Christianity*;
Professor of Psychology, *Grove City College*

"This book is a powerful and encouraging model of how one Christian psychotherapist derives his foundational insights into human personality from Scripture, and especially from the teaching and behavior of Jesus. Here is no simplistic proof-texting but careful exegesis. Along the way, numerous claims of modern psychology are confirmed, while other ones are challenged. Anyone who reads this book and still believes that Christian counseling cannot be thoroughly biblically rooted simply does not understand *the Bible,* much less Christian counseling!"

CRAIG BLOMBERG
Professor of New Testament, *Denver Seminary*

"While many authors talk about integrating psychological and theological perspectives on human personality, it is refreshing to see someone succeed. Beck has masterfully blended modern personality psychology with biblical views of human functioning, showing how each is essential for a complete understanding of how humans both *are* and *ought* to be. The science of personality can yield valuable insights into the teaching and counseling of Jesus. Conversely, Beck convincingly demonstrates that Jesus is the ultimate authority on human personality. This book is a concrete illustration of how the search for truth regarding human nature requires both revelation and experimentation. Thank you, James Beck, for showing us how to do integration the right way. This is a book to get excited about!"

ROBERT A. EMMONS
Professor of Psychology, *University of California—Davis*

Jesus &
PERSONALITY
THEORY

Exploring
the Five-Factor
Model

James R. Beck

InterVarsity Press
Downers Grove, Illinois

InterVarsity Press
P.O. Box 1400, Downers Grove, IL 60515
World Wide Web: www.ivpress.com
E-mail: mail@ivpress.com

©1999 by James R. Beck

All rights reserved. No part of this book may be reproduced in any form without written permission from
InterVarsity Press.

InterVarsity Press® is the book-publishing division of InterVarsity Christian Fellowship/USA®, a student
movement active on campus at hundreds of universities, colleges and schools of nursing in the United States
of America, and a member movement of the International Fellowship of Evangelical Students. For
information about local and regional activities, write Public Relations Dept., InterVarsity Christian
Fellowship/USA, 6400 Schroeder Rd., P.O. Box 7895, Madison, WI 53707-7895.

All Scripture quotations, unless otherwise indicated, are from the New Revised Standard Version of the Bible,
copyright 1989 by the Division of Christian Education of the National Council of the Churches of Christ in
the USA. Used by permission. All rights reserved.

Cover illustration: Byzantine mosaic: Christ blessing Duomo, Monreale, Italy (Scala/Art Resource)

ISBN 0-8308-1925-8

Printed in the United States of America ♻

Library of Congress Cataloging-in-Publication Data

Beck, James R.
    Jesus and personality theory: exploring the five-factor model/
James R. Beck.
          p.   cm.
    Includes bibliographical references.
    ISBN 0-8308-1925-8 (paper: alk. paper)
    1. Jesus Christ—Counseling methods. 2. Pastoral counseling—
Biblical teaching. 3. Bible. N.T. Gospels—Criticism,
interpretation, etc. I. Title.
    BT590.C78B43 1999
232.9'03—dc21   98-54077
                                                                                          CIP

21	20	19	18	17	16	15	14	13	12	11	10	9	8	7	6	5	4	3	2	1
16	15	14	13	12	11	10	09	08	07	06	05	04	03	02	01	00	99			

Dedicated to
our three granddaughters

Kendalyn Rebekah Beck
Kaylee Victoria Beck
Sarah Beth Erickson

1

Jesus As the Wonderful Counselor

OF ALL THE MAGNIFICENT PROPHECIES IN THE BOOK OF ISAIAH, NONE IS MORE familiar than the stirring words of Isaiah 9:6. Christians all over the world know the words of the promise; many in the English-speaking world can sing it as well.

> For unto us a child is born, unto us a son is given,
>   And the government shall be upon his shoulder;
> And his name shall be called Wonderful, Counselor,
>   The Mighty God, The Everlasting Father, The Prince of Peace.
>   (Is 9:6 KJV)

Isaiah's prophecies about the coming Messiah permeate his entire book. They deal with a wide range of characteristics of the redeemer who was to come: his suffering (chap. 53), his faithfulness (chap. 26), his pursuit of justice (chap. 42) and his ministry of deliverance and mercy (chap. 61). The famous prophecy of Isaiah 9 specifically addresses the Messiah's advent into this world (as a baby) and the name that would be given to him (a powerful statement about his character and his work).

Included in the comprehensive name for the coming Messiah in Isaiah 9:6 is a reference to him as a counselor. Is it possible that this reference connects in any way to the modern counseling movement? Could it be that the work of the Christian counselor is, in part, a reflection of a central role filled by Israel's Messiah and our Savior? Should Christian counselors seek to shape their work and ministry after the counseling of the Messiah who was called "Wonderful Counselor"?

Obviously, Isaiah knew nothing about the modern counseling movement; he knew only about the sages of Israel who performed a similar function in that ancient society. We cannot automatically assume that the English word *counselor* used to translate a Hebrew noun in Isaiah 9:6 describes a function equivalent to that filled by a contemporary counselor. So, to answer these questions, we will explore the meaning of the words used by Isaiah in this passage as well as the origin of the English word *counselor* with which we are all so familiar.

Isaiah's Original Meaning

The prophecy of Isaiah 9:6 follows important material that must be understood if we are to interpret the name of the promised Messiah correctly. Isaiah was speaking to a people whose suffering was great (1:5-7) because of their unfaithfulness to the covenant-keeping God of their fathers (1:16-17). Through the prophet Isaiah the Lord was offering them forgiveness and cleansing (1:18). In the passages that follow, God speaks to his beloved Israel with a strong and clear message through his prophet Isaiah: God is still faithful and true even though they are suffering greatly; he will forgive and cleanse if they repent; he will send a powerful deliverer to be a Messiah for them. In chapter seven Isaiah gives a sign to Ahaz: "Behold, a virgin shall conceive, and bear a son, and shall call his name Immanuel" (7:14 KJV). Isaiah 9:6, the passage before us now, expands on that promise by giving further details about the name and work of the coming Messiah.

Isaiah 9:6 presents several interpretive challenges for us. First, we must decide how many names are given here for the coming Messiah. Some interpreters have suggested that the name given here is actually one name in the style of Isaiah 8:1: "Then the LORD said to me, Take a large tablet and write on it in common characters, 'Belonging to Maher-shalal-hash-baz.' " We have already seen another example of a multiple-word single name in Isaiah 7:14: "And shall call his name Immanu-el."

Translators have often left these names in their transliterated form rather than giving their literal meaning in Hebrew ("The spoil speeds, the prey hastens" in Is 8:1; "God is with us" in Is 7:14). When translators come to Isaiah 9:6, they could also leave the name of the promised Messiah in its transliterated state, in which case the name would be even longer than that of Isaiah 8:1: Pele-joez-el-gibbor-Abi-ad-sar-shalom. It is possible, however, to do that—to leave the name as one "long, rambling name" such as "the Mighty God who counsels as the Everlasting Father and the Prince of Peace is wonderful" (Wegner, 1992, p. 183).

Other interpreters prefer to view the passage as giving us one name that is expressed in several names. In a sense this is the case with most of us: we have one name that can also be viewed as three names, a first, middle and last name. The name of the Messiah as given in Isaiah 9:6 contains eight words. Some of them are clearly linked one to another. The relationship of the first two to each other, however, is not entirely clear.

As a result, some translations give this name in five parts: Wonderful, Counselor, the Mighty God, the Everlasting Father, the Prince of Peace. Handel helped stamp the King James Version's fivefold translation of the name forever on our minds and hearts. The music to which he set this verse clearly emphasizes the five parts of the name. Other translators prefer to view these eight words as four two-word pairs. In this case, the Messiah's name has four expressions. He will be a Wonderful Counselor, the Mighty God, Everlasting Father and Prince of Peace. The advantage in this approach to the verse is that it respects poetic form by making all the terms of this name parallel.

In some ways we can view this verse and the one following as a birth announcement. It contains all the elements of a birth announcement oracle: a declaration of the birth, the announcement of the child's name, an explanation of the meaning of the child's name, and a further prophecy concerning the child (Wegner, 1992). In Isaiah 7:14 the mother names the baby. Here the name is given to the baby by those who rejoice in his arrival. The names ascribed to this baby are unmistakably the names of God. "Everlasting Father" speaks not only of the Messiah's eternal existence and his deity but also of his role as a "tender, faithful, and wise trainer, guardian, and provider for his people even in eternity" (Delitzsch, 1965, p. 253). "Prince of Peace" refers to the Messiah's commitment to remove all that would rob his people of peace and to bring peace even to the nations of the earth—an accomplishment that only God can perform. The name "Mighty God" is clearly a divine title.

But leading this list of impressive appellations are the two words *wonder* and *counselor*.

The word *wonder* is often used in the Old Testament to speak of the acts of God that were nothing short of wonderful. These acts—dividing the Red Sea, providing water in the desert, leading his people with pillars of fire and cloud—could be viewed in only one way: they clearly expressed the direct intervention of God in the course of human affairs for the blessing of his people (Young, 1965). The same will be true of the counseling that this Messiah will bring on behalf of his people. It truly will be unmistakably the work of God in our midst.

As a counselor, the Messiah will apply the wisdom of God to the "human situation" (Widyapranawa, 1990, p. 53). Specifically, the Messiah will bring to the task of governing the world all the wisdom that is needed for that job. More generally, he will plan and execute for his people wonderful things (Jensen, 1984; Kaiser, 1972; Sawyer, 1984). Harris (1980) notes that Isaiah later reveals that the Holy Spirit gives the Messiah the spirit of counsel (Is 11:2).

The word *counselor* in both Hebrew and English refers historically to an advisor to royalty. The prosperity of kingdoms and nation states depended on valid, wise and pragmatic advice given to rulers. Jethro was a wise counselor to Moses (Ex 18), and Ahithophel was a good counselor to Absalom in spite of the fact that he accepted the evil counsel of Hushai (2 Sam 17). God's counsel, the kind of counsel that the promised Messiah will give to his people, is trustworthy and sure (Ps 33:10-11). A second major use of the English word *counselor* came to be applied to lawyers, counselors-at-law. They too helped people, many more in fact than were helped by the political or governmental counselors whose wisdom was shared with just one person. In the twentieth century we have used the word *counselor* to refer to many types of helpers, primarily those who work in the mental health field and who seek to help people with the struggles of life.

Can we justifiably link the modern counseling function with the counseling function displayed by the promised Messiah who came to earth as a babe wrapped in swaddling clothes? Is the Savior thus a model for the Christian counselor? The answer is clearly yes. Not because of any one-to-one correspondence between what Jesus did during his earthly life in the first century and what the Christian counselor does in the twentieth. But because counseling, according to the Bible, is *the sharing of God's wisdom with God's people.* Jesus did it through his teaching while here on earth. The Christian counselor does it by sharing with clients the truths found in his Word and in his world.

We can identify one further way in which the counseling of Jesus is connected with the work of the modern Christian counselor. Jesus fulfilled the prophesied function of counselor during his earthly life. When he was making final preparations on the evening before his death, he promised that he would send another counselor to take his place, the Holy Spirit. Thus the Christian counselor who works and ministers under the counsel of the Holy Spirit works in direct connection with the Jesus the Wonderful Counselor. The same Holy Spirit who provided the Savior with his counsel (Is 11:2) also provides us with guidance, instruction and counsel (Jn 14:26) that we in turn can share with others.

How Did Jesus Do Counseling?

If then the ministry of Jesus is in some ways a model for the Christian counselor, we need next to determine in what manner Jesus serves as the counselor's model. Many authors have been interested in this question, and they have provided us with a large variety of answers. The first general approach has been to examine the emotional life of Jesus while he was here on earth. This interest in how Jesus displayed and handled human emotion is a foundational approach to all others because it establishes a baseline for understanding that the Lord of all history was in his incarnate state an emotional person just as we are. Thus he was not only fully divine but also fully human.

An early and major treatment of this subject appeared in a collection of essays commemorating the 100th anniversary of the founding of Princeton Seminary. B. B. Warfield's essay "On the Emotional Life of Our Lord" (1912) provides us with a thorough and critical review of the three main emotions Jesus displayed during his earthly ministry. Warfield examines the sorrow, the compassion and the anger of Jesus. Often obscured by translations that fail to do justice to the intensity of the Greek words used for these emotions, the Bible does indeed give us a rich and detailed picture of how Jesus clearly demonstrated a wide range of emotional expression that was as sinless as it was human.

> When we observe him exhibiting the movements of his human emotions, we are gazing on the very process of our salvation: every manifestation of the truth of our Lord's humanity is an exhibition of the reality of our redemption. . . . When we note the marks of humanity in Jesus Christ, we are observing his fitness to serve our needs." (Warfield, 1912, p. 89)

Many other examples of this approach to the issue could be cited. Hansen (1997) continues in the tradition of Warfield by looking at compassion, anger, grief, joy and love in the Savior's life. Mohline and Mohline (1997) encourage their readers to identify with the emotions of Jesus as a means to experiencing emotional wholeness.

A second approach to the counseling of Jesus comes from the work of Albert Schweitzer (1948), who attempted to examine the mental health or lack thereof in Jesus. Schweitzer's work utilized an approach to Scripture not in keeping with an evangelical understanding of the Bible. Hence its conclusions are hardly useful to the serious student of the Bible. Continuing in this tradition, but within a conservative view of Scripture, is the work of Hodges (1986) who attempted to conduct a psychiatric interview with Jesus across the centuries by exploring the events of his life from a psychiatric viewpoint.

Others have sought to understand the counseling of Jesus by using certain models of understanding through which they attempt to uncover the ways in which Jesus was the Wonderful Counselor. Kelsey (1982) examines Gospel accounts through a heavily Jungian model to discover how the teachings of Jesus relate to individuation, archetypes and personality types. Tyrell (1982), writing from a Roman Catholic theological position, uses his understanding of Christotherapy to look at the life of Jesus as it relates to the self and the healing of sin, neurosis and addiction. An example of this approach among evangelicals is the work of Charles Solomon (1977). Solomon uses his model of handing problems over to the Holy Spirit and the indwelling Christ as a framework for understanding and discussing the counseling of Jesus.

A fourth approach has been to look in the Gospels for examples of various counseling techniques or strategies that Jesus used when he approached various people. Carlson (1976) is the best example of this approach. In essence, Carlson was interested in determining whether Jesus represented modern counselors in a technical manner; that is, did Jesus use counseling approaches, interventions and methods that would inform the work of the modern Christian counselor?

A final approach is to examine the teachings of Jesus and to find in those teachings material that exemplifies the ways in which Jesus was the Wonderful Counselor. Cramer (1959) explored the Sermon on the Mount as a concise statement of the principles undergirding the counseling of Jesus. Cramer explored frozen rage, overconcern, the appeal of freedom and the transforming power of love, among other themes. Buchanan (1985) took a topical approach to the teachings of Jesus in order to examine the ways in which Jesus was the Wonderful Counselor by looking at fear, anxiety, anger, forgiveness and giving. Thurman (1993) took various teachings of Jesus and extracted from them a set of principles that he felt reflected the counseling of Jesus. These principles include living like an heir, cleaning the inside of the cup, solving paradoxes and loving everyone.

Another example of this approach to the counseling of Jesus comes from Alter (1994). She examined Gospel accounts to form a resurrection psychology, one that represents the ways in which the teachings of Jesus counsel us. Among other themes, Alter explores the centrality of forgiveness, the holiness of being human, the danger of certainty and the significance of scars.

Major Theses of This Book

The approach of this book is similar to this last category. Rather than understanding the teaching themes of Jesus through a pre-selected theory, and rather than exploring the counseling techniques or methods of Jesus, this book will analyze ten major teaching themes of Jesus as illustrations of his counseling to us. The wonder of his counseling will become evident as we see how these ten themes speak powerfully to the five major factors found in human personality.

The two major theses of this book are these:

1. *Jesus is a counseling model for Christian counselors in that his teachings speak directly to the five major structural components of human personality.*

2. *These teachings (Jesus' counseling) are indeed wonderful because they speak so perfectly to the composition of the human personality.*

Structure of the Book

Chapter two will complete this first section by providing a brief introduction to the five major components of human personality structure called the Big Five. The remaining sections of the book will examine how these five factors of human personality relate to ten major teaching themes from the life and ministry of Jesus. Regarding the experiential side of our personality (openness to experience), we will examine the commands of Jesus to spread joy and to experience hope. Regarding motivation (conscientiousness), we will look at the ethic of Jesus that requires us to display mercy and to pursue justice. The interpersonal side of human functioning (extraversion-introversion) requires us to learn how to show love and how to be trustworthy. Jesus addresses the personality feature that deals with attitude (agreeableness) by enjoining us to enjoy peace and to live in acceptance. Finally, we will look at emotional style (neuroticism) and how it relates to the teaching of Jesus that we must accept confession and grant forgiveness.

By looking carefully at how well the teachings of Jesus fit with human personality structure, we will be able to appreciate more fully how the counseling of Jesus is truly full of wonder and how Jesus is the Wonderful Counselor.

2

Jesus & the Big Five

JESUS AND THE BIG FIVE. WHAT BIG FIVE? THE FIVE PREPARED VIRGINS? THE FIVE books of the Law? Five loaves? Five talents? The Big Five we will discuss in this book were identified almost two thousand years after Christ's birth as the basic trait structure of human personality. Over the last fifty years studies have shown that five different factors, often called the Big Five, undergird our personalities. The Big Five can be easily remembered by the acronym OCEAN:

Openness to Experience
Conscientiousness
Extraversion
Agreeableness
Neuroticism

We can understand the Big Five better when we understand more about personality theory and personality research.

What Is Personality?
Human personality almost defies description. On the one hand we all know what it is. Every person has a personality. We think some personali-

ties are fine, others objectionable. Yet when someone tries to write a definition of personality, roughly or specifically, the task is very difficult. Personality basically refers to those non-physical features of a person's existence that give identity to the person.

As Christians we believe that there are other features of the immaterial parts of ourselves that are not part of our personality, such as our soul and our spirit (or the part of us that relates to God). The term *personality*, however, refers to those emotional and psychological features of our immaterial selves that influence and indeed govern how we relate to others. No one is able to draw a line around the personality and define it with great precision. Nor can we fairly deal with the personality as a feature of human existence as if it could be separated from other features of the person. The Bible clearly teaches us that the human person is a whole and cannot nor should not be divided into discrete spheres. However, we can identify the approximate boundaries of the personality, and we can study it to learn more about its mysteries.

Some authors define personality by saying that it is composed of two parts: those parts of the self that make a person similar to other people and those parts that make a person distinct from anyone else. We do know that all humans share a great deal when compared one to the other. We all have emotions, we all are influenced by what is inside us as well as by what is external to us, and we all have capacities to relate to other people. Yet there are also a large number of personality features that make us each quite distinct from others. No two people are exactly alike in personality. We differ in intensity of emotions, in degree of characteristics and in style of relating, to name just a few.

These personality similarities and dissimilarities have been part of the human race from the very beginning. Jacob was different from Esau, Ruth from Esther. David was distinct from Solomon. Jeremiah and Isaiah were not carbon copies of one another's personalities. Or take the twelve disciples of Jesus. We learn in the Gospel accounts about assertive, rambunctious personalities as well as quiet, reserved types. All of these biblical characters were distinct from others of God's followers even though they all shared a great deal in common as fellow human beings.

The field of personality theory within the discipline of psychology attempts to study these human similarities and differences. To put these two goals in formal language, "One venture is directed toward the study of species-typical characteristics, the other toward individual differences" (Briggs, 1989, p. 246). Other definitions limit the field to just one of these two approaches. "I have always favored the rather loose, but encompassing, characterization of personality as the general psychology of individual differences" (Wiggins, 1996, p. vii). In short, what makes us different from each other?

Some Christian critics of psychology assert that we should not bother with any such efforts to study individual differences. After all, personality theories are just that, theories. In this criticism they are using the word *theory* in a pejorative sense as opposed to the more positive term *fact*. Furthermore, personality theories are culture-bound and are mainly devised by people who have no interest in knowing what God might have to say about personality (Welch & Powlison, in press). Finally, critics argue, personality theories are not needed because we know all we need to know about humans by studying the Bible.

It is true that the Bible does give us information about the human personality. We know, for example, that human personality was created by God (Gen 1), is tainted throughout by the effects of sin (Gen 3), is renewed by redemption (2 Cor 5) and can be used as an instrument for righteousness or unrighteousness (Rom 8).

These broad themes revealed to us in the Bible regarding human personality form a general outline, but many details are not revealed. We do not find in the Bible, for example, why some people are naturally gregarious and some painfully shy. We do not know why some people are prone to certain kinds of sins but not other kinds, or why some people are capable leaders and others cannot lead. Spiritual gifts could explain some of these differences for believers but could hardly help us account for differences in interpersonal effectiveness, preference for sins, or leadership style among those who do not believe.

The number of questions regarding human personality left unanswered by scriptural revelation is massive. Some people are content not even to wonder about these unanswered issues. They take refuge in psychological agnosticism. I am not one of those; I am curious about what makes all of us different from one another. I think we can profit from studying humans to learn more about how our personalities function.

Personality Theories—Which Is Right?

Critics are correct when they charge that the field is fraught with many kinds of theory about human personality. Some of these theories can be harmonized; others are contradictory and mutually exclusive. Modern theorizing about personality began with Sigmund Freud, who developed an assumption of unconscious mental determinism. He argued that conflict and untamed anxiety were at the heart of the human functioning and that mature behavior was actually a compromise of sorts made possible because of extensive use of defenses. A distinctive contribution of Freud to the discussion surrounding personality was that behavior we can observe may not be as it seems: kindness or love may not be pure expressions of intent but in fact compromised selfish needs.

Since the days of Freud the number of personality explanations has greatly increased. Carl Jung further developed the unconscious construct and focused on character and temperament types. Adler, Fromm and Erikson all built on a psychoanalytic base but moved their emphases to the ego and to conscious behavior. The current descendants of theorizing in the tradition of Freud focus on ego psychology, self psychology, and object relations theory.

Other major strains in the field of personality include the phenomenological; these theories seek to explain what can be seen and observed rather than what has to be inferred. Allport, Lewin, Rogers and Kelly have all pursued this approach. Allport contributed to the field of personality theory by studying traits and exploring in great depth the problem of prejudice. Lewin's Field Theory, Rogers's unconditional positive regard approach and Kelly's Personal Construct Theory each make a contribution to our understanding of how humans function. Behaviorists are another group who have made a substantial impact on personality theory by examining conditioning and reinforcement principles as a major explanation of why people do what they do. Behaviorists examine cues, drives, learning, response, classical conditioning, operant conditioning, shaping, patterning, punishment, modeling and a host of other features of human functioning.

Various social learning and cognitive theories add to the variety among personality theories. Social learning theory, as developed by Albert Bandura, expands on behavioral approaches by highlighting the role of modeling or social learning in shaping behavior. Cognitive theories focus on the inner world of cognition, how it affects our mood and how it contributes to psychopathology. Cognitive-behavioral personality theory attempts to take the best of the two approaches and make them relevant to an understanding of personal functioning.

All of this theory development has resulted in wide disagreement among these various schools regarding the role of the unconscious, how responses are formed and how the mind works. Critics argue that one reason for the wide-ranging disagreement among these theories is that each one focuses on a specific feature of human functioning and so fails to be comprehensive. "One of the major shortcomings of classical theories of personality is that they often seem to address entirely different aspects of the person" (McCrae & Costa, 1996, p. 64). Each school emphasizes certain features while ignoring others. As a result they sometimes fail at giving adequate explanations for individual differences. In fact, McCrae and Costa (1996) argue that these classic twentieth-century personality theories are really armchair theories that should be studied for their historical interest but should not consume so much of our time as they currently do in most personality theory classes. Many theories that are discussed in most personality textbooks have very shaky empirical support, are more and more obsolete and have questionable heuristic value.

> It has become increasingly clear to us that the old theories cannot simply be abandoned: They must be replaced by a new generation of theories that grow out of the conceptual insights of the past and the empirical findings of contemporary research. . . . The FFM [The Big Five] cannot single-handedly replace the grand theories of personality, because it describes only one aspect of the person. It can however, form the nucleus for a theory of personality that might serve as a model for a new generation of empirically based theories. (McCrae & Costa, 1996, pp. 53-54)

The Five-Factor Model (FFM) or Big Five theory referred to above has developed out of yet another approach to personality theory, namely the study of human traits. Trait theory has roots deep in American psychology. For many years, a large number of American psychologists dismissed trait theory as interesting but not very useful in understanding human behavior. But in recent years trait theorists, especially those who work with the Big Five approach, have demonstrated that five major trait factors explain the full range of individual differences far more completely than do any of the classic theories. Although the process has consumed more than fifty years, research of human traits is now very well established in the scientific community (Goldberg, 1995).

> A series of research studies of personality traits has led to a finding consistent enough to approach the status of a law. The finding is this: If a large number of rating scales is used and if the scope of the scales is very broad, the domain of personality descriptors is almost completely accounted for by five robust factors. (Digman & Inouye, 1986, p. 116)

What Is Trait Theory?

Traits are "dimensions of individual differences in tendencies to show consistent patterns of thoughts, feelings, and actions" (McCrae & Costa, 1990, p. 23). In other words, traits are components of our personality that enable us to be consistent over time in our behavior and reactions to life (Hogan, DeSoto, & Solano, 1977). Research shows us that counseling and therapy generally do help people change in a desired direction, but traits remain rather constant for these clients (Brody, 1988). Some traits will emerge in certain situations and not in others.

Traits are related to temperaments that emerge very early in life. Buss and Plomin (1984) list three very early temperaments (emotionality, activity and sociability) that form the basis for future personality trait development. The study of traits then is one way of viewing human personality that gives us a comprehensive sweep of its structure (Buss, 1989). Not only is current trait theory, especially the Big Five, comprehensive, it is also research-based and has a very impressive array of empirical support that has been replicated countless times. By comparison, many of the classic theories of personality that have been articulated in the past century do not have extensive empirical support nor have they generated much research. The five factors emerge when studying how people rate themselves, how friends rate them and how professionals rate them (Fiske, 1949).

Research has consistently found five factors in work conducted in Spain, the Netherlands, Norway, China, Czechoslovakia, Poland and Portugal. Tests designed to measure the Big Five personality factors have appeared in Arabic, Croatian, Czech, Dutch, Estonian, Finnish, French, German, Italian, Hebrew, Icelandic, Japanese, Korean, Norwegian, Polish, Portuguese, Russian, Spanish and Swedish, so that ongoing research based on many culture groups outside of North America will continue to appear (Caprara & Perugini, 1994; Costa & McCrae, 1992c; Pulver, Allik, Pulkkinen, & Hamalainen, 1995; Yang & Bond, 1990). Recent research findings in languages from five distinct language families "strongly suggest that personality trait structure is universal" (McCrae & Costa, 1997, p. 509).

We have noted above how the establishment of the Big Five has approached the status of law in the field of personality research. Even though the fact of this underlying personality structure is widely accepted, this approach has its limitations. The Big Five principally help us understand how human personality is configured, how it is organized, what are its main themes. The Big Five personality factors do not tell us how these traits developed, how they change over time, exactly how they affect behavior or how social roles interact with the factors (McCrae & Costa, 1996).

Others note that the study of behavior ought to be more concerned with the context or situation within which it occurs than with what is inside the person who is in that situation. Also, are we justified in finding general structures of personality that apply to all people and then applying those general structures to any one, given person (Briggs, 1992)?

Another important question deals with the fact that much of the research on the Big Five has occurred within a North American context and among speakers of English. Is this theory just another example of cultural imperialism in psychology (Yang & Bond, 1990)? Some authors feel that these limitations should make us think twice before we too quickly adopt the Big Five as the law in personality theory (Block, 1995).

Some argue that the three major personality factor system of Eysenck is another major alternative to the Big Five system. British researcher Hans Eysenck developed a three-dimensional view of personality: extraversion, neuroticism and psychoticism. The overlap that exists here with the Big Five is easily noticed.

Psychoticism is related to aggressive, cold, egocentric, impersonal, impulsive, anti-social, unempathic, creative, and tough-minded characteristics. Neuroticism is related to anxious, depressed, tense, irrational, shy, moody, and emotional characteristics as well as guilt feelings and low self-esteem. Extraversion is related to sociable, lively, active, assertive, sensation-seeking, carefree, dominant, surgent, and venturesome characteristics. (Brody, 1988, pp. 103-104)

Most authors, however, feel that Eysenck's system is so similar to the Big Five system that has emerged out of research in North America that the two approaches are not alternatives to one another but that Eysenck's work is just a historical prelude to the Big Five. Eysenck was merely measuring fewer human characteristics and was using a different statistical analysis to develop his three factors.

Development of the Big Five
John Digman (1996) says that the Five-Factor Model has a curious history because psychologists began their work on this approach in the field of linguistics rather than directly in the field of psychology. The modern origins of work on the Big Five then are connected to language, lexicons and dictionaries. The linguistic foundation of modern trait theory research led directly to the two other avenues of research that have led to the current state of theory development for the Big Five: the use of scales designed on the basis of this linguistic work for (1) self-evaluation and (2) peer ratings. Once researchers identified a human personality characteristic using their search of language, they designed a question they could ask of people who were rating their own personalities or someone else's to determine if that personality characteristic was present in the person being studied. The following brief summary of Big Five's history will discuss how these three avenues of research have led to the solid research foundation that undergirds the Big Five Theory.

The Lexical Approach
At first we might think it strange that psychology would begin a study of human personality characteristics by studying words in a dictionary. But with a little reflection we can see the simple logic of the approach. Language reflects human experience. When people want to communicate with each other about some new observation, they invent words and

grammatical structures through which they can communicate that material to others. The process is both historical and current. For example, if an ancient ruler was selecting members of the court who could advise and counsel the ruler, some assessment of the personality strengths and weaknesses of the prospective advisor would undoubtedly take place. Officials would likely have to assess the person's trustworthiness, reliability and honesty, among other things. A growing and developing language to describe all of these personality attributes facilitated this endeavor. The older and more developed the language, the more sophisticated was (and is) its capacity to describe with precision these subtleties of human functioning.

The biblical languages of Hebrew and Greek both contain a large number of nouns, adjectives and verb forms that provided the human writers of Scripture with a varied vocabulary with which to describe people. We read about the guile of Jacob (Gen 27:35), the verbal hesitancy of Moses (Ex 4:10), the slyness of Herod (Lk 13:32) and the lovableness of the apostle John (Jn 21:7). We also learn from Scripture that at one time language was quite underdeveloped. Genesis 11:1 tells us that the human race had at one time only one language and that the language had few words. As God dispersed the people and confused their one language into many, languages not only multiplied, they increased in their sophistication of description.

Language not only reflects human experience, it is a vehicle with which we lift our praise to God (Ps 119:13), a vehicle through which God communicates to us (Ex 20:1) and the ultimate vehicle through which God brought salvation to a lost and dying world (Jn 1:1).

> Long ago God spoke to our ancestors in many and various ways by the prophets, but in these last days he has spoken to us by a Son, whom he appointed heir of all things, through whom he also created the worlds. (Heb 1:1-2)

We also know that studying language can aid us in understanding God's truths. In fact, we have to all be students of language in order to comprehend well the revelation God has given to us through his Word (Beck, 1993). Thus when personality theorists seek to learn about human personality through a thorough review of the language humans use to describe the personalities of themselves and of others, we can understand the logic and value of such an approach. The lexical approach gives the Big Five theory a solid foundation that is anchored to the familiar and is logical in its approach (Saucier & Goldberg, 1996).

One of the first to explore the lexical contribution to human psychology was Harvard professor and Episcopal layman Gordon Allport. Allport & Odbert (1936) published an extensive monograph in which they described their search of English language dictionaries for words that describe human personality traits. They amassed a list of 17,953 words! After eliminating terms that described temporary states, evaluation of character terms, explanations of behavior, physical quality descriptors and terms for capacities, they reduced that number to 4,504. These remaining terms in the English language characterized human behavior and personality and could be considered personal traits. They arranged many of the 17,953 words into four columns from A to Z (see table 1). The 4,504 personal trait terms all appeared in Column I. Their effort was one of the first to collect a linguistic data base from which other researchers could develop a structural system for these human traits and attributes

Column I Neutral Terms	Column II Terms for Temporary moods	Column III Judgmental Terms	Column IV Miscellaneous
Abandoned	Abashed	Abnormal	Able
Abject	Ablaze	Absorbing	Abortive
Abrupt	Absent	Absurd	Abrasive
Zealful	Zigzagging	Zany	Zebrine
Zealless		Zesting	Zooid
Zealotical			Zoophilous

Table 1. Allport & Odbert's (1936) trait names

British researcher Raymond Cattell further reduced this vast number of terms in the Allport and Odbert study by identifying 35 bipolar scales (thus reducing the 4,500 to just 70 terms). He had 373 male university students rate the personalities of students they knew well, and then he conducted a factor analysis on the results. (We will say more about factor analysis below).

We have to admire Cattell and his team of researchers who did this work in the mid-1940s. "The clerical labor involved, using the clumsy calculators of that time, was monumental, enough to dampen anyone's enthusiasm for such an undertaking" (Digman, 1996, p. 5). Cattell defined a trait as a hypothetical construct that we can infer when we observe consistent and regular behavior in a certain domain (Engler, 1985). Cattell felt that his statistical analysis yielded twelve factors to which he added on his own four additional factors (John, 1990). The resulting sixteen factors that he felt were the basis of human personality organization have become very well known through the personality inventory called the 16PF.

Later investigators have re-analyzed Cattell's data and suggest that more rigorous use of statistical principles yields far fewer factors than his 16. "Ironically, Cattell's third study . . . provided an excellent Big Five solution" (Digman, 1996, p. 6). Cattell was simply convinced that five factors were far too few. Surely, human personality must be more complicated than that. But by today's standards, Cattell's data yields only five robust factors, in keeping with later work on the Big Five.

Some critics have suggested that Cattell began his analysis with far too few descriptors (70 terms arranged into 35 bipolar scales). However, subsequent studies achieve the same five factors even when beginning with a much larger initial pool of terms (John, 1989). Hans Eysenck, another British researcher, continued in Cattell's tradition by further reducing the number of traits to three: neuroticism, extraversion and psychoticism. Eysenck's three factors can be fit with the Big Five quite well even thought the Eysenck model is not as comprehensive (Zuckerman, Kuhlman, Joireman, Teta, & Kraft, 1993). Neuroticism and extraversion in the Eysenck system fit well with factors of the same name in the Big Five system. Eysenck's psychoticism factor relates to the low poles of two Big Five factors, agreeableness and conscientiousness (McCrae & Costa, 1985).

Is this lexical approach reliable enough to yield data on which we can place confidence or is it a crude technique that should not be given much credence? The answer to this question is that the lexical approach is a sophisticated and warranted approach to the study of personality (Saucier & Goldberg, 1996). We can learn about the relative importance of human characteristics by doing a frequency analysis of words used to describe that function. We can be assured that when we gather together all the terms describing human functioning we are controlling for biases that might lead us to select some attributes as more important than others. In fact, biased selection of issues to study in the development of one's personality theory has led the classic theories into some truncated theoretical cul-de-sacs.

Furthermore, we can study language in a disciplined and methodical manner by identifying which terms are ambiguous, metaphorical, obscure, difficult, abstract or specific, idiosyncratic or universal (by studying various languages, not just one). All of these possibilities give the lexical approach a great deal of power and possibility. In addition, researchers can conduct their survey of human personality by studying various parts of speech. Normally, adjectives are selected for study because grammatically they serve as descriptors of qualities or properties. Surprisingly, however, some languages do not possess adjectives, so a different part of speech must be studied. Nouns are more frequently used in language to refer to objects or events; verbs describe process and so are not as useful in this type of research.

Comparative linguistics has also established that most of the languages of the world contain terms related to psychopathology (schizophrenia, anxiety, depression and other indications of mental illness), making linguistic study hospitable to psychology, which has a natural interest in the analysis of pathological states (Goldberg, 1981). One additional feature of the lexical approach is that it allows researchers to use single words, phrases or sentences. Research with all three of these approaches typically yields the same Big Five factors although researchers seem to prefer single-word research (Goldberg, 1992). In summary, "The English language includes thousands of terms to describe aspects of personality, and analysis after analysis has found five similar factors" (Costa & McCrae, 1992a, p. 656).

What Is Factor Analysis?

We have seen how the development of the Big Five theory includes a heavy reliance on statistical analysis to establish its empirical base. Cattell used the factor-analysis methodology devised by Charles Spearman, who developed factor analysis in 1902 (Corsini & Marsella, 1983). All subsequent researchers pursuing an understanding of human personality traits have used this same statistical procedure. The advent of computers and more sophisticated statistical procedures in the past two decades has greatly increased the use of factor analysis in psychological research and has contributed heavily to the emergence of the Big Five as a major force in the field of personality research.

Factor analysis is a statistical procedure that allows us to assess massive quantities of data as we seek to find relationships among the various findings we have gathered. It identifies clusters of variables that are related to each other and unrelated to other variables. In effect it systematizes large amounts of material into useful categories. The method has been called "the queen of analytic methods" (Kerlinger, 1973, p. 659). It enables us to locate underlying factors and thus reduce the number of variables we are trying to study. Thus we can eliminate duplication and unnecessary measurements.

For example, we might identify 25 different issues related to human functioning. Twenty-five topics represent a sizable task for the investigator, so we would conduct a factor analysis using powerful statistical techniques. In the process we discover that several factors in this list of 25 rise and fall together. People who score high on item 3 may also tend to score high on items 14, 17, 21 and 25. Those who score low on one of these five tend also to score low on the other four. These five items tend to score in a similar fashion among subjects irrespective of what these individuals might score on the other twenty items. Hence we can identify these five as reflective of a common underlying factor. Of course, these findings must be replicated many times by many different researchers studying many different kinds of populations before we can confidently assert that we have identified a stable factor.

The researcher then would examine the five items we have found to be clustered into one factor. Perhaps they all refer to some type of interpersonal functioning skill that is not represented in the remaining twenty items. We might label this underlying factor an "interpersonal" factor. We might find that a total of four such underlying factors account for most all of the variance in this set of twenty-five items. Our fictional factor analysis then would lead us to conclude that we have identified four factors on which we can concentrate our work rather than having to analyze all twenty-five items that we had originally identified.

Obviously, the procedure is much more complicated than these few paragraphs can convey. Data, for example, is displayed in matrices for analysis, and various procedures to "fine tune" the data, called rotations (oblique, orthogonal, Varimax, orthoblique), are performed. Many of the relatively small differences among the various five factor solutions that have emerged in recent decades seem to be related to minor differences in statistical techniques, such as these rotations, that are used with the data. When consistent statistical techniques are used with these data sets, however, the results are consistently congruent with the Big Five factors.

Further Developments

Two researchers working for the United States Air Force in the early 1960s were the earliest team to document with certainty the five factor solution at which many previous research studies had hinted. Ernest Tupes and Raymond Christal, using factor-analysis techniques as described above, published their work in government technical reports, so their discoveries were seen by very few personality researchers. "Despite this obscurity, the report marks the beginning of a serious interest in the Five-Factor Model, at least on the part of a few researchers" (Digman, 1996, p. 9).

Tupes and Christal were able to demonstrate to the Air Force that peer ratings were a highly reliable predictor of officer success (Christal, 1992). They examined peer ratings of persons who had known each other three days, persons who had known each other for over a year, persons in military training courses, members of a fraternity house, people with high-school educations as well as those with college or graduate level educations, and untrained as well as highly trained mental health personnel. In effect they conducted a meta-analysis and concluded that five main factors underlie human personality. They concluded that the five factors possess a "fundamental nature and probable invariance" (Tupes & Christal, 1992, p. 250). Their report was "the pivotal work that summarized and crystallized previous research and laid the foundations for future elaborations on the Five-Factor Model" (McCrae, 1992, p. 217).

Norman (1963) was the next major researcher to elaborate on and confirm the Five-Factor Model. Soon researchers discovered that people rated their peers by using an implicit personality theory as well as their personal knowledge of the other person. In other words, people seem to know that certain personality traits go together, traits such as talkativeness and extraversion. So when a rater observes one trait in a stranger or in someone known only for a short time, it is rather likely for the rater to rate the near-stranger as possessing the other trait (Passini & Norman, 1966). We tend to use reality when rating friends and our implicit theory of personality when rating people we do not know (Cloninger, 1996).

For a while, critics felt that this discovery of an implicit personality theory discredited the Big Five because ratings of others are skewed away from reality by this implicit schematic. However, as Borkenau (1992) has demonstrated, the implicit theory of personality that we all seem to possess is nothing but a mirror of reality. The ratings we make on the basis of our implicit theory are surely accurate for some people in the world, even though they may not perfectly match the person we are trying to describe. All of this theory development surrounding the Big Five in the last fifty years has resulted in a model that "has shown robustness across cultures, . . . across media, . . . across age groups, . . . and which offers a model for unifying the field of personality attributes" (Digman, 1996, p. 16).

At this point let us note the characteristics of the Big Five.

Is Personality Genetically Based?

One of the most surprising findings in recent decades is that a significant influence on personality traits comes through a genetic influence as opposed to an environmental impact of our surroundings. (Jang, Livesley, & Vernon, 1996). Most of the classic personality theories have argued that much of our personality makeup is attributable to the learning that occurs relative to parenting styles, early experiences, bonding, attachment and separation, individuation, trauma or other environmental effects.

The first line of evidence that these Big Five personality factors have a strong degree of genetic influence comes from the observation that the five factors are found in many cultures. Some studies indicate that as much as 41 percent of the variance among the factors is attributable to genetic influence (Costa & McCrae, 1992a). Estimates of the heritabilities of the Big Five factors are: extraversion, .36; agreeableness, .28; conscientiousness, 28; neuroticism, .31; and openness, .46 (Cloninger, 1996). In each case these numbers are higher than the corresponding effect of the environment.

Cloninger concludes, "Although, presumably, there are not specific genes for such attitudes, a variety of biological mechanisms could ulti-mately affect these attitudes. These may include the senses, hormones, intelligence, temperament, and emotionality. . . . Genetic effects reach deeply into our social behavior" (1996, p. 395).

Brody writes that genetics has a "pervasive influence" on personality (1988, p. 89). Unfortunately, many mental health workers still do not realize that such a dramatic shift has occurred in recent years; whereas we all thought that learning was at the heart of personality development, we now know that genetics has an even more powerful role to play in the formation of our personalities.

Genetic personality research consists of twin studies, family research and adoption research designs. By studying identical and fraternal twins reared together and apart, geneticists can formulate approximate ratios to help us understand the relative role of environment and heredity (Bergeman, Chipuer, Plomin, Pedersen, McClearn, Nesselroade, Costa, & McCrae, 1993). We do know that at least three personality traits emerge very early in a child's life: emotionality, sociability and activity (Pervin, 1989). All three are heavily influenced by genetic factors.

Loehlin (1992) conducted a large-scale review of genetic studies and found that for adults genetic factors (both additive and nonadditive) accounted for between 33 and 65 percent of the variance on the Big Five factors whereas family environment accounted for between 0 and 11 percent. The implications for child rearing are monumental. Perhaps we need to focus our parent education on helping parents *shape* the temperament patterns of their children rather than try to *create* these patterns.

Assessment

Several instruments have appeared to help researchers gather data on the Big Five and build a data pool that describes how these factors appear in the general population. The Big Five Questionnaire (BFQ) is a 132-item questionnaire that explores the five factors (Caprara, Barbaranelli, Borgogni, & Perugini, 1993). The NEO PI-R contains 240 items designed to assess the Big Five factors. The test yields data on all five factors and on components that comprise each factor (Costa & McCrae, 1992c). The NEO PI-R has a form to be used by persons rating themselves and a different form to be used by raters who are describing some other person. Other research tools include the Hogan personality inventories, the IASR-B5, Goldberg's 100-item measure (Briggs, 1992; Goldberg, 1992) and the Personal Factors Rating Scale, which is derived from the Adjective Check List.

As part of preparing to write this book, I asked two respected New Testament scholars to rate the personalities of Jesus and the apostle Paul using the NEO PI-R test instrument. Table 2 contains the results of these very interesting test administrations. Both of these New Testament scholars are very familiar with Scripture but unacquainted with the Five-Factor Model of personality; hence their ratings are not based on any motivation to make the results turn out in any predetermined fashion. We will discuss these results more fully in later sections of the book. The results comparing the personality of Jesus to the five factors of personality are quite similar to results obtained from a large sample of lay persons, who rated Jesus as low in neuroticism and average in extraversion and openness to experience (Piedmont, Williams & Ciarrocchi, 1997).

Big Five Factor	Jesus	Paul
O (Openness to experience)	53 AVERAGE	47 AVERAGE
C (conscientiousness)	71 VERY HIGH	62 HIGH
E (extraversion)	49 AVERAGE	54 AVERAGE
A (agreeableness)	49 AVERAGE	41 LOW
N (neuroticism)	44 LOW	57 HIGH

Table 2. A Big Five assessment of Jesus and Paul

Changeability and Comparability

Do traits change over time or are they stable? Most research suggests that these five basic traits are very stable. That is, they remain at approximately the same level during an entire lifetime. When a person begins adult life as a highly conscientious individual, the likelihood is that the person will remain that way during her or his entire life. Testing and retesting have determined that traits decline slightly over an entire lifetime but only at the same rate as intelligence declines (Brody, 1988).

A strong reason to give serious consideration to the Big Five as an important, foundational theory regarding human personality is its comprehensiveness (Schultz & Schultz, 1994). The five factors encompass most all the material developed during this century by proponents of the classic personality theories. For example, openness to experience, the first of the five factors that we will consider, has consistently correlated positively with intelligence. Other factors among the Big Five correspond to other well-known concepts. For example, agreeableness compares closely to Adler's concept of social interest, a motivation that Adler posited at the heart of his theory.

Another way of exploring the comparability and resulting comprehensiveness of the Big Five in relationship to other personality theories is to examine other existing tests designed to measure human personality characteristics. We will explore only one example. The Myers-Briggs Temperament Inventory (MBTI) is the most famous of all inventories designed to measure the theories of Carl Jung. The test has received more widespread approval among the mental health consuming public than among professional researchers. Nonetheless, when its scales are analyzed by factor analysis, four of the Big Five factors clearly emerge from the MBTI (MacDonald, Anderson, Tsagarakis, & Holland, 1994; McCrae & Costa, 1989b).

"Extraversion is similar in both systems. Openness corresponds to Intuition (versus Sensation). Agreeableness is akin to Feeling (versus Thinking), and Conscientiousness resembles Judging (versus Perceiving)" (Costa & McCrae, 1992c, p. 52). The fifth factor of the Big Five, neuroticism, is conspicuously absent in the MBTI items. This gap of personality measurement is due not to Jung's naivete about whether humans possess undesirable characteristics but to Myers and Briggs's attempt to make all results of the MBTI equally desirable. By including items that measured undesirable features of the human personality they could not have achieved their stated goal. As a result the Myers-Briggs inventory does not completely measure the full range of human traits.

Advocates of a psychodynamic view of human personality have had a difficult time accepting the comprehensiveness of the Big Five theory (Block, 1995). After all, the psychodynamic family of theories (self psychology, object relations theory, ego psychology and others) has prided itself on its richness of explanation. Origins of behavior are early, deep and highly linked to environment. Given these commitments, how can a psychodynamically oriented person come to believe that human personality is basically structured around five basic trait factors?

Block made a gallant effort to construct a personality assessment tool that would measure the large variety of traits and character domains that psychodynamic theory would predict. But when his inventory was submitted to factor analysis, the same basic five personality factors emerged, despite a conscious attempt by the originator of the test to achieve a different outcome (McCrae, 1989).

In summary, the Big Five can serve a *lingua franca* among personality researchers and as a prototype for a new generation of personality theories (McCrae & Costa, 1996), and the Big Five factors can serve counselors and mental health personnel in wide-ranging ways (Costa, 1991; Costa & McCrae, 1992b; McCrae, 1992). The Big Five are not the sum total of what we need to affirm about human personality, but everything we affirm about human personality must somehow explain and account for the Big Five.

The Big Five and the Teachings of Jesus

We are now ready to examine the teachings of Jesus in light of the Big Five theory of personality structure. We have seen how Jesus clearly was the Wonderful Counselor during his earthly life. He fulfilled Isaiah's prophecies by being for his people a source of counsel that was truly full of wonder. When Jesus left this earth he gave another Counselor to continue this strategic work with the people of God. As we live our lives, give counsel to other people and receive counsel from other people, we can do so led by the Spirit of God who is now the Wonderful Counselor in our midst. The Holy Spirit teaches us all things, especially the things Jesus taught us.

We have always known that the teachings of Jesus are powerful and beyond wonder. This book suggests that one reason for the powerful nature of his teachings is that they speak so directly to the five basic features of human personality. Table 3 lists these factors, the personality theme represented by each of the five, and two teaching themes of Jesus that address each of these five factors.

Christlikeness

We need to highlight one additional issue before we begin. What is Christlikeness? Throughout the New Testament we read of the need we have as fallen, lost people to be reconciled to God (Mt 11:28-29; Jn 3:16). We are not only to be reconciled to God but we are to become like him (Mt 5:48). We are to be holy as God is holy (1 Pet 1:16). We are to follow

Big Five Factor	Theme	Teaching of Jesus
O (openness to experience)	The Experiential Life	Spread Joy
		Experience Hope
C (conscientiousness)	The Motivational Life	Display Mercy
		Pursue Justice
E (extraversion)	The Interpersonal Life	Show Love
		Be Trustworthy
A (agreeableness)	The Attitudinal Life	Enjoy Peace
		Live in Acceptance
N (neuroticism)	The Emotional Life	Offer and Accept Confession
		Seek and Grant Forgiveness

Table 3. The Big Five and the teachings of Jesus

in the steps of Jesus (1 Pet 2:21). We are to learn from Jesus (Mt 11:29) and to follow him (Mt 16: 24). Jesus is our example in service (Jn 13:15) and in attitude (Phil 2:5). Our Christlikeness will be proof of our profession (1 Jn 2:6). In short, the follower of Jesus is to become like Jesus. The very term applied first in Antioch to the followers of the Way was *Christian,* a diminutive word literally meaning "a little Christ" (Acts 11:26). Most New Testament scholars believe that the goal of sanctification is Christlikeness (Col 3:10).

But what does this Christlikeness mean? Are we to strive to develop a personality configuration that makes us a clone of Jesus? If we can determine that Jesus was mildly an introvert, highly conscientious, with very low neuroticism, does that mean we should all try to replicate that personality pattern? The thesis of this book is that Christlikeness does not consist of personality similarity to Jesus but behavioral similarity to Jesus. For example, even though we may differ greatly from Jesus in degree of extraversion, we still have the obligation to function interpersonally as he did: to show love and be trustworthy.

The wonderful counsel of Jesus, his teachings for first-century listeners as well as for us, is that we must strive to use our personalities—no matter how they might be individually constituted—to do the same work he did, to behave and act as he did. When we spread joy, experience hope, display mercy, pursue justice, show love, are trustworthy, enjoy peace, live in his acceptance, offer and accept confession, seek and grant forgiveness, we are using our personalities and our very beings to be Christlike.

Section One

Openness to Experience

Introduction

Jesus & Our Experiential Life

THE CLASSIFIED JOB ADS DEMAND IT. HIGH-SCHOOL STUDENTS TAKE BURGER-flipping jobs to get it. And it teaches us all valuable lessons about navigating well through life. *Experience*. The interactions we have with the world, what it does to us, what it seeks to teach us, and what we need to learn from it are all components of experience. Coan defines it as a "total network that includes behavior, biological processes, and past and present environmental stimulation" (1974, p.8). Experience then is just a sophisticated word for life itself.

We can be either open to experience or closed to it. We can learn from what happens to us and grow thereby, or we can resist change and remain relatively unaffected by experience.

One of the five basic domains of personality deals with this very issue: openness to experience. In other words, one important way in which we can understand ourselves and others is to rank ourselves according to how open we are. To accomplish this sorting we would administer questionnaires to ourselves and others in which we would describe how we score on this cluster of traits. Openness to experience is one of the five basic ways in which we can characterize human personality.

We have already seen that trait theory bases itself partly in linguistics and in a lexical approach. Researchers have found that the importance of a trait seems to be reflected in the number of words reflecting that trait in a language. For example, one of the Big Five, agreeableness, is represented in the English language by a large number of descriptive adjectives ranging from "abusive" and "acrimonious" to "amiable" and "approachable" (Costa & McCrae, 1992a). But openness to experience is reflected, in English and in other languages, by the fewest number of descriptive terms of all the Big Five. Most of the terms that apply to openness refer to the cognitive aspects of human intelligence. Thus some researchers have named this factor "intellect."

We also know that this cluster of traits seems to be the one that is most affected by culture and has been the most difficult for researchers to name. The label "intellect" is confusing because it is so similar to the familiar concept of intelligence. Intelligence as represented by results of an I.Q. test, however, is more of a capacity and ability than an aspect of personality, even though intelligence correlates very highly with the openness factor. Most authors have now abandoned the label "intellect" as an apt and useful name. Others have suggested the label "culture" (Norman, 1963). The weakness of "culture" is that it suggests a sophistication that is not central to the factor. In spite of the variation of names attached to this factor, "openness to experience" is now a standard label (Cloninger, 1996; John, 1989). By examining the content of openness to experience as a personality domain, we will begin to understand why it has been the most difficult to define and name.

What Is Openness to Experience?

Bergeman et al. define the openness domain as "a proactive seeking and appreciation of experience for its own sake, based on characteristics such as openness to feelings, new ideas, flexibility of thought, and readiness to indulge in fantasy" (1993, p. 160). Adjectives that describe this factor include "knowledgeable," "perceptive," "imaginative," "verbal," "original" and "curious" (Digman & Inouye, 1986). People who score high on the openness factor engage the world with a spirit that is eager and keenly interested. Open individuals are characterized by a "broader and deeper scope of awareness and by a need to enlarge and examine experience; they are imaginative, aesthetically responsive, empathic, exploring, curious, and unconventional" (McCrae & Costa, 1991, p. 227). Persons who score low on this cluster of traits tend to be closed, prosaic and conventional.

They prefer the familiar rather than the unknown, and they have a rather narrow range of interests (Costa & McCrae, 1992c). Both high and low scorers can be mentally healthy or unhealthy, authoritarian or nonauthoritarian, and extraverted or introverted (McCrae, 1993).

We need to remember that a high score on openness to experience may seem very commendable to some groups of people and very undesirable to others. For example, mental health personnel may view a very open person as a mature, healthy person. Many people in our contemporary world admire persons who can accept everything, can change any value at any time, and can tolerate any and every thing. But we need to remember that this much openness may render people useless and ineffective when action is needed that is predicated upon principles of highly held values. Conversely, some evangelical Christians or other conservative types might automatically assume that openness is the equivalent of liberal attitudes, so that a low score on this factor might be the far preferred test outcome. Again, we cannot assume that this factor that ranges from open to closed attitudes is the same as a liberal-to-conservative measure. The domains are not equivalent.

Recent research has identified the components of this factor. Openness to experience is composed of six subfacets: fantasy (a vivid imagination that creates a rich inner life), aesthetics (a responsiveness to poetry, art and beauty), feelings (an awareness of intense emotion), actions (an interest in doing new and different things), ideas (intellectual curiosity) and values (a readiness and willingness to reexamine values) (Costa & McCrae, 1992c). Table 4 gives the scores on Jesus and Paul that are the result of how scholars rate them on openness to experi-

Openness Facets	Jesus	Paul
Fantasy	AVERAGE	LOW
Aesthetics	AVERAGE	AVERAGE
Feelings	VERY HIGH	AVERAGE
Actions	AVERAGE	HIGH
Ideas	HIGH	HIGH
Values	VERY LOW	VERY LOW

Table 4. Jesus and Paul on openness to experience

ence. Readers will notice how the total scores on this factor (see table 2) for both Jesus and Paul are composed of widely differing scores on the subfacets. Scores on any of the Big Five domains for any of us would likewise be composed of a complex configuration of the composite facets.

What Do We Know About Openness to Experience?

Of all the Big Five factors that undergird the human personality, openness to experience apparently has the highest level of genetic influence (Cloninger, 1996). In a major twin/adoption study in Sweden, researchers examined a large number of identical twin pairs (82) and fraternal twin pairs (171) who had been reared apart and identical twin pairs (132) and fraternal twin pairs reared together (167). Major studies of this type allow investigators to form estimates of the relative role of family environment and social learning on various facets of personality configuration as opposed to the influence of genes. Identical twins possess the exact same genetic inheritance whereas fraternal twins are genetically similar only to the degree that other siblings are alike.

One could well assume that openness to experience as we have described it above might be very much influenced by early childhood experiences and parental influence. In fact, most personality theories have predicted such a heavy influence from the environment on openness. However, results in the Swedish twin study indicate that openness of experience shows "moderately high heritability and little evidence of shared rearing environment effects" (Bergeman, et al., 1993, p. 171). Shared rearing environment effects included, for these researchers, style of child-rearing, religious influences, education, peer influences, and socioeconomic status. The genetic influence on openness is startling and quite unexpected. We need to realize that genetic research is an ongoing enterprise and that only time and replication will remove all the tentativeness from these early findings (Loehlin, 1992). Nonetheless, the role of genetics on how open we are to experience is apparently quite high.

We know that openness to experience is an excellent predictor for vocational success in jobs that require exactly this type of attitude toward the world (Costa & McCrae, 1992a). We know that individuals scoring high on the openness scales will likely influence how they respond to counseling. They will be much more responsive to innovative approaches.

Persons who score low on openness will likely need more directive, sensible therapies (Costa & McCrae, 1992b). We also know that openness is a major factor in predicting how pastors will respond to Christian counseling as a ministry to hurting people and how often they will refer to professionals (Rumberger & Rogers, 1982). We know that individuals with high openness scores experience emotions more intensely and that individuals with low openness scores report lower levels of both negative and positive emotions (McCrae & Costa, 1991).

Finally, we know that this characteristic of openness is a significant feature in the psychological maturity of many persons (Coan, 1977). The interactions we have with experience and how we deal with life are central to the level of psychological maturity we possess. When we are relatively open to experience we can enjoy a richness and fullness that we otherwise would miss. The alternative to this openness is a closedness that may give us some freedom from distress but which will ensure that our lives are not as rich and varied (Coan, 1974).

Jesus and Openness

How can we understand openness to experience from the vantage point of our Christian faith? We can be glad that the gospel does not demand of the followers of Jesus a certain level of openness to experience. If it did, and if our level of openness is primarily determined by genetic factors, we might be unable to change our personal degree of openness in the direction demanded of us by our faith. I do not believe that mature, Christlike followers of Jesus should all strive toward a certain level of openness as an optimal level for the believer. Rather, whatever our level of openness may be, God requires us not to change that level but to face life (experience) with two major experiential characteristics: joy and hope. In the next two chapters we will examine joy and hope as they appear in the Gospels and in the life of Jesus.

God does call us all to be a people of closely held values, and he honors those who are deeply convinced of the core issues of the Christian faith. Yet he may not be as pleased with persons who are dogmatic about peripheral values. God honors some in his kingdom who are open to beauty (aesthetics) and use their gifts for the glory of God, as he did with the artisans who made the tabernacle and those who worked on Solomon's temple. Yet many of us may not have the same interest in aesthetics, so our trait scores on this facet might be very low. God can use people with different configurations on this openness cluster of traits if they are able to live life with the two distinctly Christian approaches to experience: joy and hope. In the next two chapters we will explore these two themes.

3

Spread Joy

AS LIFE COMES OUR WAY, AS EXPERIENCES UNFOLD BEFORE US, WE ESSENTIALLY
have two different options: We can welcome and embrace the experiences,
or we can shun them and retreat from them. The responses we make to
experience will vary somewhat from time to time and from situation to
situation, but, overall, each of us a characteristic pattern of reactions to
life and what it brings our way. We have seen how this response is basic
to our personalities and how it is heavily influenced by genetics and
hereditary factors that are beyond our immediate, personal control. But
Scripture clearly requires the followers of Jesus to include in our experiential lives two sets of Christlike behaviors, no matter what our individual
scores might be on the openness to experience domain of our personalities.
Those two behavioral sets are to spread joy wherever we go and to
experience hope as we encounter life.

Spreading joy is a privilege of the follower of Jesus that many people
fail to practice. Although spreading joy is built on a foundation of knowing
how God has acted toward me and in my behalf in the past, and although
spreading joy also anticipates what God is going to do in the future, the
task of being joyful primarily concerns itself with the present. Likewise,
experiencing hope is obviously oriented toward the future. But hope too
is anchored in the goodness of God in the past, and hope too takes account

of the present. So both of these behavior sets deal with the full range of time, even though spreading joy is very much present-focused and hope is very much future-oriented.

Joy is a prominent theme in the Bible. "The Bible is a book of joy" (Wirt, 1994, p. 9). God's people have always had the capacity to rejoice in the good works of God on their behalf, even though at times they grumbled instead (Num 14). From the sheer joy of Hannah as she learned about how God was going to work miraculously in her life (1 Sam 2) to the exuberance of David as he danced in celebration of the arrival of the ark in Jerusalem (2 Sam 6), God's people have had much to celebrate. Their joy can be so unhindered as to cause them to lose their dignity (2 Sam 6:22). But when God acts in mighty and powerful ways, a natural and spontaneous response is to break out in joy.

The English word *enjoy* means to experience something with joy. Joy is an inward response to some experience that we have. The book of Psalms, the worship book of ancient Israel, is replete with joy as the people of God brought to him due praise.Often as we praise God we experience inward joy. "Now my head is lifted up above my enemies all around me, and I will offer in his tent sacrifices with shouts of joy; I will sing and make melody to the LORD" (Ps 27:6). Ancient worshipers sang "Let my tongue cling to the roof of my mouth, if I do not remember you, if I do not set Jerusalem above my highest joy" (Ps 137:6).

Joy is massively present in the New Testament. As the church spread throughout the Mediterranean world, it carried with it the gospel of joy. Joy is the theme of Paul's epistle to the Philippians, a book in which the word *joy* and its cognates occur over and over again. The New Testament closes with scenes of great joy and rejoicing in heaven.

> Then I heard what seemed to be the voice of a great multitude, like the sound of many waters and like the sound of mighty thunder peals, crying out: "Hallelujah! For the LORD our God the Almighty reigns. Let us rejoice and exult and give him the glory, for the marriage of the Lamb has come, and his bride has made herself ready." (Rev 19:6-7)

Our focus in this book, however, is on the Gospels, where joy likewise has a large and importance presence. Joy forms a giant parenthesis around the life of Christ.

As the opening half of these parentheses, we find a concentration of joy in the birth narratives both of John the Baptist and of Jesus himself. When the angel appeared to Zechariah to announce the birth of a son, the angel said, "You will have joy and gladness, and many will rejoice at his birth, for he will be great in the sight of the Lord" (Lk 1:14-15). Elizabeth said to Mary, the soon-to-be mother of Jesus, "For as soon as I heard the sound of your greeting, the child in my womb leaped for joy" (Lk 1:44). When Mary sang what we now call the Magnificat, she said "My soul glorifies the Lord and my spirit rejoices in God my Savior" (Lk 1:46). The angel of the Lord, appearing to shepherds in the fields near Bethlehem, said to them "I am bringing you good news of great joy for all the people" (Lk 2:10), and when the Magi saw the star "they were overwhelmed with joy" (Mt 2:10).

Into the tired old Roman world of Caesar came tidings of great joy. "What the Stoics, the Epicureans, and the mystery religions had all failed to do, Jesus Christ did" (Morrice, 1984, p. 14). Clearly the births of these two little boys, John and Jesus, marked a magnificent time in the drama of redemption. Widespread joy among all the participants was the only logical response.

The closing half of the parentheses occurs on the Sunday of the resurrection. As soon as Mary Magdalene and the other Mary heard the angelic announcement that Jesus was alive, "They left the tomb quickly with fear and great joy, and ran to tell his disciples" (Mt 28:8). Later when Jesus appeared to his disciples and showed them his hands and feet, they still did not believe it; "in their joy they were disbelieving and still wondering" (Lk 24:41). When Jesus later ascended into heaven, "they worshiped him and returned to Jerusalem with great joy" (Lk 24:52). The life of Jesus began in an atmosphere of joy, and his ascension into heaven—the event that ended his earthly life—was likewise a time of great joy for his followers.

The Gospel writer who uses words for joy most frequently is Luke. Some have even called Luke's Gospel "the Gospel of joy." Physician Luke might have scored high on the openness to experience scale, given his interest in conveying the joy that the life of Jesus brought the world. Luke uses various words for joy a total of 53 times in his Gospel; the closest rival is Matthew, who refers to joy 29 times (Morrice, 1984). From Luke's Gospel and the other accounts of the life of Jesus we learn that joy has at least six components that roughly correspond to the six facets of the openness to experience personality factor (see chapter two). Before we discuss these six, we will examine one of most joyful events in the earthly life of Jesus, the triumphal entry.

The Joyful Ride of Jesus

On the Sunday before his death, Jesus approached Jerusalem on what would be his last trip into the city. The pilgrimage of faithful Jews to the holiest of cities for the various festivals of the Jewish calendar was a noteworthy happening, and this trip was no exception. Luke's account of the events of Palm Sunday immediately follows the parable of the ten minas, sometimes called the parable of the pounds (Lk 19:11-27). The parable suggests three different responses to the nobleman's return: joy (the first two servants), distress (the third servant) and uninvolvement (the remaining seven). Apparently these same three types of people witnessed the triumphal entry. Jesus rode into the city as a king. The whole crowd of disciples was overjoyed (v. 37), the Pharisees were distressed (v. 39), and others observed only as silent and uninvolved witnesses. Is joy spread among us in these same proportions, with a few experiencing it while most do not? The powerful message of the triumphal entry is that we can all choose to join the throng of those who experience joy in the presence of Jesus.

What was this joyful ride of Jesus all about? His disciples recognized it as a symbolic, kingly act. Roman officials would sometimes press into service the animals of local people. So when the owners of the donkey's colt asked what they were doing, the disciples said, as they had been instructed to say, "The Lord needs it" (Lk 19:34). A donkey's colt would be used for civil not military purposes (Keener, 1993); Jesus might have been arrested prematurely if his enemies had perceived him as making a military statement with his ride into the city.

The disciples spread their own clothing on the animal and placed Jesus on this colt that had never been ridden before. They spread garments on the road as Jesus and the animal went along. These acts are what common people would do for a king. As they approach the city, with all its beauty and splendor in full view, "the whole multitude of the disciples began to praise God joyfully with a loud voice for all the deeds of power that they had seen" (Lk 19:37). "Spontaneously and irresistibly they now give vent to their excitement" (Geldenhuys, 1966, p. 480). With the miracles of Jesus giving sight to blind Bartimaeus and life to dead Lazarus freshly on their minds, these disciples spread joy to all the pilgrims along that road. What a festive, brave witness they gave to the glory of the beloved king.

Could there be a comic, jesting side to this story? Harvey Cox highlights several features of the life of Christ that do seem to show more irony than we sometimes recognize in the text.

> Like the jester, Christ defies custom and scorns crowned heads. Like a wandering troubadour he has no place to lay his head. Like the clown in the circus parade, he satirizes existing authority, by riding into town replete with regal pageantry when he has no earthly power. Like a minstrel he frequents dinners and parties. At the end he is costumed by his enemies in a mocking caricature of royal paraphernalia. He is crucified amidst sniggers and taunts with a sign over his head that lampoons his laughable claim. (Cox, 1969, pp. 140-141)

While this jesting view undoubtedly exaggerates the point, it does help us see the poignancy of this account. Jesus is allowing his disciples to credit him with regal status in front of the watching Pharisees, who quickly became joy-killers. "Some of the Pharisees in the crowd said to him, 'Teacher, order your disciples to stop'" (Lk 19:39). By this time the crowd was shouting, "Blessed is the king who comes in the name of the Lord! Peace in heaven, and glory in the highest heaven!" (v. 38). Their language was reminiscent of the account of the shepherds at the birth of Christ (Marshall, 1978). Jesus refused the request of the Pharisees and rebuked these critics by saying that his followers had no choice but to give him praise. "If these were silent, the stones would shout out" (v. 40). The enemies of Jesus clearly tried to get their revenge for this defeat by seeing to it that, at his trials and crucifixion a few days later, Jesus was mocked as a king whom they thought really was not a king.

What Is Joy?

People have had a difficult time knowing just what joy is. Some authors call it a gift from God. "Joy is a gift of God, and like all of his other inner gifts it can be experienced even in the midst of extremely difficult circumstances" (Davis, 1984, p. 588). Others say that God does not give joy to us; rather, joy is our response to what God does give us: salvation and new life in God (Miller, 1975). Swindoll (1991) refers to joy as a choice we make. This choice is exemplified by the oft-quoted poem of Ella Wheeler Wilcox, "The Winds of Fate": "One ship drives east and another drives west with the selfsame winds that blow. 'Tis the set of the sails and not the gales which tells us the way to go" (Kauffman, 1962, p. 112). In other words, we can *choose* to respond to life's experiences with joy or with despair. Other authors make the clear and simple point that joy is the fruit of the Spirit's work in our lives (Gal 5:22-23) and that when we evidence it we are displaying the maturity that God wishes to produce in his children (Flynn, 1980).

Who is right? Probably they all are. Joy is a gift from God, it is our choice to make, it is our response, and it is produced by the Spirit's work in our lives. Unlike happiness, which is determined by circumstances, joy is independent of circumstances.

Our discussion will focus on six behaviors or experiences in life in which we can experience God's joy in our lives. Six different aspects of joy spill out of the happy occasion we call the triumphal entry. We will explore each briefly.

1. The Joy of Finding
One of the facets of openness to experience is action. People who are open to experience are behaviorally willing to try new and different activities and enjoy change. They are energized by their actions rather than exhausted by them. Luke's Gospel links joy with a particular type of action, that of finding. Luke 15 is this Gospel's joy chapter. There Luke records for us three famous parables: the lost sheep, the lost coin and the prodigal son. The point of all three parables is not that these three were lost but that they were found! Luke teaches us through the words of Jesus that there is great joy in finding.

The finding of the sheep. In our throw-away society the loss of one out of a hundred can seem paltry and hardly worth the trouble. Why bother? The power of this first "finding" parable is that God does bother. We are the sheep of his pasture, and God cares for each of his sheep. John's Gospel also makes extensive use of this metaphor to convey the amazing and awesome care of God for his own (Beck, 1993). The Pharisees and the teachers of the law had quite a different concept of who God was. God would never seek out a sinner, let alone a tax collector, and these were the very people who were crowding around Jesus that day (Lk 15:1). But Jesus not only allowed these people near him, he welcomed them and ate with them! So when Jesus told them about a shepherd who actively sought out a lost, helpless, doomed sheep, they were hearing about a God that they did not know well.

Jesus made the point even more powerfully since shepherds were regarded by the religious establishment as a poor and lowly lot (Keener, 1993). Jesus chose a shepherd to be a metaphorical representative of God himself, another jibe at the enemies of Jesus. The shepherd does not abandon the ninety-nine other sheep; hearers would naturally assume that several shepherds were likely on duty with a flock this size. When the shepherd finds the lost and helpless sheep, "He is full of joy at his success" (Marshall, 1978, p. 601). And, as with all sorts of finding joy, it has to be shared. He calls together his friends and neighbors and says, "Rejoice with me, for I have found my sheep that was lost" (Lk 15:6). The joy of finding is so great that it overshadows by far any joy God may have in the already-found. Jesus said, "I tell you, there will be more joy in heaven over one sinner who repents than over ninety-nine righteous persons who need no repentance" (Lk 15:7).

The finding of the coin. A poor woman lost one of her ten silver coins (Lk 15:8-10). Perhaps these coins were part or the whole of her dowry, a treasure that she had to guard carefully. It was, no doubt, her only insurance, her retirement and her savings—all in one small bag of ten coins. She likely lived in a small home with small windows such that she had to use a lamp even in the daytime to search for the coin that had fallen somewhere between the stones of her humble floor. Archeologists are still finding such coins that got lost in ancient homes. This woman's joy is full when she finds the coin; such finding joy must be shared, so she too calls her friends and neighbors and asks them to rejoice with her.

The finding of the son. The story of the prodigal son is likely one of the most beloved in the Gospels. Like the finding of the woman's lost coin, we find this parable only in Luke's Gospel. Luke's interest in helping us learn the joy of finding is impressive. Now the ratios have changed again. We first learned about the joy of finding when the loss was 1 percent of the total. Then we learned about loss that was 10 percent of the total. In both cases, finding joy was great. Now we learn how a father who has lost 50 percent of his heirs feels when that son returns to him. What a great scene of joy when the father saw the wandering son coming back home. He "was filled with compassion; he ran and put his arms around him and kissed him" (Lk 15:20). Immediately he expressed his finding joy in actions of celebration. "Let us eat and celebrate" (Lk 15:23-24). The word Luke uses here is a joy word that speaks of merrymaking. Often this kind of merrymaking is crude, raucous and ribald, as in Revelation 11:10. Here, however, the celebration is right and honorable. "We had to celebrate and rejoice," the father told the older brother, "because this brother of yours was dead and has come to life; he was lost and has been found" (Lk 15:32).

The parable of the prodigal son is open-ended. We leave the story without knowing how the older brother reacted. In the first two parables, all of the participants shared in the finding joy of the shepherd and the woman. In the story of the prodigal there is much rejoicing with the father, but we are left with a glum-sounding older brother who initially became angry and sullen at the celebration given for his irresponsible and wayward brother (Lk 15:28). The story could not be clearer. The Pharisees and the teachers of the law, who most strenuously objected to the association Jesus was having with wayward, despised, hopeless people, were like the older brother. They did not know the joy of finding. Perhaps the older brother came to share later in that joy; we do not know. "The important fact is that the invitation remains for all who hear or read and are willing to respond and rejoice" (Blomberg, 1990, p. 179).

People who obtain high scores on the openness factor and especially on the actions facet of that factor will likely have the easiest time learning how to spread joy when finding new evidences of God's love and caring. People who are more closed to responding to experiences around them may have to exercise more discipline to experience the joy of finding and to spread it around to neighbors and friends. God's goodness is abundant. When we are deficient at finding it, rejoicing in it and talking about it with others, we will miss out on the exuberant joy we have read about when the shepherd, the woman and the father found new evidences of God's goodness.

2. The Joy of Worship

On that first Palm Sunday, the disciples broke out into spontaneous and heartfelt worship of their King who had come to them in the name of God himself. Sadly, we sometimes have totally missed the joy of worship in our contemporary church settings. Sometimes the only joy comes from sermon jokes or unintended mistakes. A song leader was trying to get one particularly grumpy man to be more animated in singing the praises of God. He said, "Will you please stand and lead us in a frown?" (Flynn, 1980, p.21). And then there are the bulletin typos that are funny only at the expense of church secretaries or pastors who write copy with poor grammar ("Today in the sanctuary babies will be baptized at both ends"). Why does joy come only from the incidental, accidental or unintentional? Why cannot our joy stem from our worship of our joy-filled God? The psalmist wrote, "I was glad when they said to me, 'Let us go to the house of the LORD' " (Ps 122:1). We sometimes approach worship with more of a dirgeful than a joyful mind set.

Early church worship. As soon as the church was founded on the day of Pentecost, believers began to gather together in worship and praise (Acts 2:46-47). The church has never existed without worship as a central feature of its identity. The worship of the early church was as joyful as are the New Testament records. "The earliest Church, though she worshiped in very humble meeting-places, reached out her arms toward a fellowship that was world-wide and heaven-high; and the joy of her worship on earth was attuned to the majestical Joy of the worship above" (Macdonald, 1935, p. 39).

The joy of the Eucharist. We have lost somewhere the important component of joy when we celebrate the Lord's Supper. "Joy was an original emphasis of the Eucharist, but it is one that has not been characteristic of its celebration for many, many centuries" (Davies, 1993, p. 90). The Lord's table is a Christian celebration. Just as we regularly gather together with family and friends to celebrate birthdays, anniversaries or other important milestones, followers of Jesus gather together regularly to celebrate the joyful resurrection of our Lord. Luther spoke of *risus paschalis* (Easter laughter); it is all too often missing in our churches. "There is no question that our Western worship at the Eucharist has become far too dolorous, dominated by the cross rather than the Resurrection" (Davies, 1993, p.

122). When we recognize that component of the Lord's Supper, we will be well along in bringing joy back into our worship.

Joy, beauty and worship. We have seen that one of the facets of openness to experience is aesthetics, the capacity for appreciating art, beauty, poetry and music. Low scorers on openness to experience are usually relatively uninterested in and insensitive to art and beauty, perhaps artistically challenged. Readers of the Bible will immediately recognize that worship in Scripture is associated with art and beauty.

The makers of the tabernacle were artisans gifted by God to create a worship center of splendor and brilliance (Ex 35:30-35). These artisans worked with gold, silver, bronze, precious stones and blue, purple and scarlet yarns. The tabernacle contained objects of fine craftsmanship in wood and metal. The priests were resplendent in garments of striking beauty. The linens, the silver and the bronze made it a striking place in which to worship Jehovah.

And it was just a prelude to the temple that was built years later by Solomon. The temple was palatial (1 Chron 29:1), built with silver, bronze, iron, wood, onyx, turquoise, marble and precious stones. After its dedication, King Solomon "sent the people to their homes, joyful and glad in heart for the good things the LORD had done for David and Solomon and for his people Israel" (2 Chron 7:10 NIV). Beauty brought joy to their worship. For those of us who may be artistically challenged, how will we appreciate heaven? The look of heaven was nearly beyond words for the apostle John, who was given a glimpse of it. Its carnelian, onyx, jasper, emeralds, gold and crystal are nearly beyond description (Rev 4:1-8). To worship God fully we must all have at least some sense of beauty if we are to experience the true joy of worship.

3. The Joy of Modeling

Jesus was the joyful Christ. On that Sunday when he entered the city of Jerusalem on the back of a colt, the worshipers along the way could no doubt see joy in his face as he received their praise and worship. "Hosanna to the Son of David! Blessed is the one who comes in the name of the Lord! Hosanna in the highest heaven!" they shouted (Mt 21:9). The joy of the crowd was modeled after the joy of the Savior. Yet most people picture in their head a sober, sad Savior.

When Elton Trueblood wrote his 1964 book called *The Humor of Christ,* many readers could appreciate for the first time a side of Jesus that they had never before seen. The humor of Jesus is there for us to read, but our mindset or our mental picture of who Jesus was sometimes interferes with our ability to read about blind guides leading the blind as humorous. Jesus began his ministry by facilitating the joy at a wedding. When the wine ran out, he created more for the festivities (Jn 2). Could a dour, humorless, dyspeptic Messiah have performed this miracle? No, yet we sometimes act as if Jesus turned the water into vinegar instead of wine.

Cal Samra (1985) set out on a quest to locate portraits of Jesus that portrayed him smiling. His book reproduces six pictures that he found, and those who look at these beautiful portraits of a smiling Christ are inevitably struck by how much they contrast with the pictures that we all tend to carry around in our heads—sober and somber visages of Jesus. No one can question that Jesus did have serious, angry and even sad moments. But when we cannot envision happy, joyful or smiling twinkles on his face we have surely missed a substantial part of his humanity that we need to appreciate and model (Warfield, 1912).

One of the facets of the openness to experience scale is labeled fantasy. Costa and McCrae (1992c) define fantasy, as used here, as a vivid imagination and active fantasy life in which people daydream as a way of creating an "interesting inner world" (p. 17). Fantasizing has a bad name among Christians. We normally associate it with lust and other indulgences of the mind that the Bible strictly forbids. But fantasy can serve useful and even righteous purposes, for we know that the parts of our body can be offered to God as "instruments of righteousness" (Rom 6:13). We are to envision Christ (picture him in our inner worlds) so that we can become increasingly Christlike. "Let the same mind be in you that was in Christ Jesus," writes the apostle Paul (Phil 2:5). The familiar hymn "Jesus, Thou Joy of Loving Hearts" is based on an old Latin poem and contains a striking verse: "Our restless spirits yearn for thee, where'er our changeful lot is cast, glad when thy gracious smile we see, blest when our faith can hold thee fast."

The New Testament makes three specific references to the joy of Jesus. The first occurs, not surprisingly, in Luke's Gospel. When the seventy-two returned from their important missionary journey, they were thrilled and filled with joy at what God had chosen to accomplish through them, especially at how the demons had responded to their rebukes (Lk 10:17). Jesus told them to keep on rejoicing, not in the fact that the demons retreated in the face of the powerful name of Jesus but in the fact that their "names are written in heaven" (Lk 10:20). At that point in his description, Luke writes that Jesus was full of joy (v. 21). This joy of Jesus was inspired by the Holy Spirit. His joy was not the same joy reported by the disciples.

> Rather was it the additional evidence provided of the method of revelation chosen by God that thrilled his heart (Lk 10:21). The knowledge of God was no longer the preserve of a select few—such as the rabbis, who were specially trained to understand it. It was open to simple-hearted people, such as those to whom the seventy-two had been sent. In other words, Jesus rejoiced that religion as a first-hand experience of the divine by mankind required no elaborate instruction, but simple trust and confidence in God as heavenly Father. (Morrice, 1984, p. 87)

4. The Joy of Obedience

One facet of the openness personality factor deals with *values*. People who score high are open to reconsidering basic values and exploring new ones. People who are committed to a belief system that is quite well defined will probably score much lower. The conjectured scores for both Jesus and Paul are "very low." Why? Paul and Jesus were deeply committed to their religious views. Faith in these core convictions was firm and certain. Neither one of them had a need to re-examine their faith in God, the reality of the supernatural or the fact that God has revealed his will for humans in Scripture. Followers of Jesus will also have made commitments that are foundational and basic and will likely score low.

A key value for the believer, one that does not allow much room for variance, is the implicit promise to obey God. Fundamental to the Christian faith is the expectation that the disciples of Jesus will follow his commands and obey the precepts of God. Therein, says Scripture, is found joy. Nowhere is this principle more clear than in the Upper Room Discourse. Jesus said in John 15,

> As the Father has loved me, so I have loved you; abide in my love.
> If you keep my commandments, you will abide in my love, just as I

have kept my Father's commandments and abide in his love. I have said these things to you so that my joy may be in you, and that your joy may be complete. (Jn 15:9-11)

This reference to the personal joy of Jesus is one of several in the New Testament. Here we also learn the secret of his joy: obedience. A distinction of Christianity is that obedience to God's commands does not yield constraint; it gives freedom. And obedience to God's commands does not breed resentment; it produces love. Jesus obeyed the Father and remained in the care of his Father's love. Such will also be true for the followers of Jesus; when they obey his commands, they remain in his love and experience complete joy. Here the values of the Christian faith run counter to what is intuitive and what is true of value systems apart from biblical faith.

John's Gospel also deals with the unusual connection between sorrow and joy, again counterintuitive. Jesus told his disciples, on the night before his death,

Very truly, I tell you, you will weep and mourn, but the world will rejoice; you will have pain, but your pain will turn into joy. When a woman is in labor, she has pain, because her hour has come. But when her child is born, she no longer remembers the anguish because of the joy of having brought a human being into the world. So you have pain now; but I will see you again, and your hearts will rejoice, and no one will take your joy from you. (Jn 16:20-22)

In this passage Jesus reminds his followers that on occasion the joy that comes from obedience may be delayed—the "not yet" of God's economy. The delay in no way abrogates the promise, however. The delay due to temporary sorrow was connected to the impending death of Jesus which was to come the following day. The prophetic utterance of John 16:22 was precisely fulfilled not many days afterward.

When it was evening on that day, the first day of the week, and the doors of the house where the disciples had met were locked for fear of the Jews, Jesus came and stood among them and said, "Peace be with you." After he said this, he showed them his hands and his side. Then the disciples rejoiced when they saw the Lord. (Jn 20:19-20)

Obedience then leads to joy. The final contribution that the Gospel of John makes to this theme comes in a concept Jesus referred to as "fullness of joy." We have already seen that he spoke of "complete joy" (Jn 16:24). In the prayer which he spoke in the hearing of the eleven disciples on the last night of his life, Jesus makes reference again to this fullness of joy. "I am coming to you now, but I say these things while I am still in the world, so that they may have the full measure of my joy within them" (Jn 17:13 NIV). The disciples would soon experience higher levels of joy that could occur only as they related to the resurrected and ascended Jesus. While we might be tempted to believe that no joy could be higher than to have physically been with Jesus when he was here on earth, Jesus is here saying that such joy does not compare to the fuller, more complete experience of joy that we can now enjoy with the risen Christ who has ascended to the throne of his Father.

This fullness of joy is also connected with prayer. "Until now you have not asked for anything in my name. Ask and you will receive, so that your joy may be complete" (Jn 16:24). "On the basis of this communion with God, the disciples of Christ can expect an answer to prayers offered in the name of their Master, that is, prayers that are in accordance with his will" (Morrice, 1984, p. 108). Fullness of joy emerges from faithful obedience that has outlived sorrow; that joy is made even more complete as the disciples of Jesus receive answers to their prayers.

5. The Joy of Taking Courage

One of the eleven words for joy found in the New Testament is a word we might not connect with joy merely by reading our English translations. When *tharsein* appears as an imperative, translators render it "take courage" or "cheer up." In the Septuagint the word is used in Exodus 14:13 where Moses says to the people, "Do not be afraid, stand firm, and see the deliverance that the LORD will accomplish for you today." In the Gospels and the book of Acts this word for joy appears seven times. Six of these occurrences are on the lips of Jesus and the seventh occurs in connection with what Jesus said. An obvious feature of the ministry of Jesus to hurting people was to lift their spirits, to bring them encouragement and a measure of hope.

One of the facets of the openness scale deals with feelings. We each have different styles of incorporating feelings into our experience. Some people are deeply and intensely aware of different emotions they experience; others are quite disconnected from them. Some people are threatened even by their own feelings; others actively seek to cultivate various emotions as a part of their sense of well-being. We have seen how Jesus scored very high on this facet whereas our conjectured score for Paul was rather average. Similar differences in how emotions are handled will appear among groups of believers and those not associated with the Christian faith. However, the message of Jesus to all of us, no matter what our scoring here may be, is *tharsei,* "Take courage!"

At the very beginning of his ministry, Jesus made it crystal clear that he had come to earth for specific purposes. When visiting his home town of Nazareth one Sabbath, he stood up to read Scripture and prophetically proclaimed:

> The Spirit of the LORD is upon me, because he has anointed me to bring good news to the poor. He has sent me to proclaim release to the captives and recovery of sight to the blind, to let the oppressed go free, to proclaim the year of the Lord's favor. (Lk 4:18-19, quoting Is 61:1-2)

To these very people, the blind, the poor, the oppressed, the prisoners, Jesus said *tharsei,* "Take courage."

One day Jesus returned to his home village of Capernaum. There some men brought a paralytic to Jesus. On the basis of the faith of those who brought the disabled man to him, Jesus said, "Take heart *[tharsei],* son; your sins are forgiven" (Mt 9:2). After an exchange with teachers of the law in the crowd regarding the theology of forgiving sins, Jesus healed the paralytic, telling him to stand up, pick up his mat and go home. As he shakily obeyed and then found that his legs suddenly worked again, what new courage and what joy he must have felt!

Shortly thereafter Jesus turned and saw a woman who had touched the edge of his cloak. The woman was ill, bleeding for twelve years. Jesus said to her, "Take heart *[tharsei],* daughter; your faith has made you well" (Mt 9:22). Jesus gave the same encouraging word to the disciples who saw what they thought was a ghost approaching them on top of the waves of a storm. To calm them, Jesus said, "Take heart *[tharsei],* it is I; do not be afraid" (Mt 14:27).

One can imagine that all these people and probably many others were greatly heartened by taking courage at the command of Jesus. Likely some or all of them were in the crowd that day waving palm branches as Jesus, the coming king, rode into Jerusalem on the colt's back. They, of all people whose lives were touched by the Savior, had great reason to be joyful. They had their mobility, their calmness of heart, their healing and their sight.

Counselors have a sacred privilege of speaking *tharsei* in the name of Jesus to hurting, discouraged, defeated and despairing clients. The message we have to share comes from Jesus himself in John 16:33: "I have said this to you, so that in me you may have peace. In the world you face persecution. But take courage *[tharsei]*; I have conquered the world!"

6. The Joy of Suffering

The final facet of the openness factor has to do with ideas. This feature of openness to experience, as we have already seen, has led some researchers to label the openness factor as "intelligence" or the "intellective" factor. High scorers on this facet are intellectually curious; they love to philosophize about the mysteries of life. Low scorers, even those whose intelligence levels may be quite high, tend to have a constricted range on intellectual interests. This fact is particularly germane to the last component of joy presented to us in the New Testament, the joy of suffering.

One of the greatest mysteries of Christianity is the teaching that we can learn to experience joy even though we are enduring suffering. If people want to wrestle with a challenging idea, this mystery will tax all of their intellectual curiosity. The crux of this cardinal tenet of biblical Christianity comes to us through Hebrews 12:2: "looking to Jesus the pioneer and perfecter of our faith, who for the sake of the joy that was set before him endured the cross, disregarding its shame, and has taken his seat at the right hand of the throne of God." This reference to the joy of Jesus is the third we have examined in this chapter. The word pictures used here by the author of the book of Hebrews almost remind readers of the triumphal entry. It is as if Jesus rode into Jerusalem surrounded by the joyful shouting of the crowds and continued right on through his week of incredible suffering with that joy ringing in his ears. The author is also referring to the joy of an accomplished and fully completed redemption—a joy that Jesus knew he would be able to take back to heaven and to his heavenly

Father because of the events of Passion Week.

Can we too experience joy through suffering, or is this teaching of the New Testament just a twisted form of unhealthy masochism? If Christianity were to teach that we somehow had to deny the suffering, pretend it was not real, or otherwise discount the reality of the suffering, we might indeed have to examine the teaching for signs of psychological unhealthiness. But such is not what the New Testament proclaims. Given the reality of the suffering, given its pain and agony, God can still produce in us joy based on larger realities that transcend the pain of the moment. Peter writes to his readers, "In this you rejoice, even if now for a little while you have had to suffer various trials" (1 Pet 1:6). Mother Teresa said, "Never let anything so fill you with pain or sorrow, so as to make you forget the joy of Christ risen" (Egan & Egan, 1994).

The Italian poet Dante Alighieri is best known for his epic poem *Divine Comedy*. The work deals with a soul that is guided through hell and purgatory by Vergil and through paradise by Beatrice. His descriptions of the suffering and torment of hell and the uncertainty and struggles of purgatory are often the sum total of what people remember about Dante. Yet Dante's message is a Christian witness to the truth that God will bring us joy through suffering.

No one has expressed this view of Dante more clearly than twentieth-century British writer Dorothy Sayers. She calls Dante a poet of supreme joy. Sayers encountered Dante's epic poem one night during an air raid in London. She picked up the book just as she was heading for the shelter. "The effect was dynamic" (Reynolds, 1994, p. 266). She found that Dante had come face to face with the reality and horror of evil and had brilliantly described that terror in the first sections of the epic. But then when he burst forth into celestial heaven, joy emerged in a radiant fashion. "The higher Dante ascends and the more ecstatic his joy becomes on beholding the perfection of Heaven, the model of what the Kingdom of God could be on earth, the more fiercely he denounces those who betray that ideal" (Reynolds, 1994, pp. 270-71). So from the heart of a medieval poet comes yet again a marvelous witness to the Christian truth: God brings joy out of suffering, as difficult a concept as that may be for us to understand fully.

That joyful ride of Jesus into Jerusalem on Palm Sunday is a graphic picture of this truth. Jesus knew what his future was. He had told his disciples many times about the suffering that the Son of Man was going to endure soon. He had been very specific: he would be handed over to Gentile authorities, mocked, insulted, spit upon, flogged and killed (Lk 18:32-33). Of course, he had also informed his disciples that he would rise again after three days, but this joy of resurrection could come only after the intense suffering that none but the basest of criminals could deserve. Jesus was aware of all of this imminent suffering as he rode that day joyfully into Jerusalem. Counselors, therapists, helpers and friends can all be witnesses to this principle with those who suffer: God can bring joy out of suffering.

Conclusion

C. S. Lewis describes his conversion first to theism and later to biblical Christianity as a process in which he was surprised by joy.

> No slightest hint was vouchsafed me that there ever had been or ever would be any connection between God and Joy. If anything, it was the reverse. I had hoped that the heart of reality might be of such a kind that we can best symbolize it as a place; instead I found it to be a person. For all I knew, the total rejection of what I called Joy might be one of the demands, might be the very first demand, he would make upon me. (Lewis, 1955, p. 230)

Instead, Lewis found true and lasting joy in his relationship with God.

We have not been examining a false, misleading joy. We read in the Gospels that the enemies of Jesus temporarily experienced "joy" when they were finally able to arrest Jesus and begin the process of his torment. Judas Iscariot was negotiating with the religious leaders of the nation. "When they heard it, they were greatly pleased, and promised to give him money" (Mk 14:11). Their joy was short-lived. They could not defeat the Son of God, who burst forth from the grave in spite of every possible human effort to prevent his triumph. By way of contrast, the joy Jesus gives is complete and lasting. Hence the command of 1 Thessalonians 5:16 (the shortest verse in the Greek text of the New Testament) is vitally important for all of us: "Rejoice always."

4

Experience Hope

THE SERVICE WAS JUST ABOUT FINISHED. WE HAD WORSHIPED FOR THREE HOURS with a congregation of South Africans in Capetown on June 16, 1989. The service was held in commemoration of the Soweto uprising thirteen years earlier when many people had lost their lives. The service of songs and sermons was somber and serious. Yet we felt privileged as a group of theological educators to join with these four hundred people in commemoration of the Soweto slaughter. The service at the African Methodist Episcopal church in Hazendal was thoroughly Christian and heartfelt. And just as it was ending, the worship leader announced that the building was surrounded on two sides by South African police.

The political climate in South Africa in 1989 was tense. Little did we know how much longer the apartheid government would be able to stay in power. Worries abounded about a violent revolution, about a bloodbath, about an extended reign of terror that might occur if a peaceful transition to majority rule did not occur soon. We had heard about police violence from the victims themselves, and the announcement that the police had arrived outside the building struck us with a thud.

The only unusual event in the three-hour worship service was a rush of students at one point to the center of the church. At first we thought they were all going to look at something; but it soon became evident that

they were encircled to perform a chanting dance, a dance that was banned
in the country at that time. The dance was a freedom dance, a guerilla
dance to which various chants can be attached. The dance was a taunt to
the authorities, but the students could indulge in doing it in the safety of
the church. We later learned that they had been denied a permit of their
own to commemorate the day and so had joined in with the church service
instead. They participated in the worship but took an opportunity to chant
dance during a quiet moment.

Just before the benediction the pastor made one additional announcement. The police had now completely surrounded the building. He
made an ardent plea for everyone to leave peacefully. People who needed
to walk to their buses were to be the first to leave the sanctuary. Our group
of twenty North Americans was ushered out of the church and down the
street toward the waiting buses. It soon became apparent that the leaders
of the commemorative service wanted us to line the curb between the
exiting worshipers who were walking to their buses and the police who
were in the field behind us. Now we knew what the pastor meant when
he invited the visiting clergy to go out and "witness what happens here."
We were human shields.

The police had arrived in their "yellow mellows," armed vehicles used
for riot control. Several police officers in their crisp blue uniforms were
milling around. We could take some comfort in the fact that they did not
have any guns drawn. Now the worshipers were exiting and passing in
front of us. The students seized the opportunity to dance and chant in the
street, the very same chant dance that had occurred in the church. Students
danced in a tight circle, slowly moving in front of us. A police official
approached the leaders of the worship service and said they did not want
this to continue. He quietly said, "It is disorderly."

Meanwhile the students were telling the world through these witnesses
that their quest for freedom and liberation could not be quelled by an edict
from Praetoria or by a request from a police officer. Their aspirations and
hopes were too powerful to be stifled and squelched by power, by displays
of authority or even by brutal force. Their dance was hopeful, and for a
moment of time I was able to see clearly what hope can do in the face of
adverse circumstances: it can keep the human spirit alive and energized
and equip it for eventual victory.

The outcome was peaceful. We were a thankful busload of frightened visitors as we headed across town to meet in person with Archbishop Desmond Tutu. The Capetown newspaper reported in the next day's issue that "the service passed without incident, although a heavy police presence was maintained outside the church grounds." We hadn't imagined it; it was a heavy show of force indeed.

Our reactions in the face of this unanticipated event were varied. We had witnessed only one event out of thousands that had occurred as the people of South Africa struggled for majority rule. We had not witnessed violence, although the potential for it was as much in the air as was the chanting song of the dancing students. I recall feeling a mix of inner determination to hold my place on that curbside and rage that justice and peace were so long in coming to this massive nation.

Later that night I sensed that I had done one small thing to help encourage these students in their quest for liberation. A colleague of ours, who stood in the line as well, was traumatized by the event. The sheer risk and potential for harm overwhelmed her so that to this day she reflects on that event with a sense of intensity that has diminished only slightly in the years that have ensued. Why did we have such strong reactions to this thirty-minute experience? Because in the midst of the experience of human bondage and suffering, in the presence of great potential for violence and mayhem, we had also seen human hope in these students. Hope can transform life and our experience of it. Hope is a distinctively Christian grace that equips us all to deal with life's experiences.

Hope and Openness

We have seen how both Paul and Jesus hypothetically scored in the average range for openness to experience. When we examine their conjectured scores on the subfacets of the openness scale, we can see that the reason for their average on the total is related to the wide range of scores they obtained on the component scales of openness (see Table 4). Jesus ranged from very high on openness to feelings to very low on openness to values; Paul scored high on openness to actions and ideas but very low on openness to values.

Those of us who are followers of Jesus will also likely have subfacet scores that vary greatly. Thus we will have varying degrees of openness to experiences that come our way, depending on the nature of those experiences. If the experience before us forces us to waver in our commitment to the core of our biblical faith, we are not likely to be very open to it. But if we can explore new actions, ideas or feelings without jeopardizing our faith commitments, some of us will be open to those experiences, some closed, depending on our genetic makeup and history of past experiences.

No matter how we might individually vary on how open we are to experience, we all can share a basic core attitude toward those experiences: we can respond with hope to the experiences of life. Hope, along with the joy that we have already examined, is to be a hallmark of the believer. "And now faith, hope, and love abide, these three" (1 Cor 13:13). How does hope affect the experiential life? How can the Christian's hope make a distinctive contribution to how we cope with experience, even though we might all individually vary on degrees of openness to it?

The believer views experience as only one segment of reality. Many people today do not have a theistic worldview or a belief in life after death. For them the experiences of life that come along are basically all there is to life. Experience is the sum of reality. For the believer, however, experience is only one component of what is real and true. God exists beyond the experiences of life, supernatural power is his to execute on our behalf, our life on earth is but a prelude to what is to come, and God is active in the world both in and above the laws of nature. The Christian sees experience as a valuable and necessary feature of life. The believer does not seek to deny experience, to relegate it to the unreal or to diminish its importance. The believer simply sees experience in its larger context.

The more specific the object, the more likely it is that wishing is indulged. In contrast, the object of hoping is a global, more or less existential condition rather than a thing: one can hope to be delivered, to be set free, to become enlightened, to be understood, to be reconciled with others, to be forgiven, to die a good death, no matter how grim the present reality is. (Brainerd, 1990, p. 533)

Another way to describe the overlay of hope and openness is to view one's openness to experience as a basic attitude or posture toward life that is surrounded by a larger meta-attitude of hope. Believers will vary from one another on the former but should be similar to one another on the latter, since we have all been given the same basis on which to build our

Christian hope. This hope is to be a conviction, a belief and a powerful influencer on how we respond to experience. It is not enough merely to have Christian hope; it is also vitally important that we allow that hope to shape our responses to experience. Theology confined to the head, no matter how accurate, is not a complete theology until it permeates the heart and affects our daily living. Only then will we be able to understand fully what the Scripture means when it promises that our hope will make the present sufferings tolerable (1 Pet 1:3-7).

Hope in the Bible
Hope is a central theme in the Bible. "The Christian faith is an eschatological faith" (Kirkpatrick, 1994, p. 33). In exploring how Jesus would have us respond to life's experiences, we learn that as we encounter life's experiences, we are to adopt a meta-attitude of joy regarding our present circumstances and a meta-attitude of hope regarding the outcome of our present circumstances. Joy is focused on the present; hope is future-oriented.

Hope Before the First Advent
The Old Testament contains scores of promises and covenants that, from the very beginning, God made with his people. To rebellious Adam and Eve he promised toil and pain (Gen 3). To Joshua he promised victory (Josh 23). To barren Hannah he promised a son (1 Sam 1). Jehovah proved his faithfulness by keeping his promises, never breaking them. On the basis of the faithfulness of God, Israel was to put its trust and hope in the same promise-keeping God. On a more formal level, God entered into agreements or covenants with his people. He promised Noah never again to destroy the world by flood (Gen 9). To Abraham he promised that a nation would come forth from his loins (Gen 12; 15; 17) and that they would dwell in the land that God would give them. To David he promised a throne that would never end (2 Sam 7). To Jeremiah God made a new covenant that would be written on the hearts of his people (Jer 31).

Throughout the Old Testament God gave his people hope. As times worsened, as oppression nearly snuffed the life out of the nation, as exile, war and famine almost totally consumed them, God was faithful to give prophetic utterances through his prophets about the future. These promises included hope for a deliverer (Is 53) who would relieve their suffering and bring them liberation. This messianic hope sustained the faithful through terrible centuries of God's wrath over their disobedience and his apparent abandonment of his people.

Israel's hope was clearly linked to the coming kingdom of God when God would rule as he promised to David. "Israel celebrated the consistent faithfulness of God's activity in history as she projected her expectations of fulfillment upon the screen of her immediate future. God alone was Israel's hope" (Kirkpatrick, 1994, p. 34). The prophet Amos foretold how God would restore the fortunes of the nation (Amos 9:11-15). God will raise up David's fallen booth and will repair the breaches of Jerusalem. In that day prosperity will return and they will prosper in the good favor of Jehovah. "I will plant them upon their land, and they shall never again be plucked up out of the land that I have given them, says the LORD your God" (Amos 9:15).

Hope After the First Advent

The messianic expectations that Jesus encountered while here on earth represented the hopes of a nation that were based on centuries of prophecy and promise. What the faithful first-century Jew could not have known is that God's prophesied plan was to be only partially fulfilled in the first advent of Christ, with the balance of fulfillment coming when Christ would come again.

Jesus did inaugurate the kingdom of God as John the Baptist had foretold when he said, "Repent, for the kingdom of heaven has come near" (Mt 3:2). Jesus became the suffering servant described by Isaiah and provided deliverance for the people of God. Their deliverance was spiritual—deliverance from the power of sin. Political deliverance and freedom from the presence of sin would come later. Thus the church that was built on the foundation of the apostles and prophets (Eph 2:19-20) also lived in hope.

Their hope, like the hope of the nation of Israel earlier, was based on the promises of God and on the actions of God in history. For the Old Testament saint, the surety of God's promise was his faithfulness in delivering the nation from bondage in Egypt (Ps 78). For the New Testament believer, the surety of God's promise is the mighty act of raising Jesus from the dead (1 Cor 15). The resurrection of Jesus was and is the cornerstone of hope. "If Christ has not been raised, your faith is futile and you are still in your sins" (1 Cor 15:17). Even though the kingdom of God has been inaugurated by the first advent of Christ, the believer hopes still for a fuller and more complete fulfillment of the kingdom that is yet to come. For the faithful of God there has always been a "not yet" that looms ahead of us, giving us hope, and prompting us to trust God in spite of present circumstances.

Hope for the believer includes hope in the resurrection of the body (1 Cor 15), in the return of Jesus (1 Thess 4) and in the glories of heaven reserved for those who know God (Rev 21—22). This hope is realistic and stable.

> Biblical hope is entirely realistic. . . . Christian hope starts . . . with the recognition that it *will* happen—the worst may well occur, indeed it has already occurred and its results are continually bound to recur. Christian hope (in its most distinctive form) never resorts to the mere optimism of "Keep hoping—things may get better." . . . Christian hope says, rather, "Things *will* get worse: anything may happen; but God . . ." Such hope is essentially a stable one, because it is grounded in nothing so fluctuating and uncertain as circumstances, still less in moods, which change, but in the undeviating reliability of God's character. (Moule, 1963, p. 17-18, italics original)

What does this hope do for us? It builds patience (Rom 8:25), it enlivens our faith (Gal 5:5), it stimulates godliness (1 Jn 3:3), it builds steadfastness (1 Thess 1:3), it breeds confidence (2 Cor 3:12) and it brings joy (Rom 5:1-5). In short, "Christian hope directs present life" (Parsons, 1991, p. 407).

All too often believers focus not on how hope should be directing their daily life in the present but upon the details, timetables or specifics of how God will act in the future. This interest is how the future will unfold will no doubt increase as believers see more and more reason to despair about the state of the world (Travis, 1980). The Bible does indeed give indications of what will happen in the last days, but the emphasis of the New Testament is not on the chronology of God's actions; it is on the need for believers to live day by day with an attitude of hope regarding the present and the future.

The value of hope is not always recognized. Some people would dismiss hope as nothing more than self-delusion. Hope can sometimes be nonsensical to those who do not believe—but absolutely transforming to those who do.

> The nonsense of the resurrection became the hope that shook the Roman Empire and established the Christian movement. The nonsense of slave songs in Egypt and Mississippi became the hope that let the oppressed go free. The nonsense of a bus boycott in Montgomery, Alabama, became the hope that transformed a nation. . . . Hope is believing in spite of the evidence and watching the evident change. (Wallis, 1994, p. 19)

Hope is an integral part of Christian experience and is to be a major component of our response to experience. Whether the times are hard or easy, whether circumstances are positive or negative, the believer is to hold fast to the promises of God. God will act in the future. Justice will prevail. Suffering will end. God will continue to reign on his throne.

Hope During the First Advent

While Jesus was here on earth, hope was an important component of his ministry. Not only were faithful Jews hopeful that the Messiah would come (Lk 2:22, 36-38); Jesus instilled hope in those who followed him that he would come *again* (Mt 24:29-31). Throughout the biblical drama of redemption, however, hope has always occurred in the context of suffering. Just as we saw previously with joy in spite of suffering, hope in the midst of suffering is a familiar biblical theme (Tutu, 1983). The nation of Israel suffered greatly as nations which defeated them carried them into captivity and devastated the city of Jerusalem. The believers of the first century who lived with a living hope burning in their hearts (1 Pet 1:3) suffered immensely under the relentless persecution of the Roman government. Hope and suffering coexist in Christian experience. The same was true for those who were touched by the ministry of Jesus.

The incident we will examine as an illustration of hope among those to whom Jesus ministered is recorded in John 5. The occasion was one of celebration in Jerusalem at a religious festival. But there was no celebration for a crowded group of desperately ill people that day who gathered at a pool near the Sheep Gate. The pool is often known as the Pool of Bethesda, although various translations render the name differently. The pool was surrounded by covered porticoes, five in number, that apparently gave shelter to those who waited there.

> In these lay many invalids—blind, lame, and paralyzed. One man was there who had been ill for thirty-eight years. When Jesus saw him lying there and knew that he had been there a long time, he said to him, "Do you want to be made well?" The sick man answered him, "Sir, I have no one to put me into the pool when the water is stirred up; and while I am making my way, someone else steps down ahead of me." Jesus said to him, "Stand up, take your mat and walk." At once the man was made well, and he took up his mat and began to walk." (Jn 5:3-9)

We do not know much about this pool. Verse 4, which is familiar to those who grew up on older versions ("For an angel of the Lord went down at certain seasons into the pool, and stirred up the water; whoever stepped in first after the stirring of the water was made well from whatever disease that person had" [NRSV footnote]), is not included in most modern versions because it is likely not a part of the original text. The pool may well have been formed by an intermittent spring that at times would replenish the pool with water rich in minerals. To receive the benefit of the fresh input, ill people would try to get near the inflow before it was dispersed and thus diluted by the rest of the water in the pool (Macgregor, 1929; Westcott, 1954).

Jesus was moved with compassion when he saw this sick man. An illness of thirty-eight years, probably some form of paralysis, was a terrible burden of suffering in the first century just as it would be today. "Jesus sees that for him there will never be healing by waiting there" (Dods, 1901, p. 178). The hint of the text is that Jesus selected the most difficult illness and the most needy person as the object of his healing power. Faithful Jews who knew their Scriptures expected that the Messiah would make the lame leap for joy (Is 35:6; Jer 31: 8-9). And so this healing was yet another sign that the Messiah had come (Hoskyns, 1947). The thirty-eight years proves the gravity of the disease, and the man's getting up and walking away at the command of Jesus proves the power of the miracle (Barrett, 1978).

Sadly, the immediate outcome of the healing among those who witnessed this miracle was not the glad praise of God but instant criticism. The Jews first criticized the healed man for carrying his pallet on the Sabbath, a violation of the law (Lightfoot, 1957). Then they criticized Jesus for working (healing) on the sabbath. Jesus had deliberately brought fulfilled hope into the life of this ill man on the sabbath to prove to all who would believe that Jesus was working with his Father to bring healing to the world (Jn 5:17).

Varieties of Hope

Our purpose now is to explore what must have gone through the mind of this nameless man during the years he sat by the pool waiting for healing. Of course, we cannot know with certainty that any of these varieties of hope crossed his mind; but if we assume that he was normal in all ways other than physical, we can reconstruct what he must have experienced. He was like us; we are like him. Despite our firm belief in the power and value of hope, the form hope takes at any given time will vary with us just as it must have for him.

Hope Floundering: The Experience of Ambivalence

We are assuming that hope is an inner attitude that powerfully affects the way we internalize experience. If we think about this man sitting by the pool, we can imagine that at first he had high hopes that his condition would be changed and that he would improve. He had not been sitting under the porticoes for thirty-eight years, but the implication of the text is that he had been there for some time. The experience of being there, however, must surely have presented ambivalent messages to him. The pool did not stir as often as he would want; others were faster at getting into the pool and benefiting from the stirring of the water. No matter what he did to position himself differently, to try harder, to move faster, to concentrate more, he could not get into the water. *Does this work or doesn't it? Were the friends who bring me here every day right or were they misled? Why do I feel encouraged some days and discouraged other days? Have I done the right thing by coming here to the pool for healing?*

Experience comes our way sometimes in inconsistent forms. Life can be very ambivalent as we interact with it—a mix of good and bad, encouraging and discouraging, affirming and denouncing, strengthening and weakening. This unpredictability and occasional inconsistency make it difficult for us to respond with certainty and confidence. When the experiences of life are ambivalent, hope flounders. This very ill man sitting by the pool under the porticoes must surely have had days when his hope floundered.

Several of the major pathologies that beset the emotional lives of humans are likewise inner responses to ambivalent stimuli in the environment. We do not yet know the precise way in which certain pathologies are influenced by *past experience,* by *genetics,* or by *present experience.* Some pathologies may have their origin in all three. Some forms of mental illness may be influenced predominantly by one and only in a minor way by the other two. Yet we can say with some degree of confidence that all the forms of mental distress are likely influenced by all three factors even if one or two are relatively minor contributors to the mix.

One example is anxiety. When we are consumed with worry, or with fear, or with an obsession or compulsion, we are suffering from an anxiety disorder. The inconsistent stimuli coming from the environment all affect the anxious person. The working out of an anxious disorder often requires that the client, with professional help, begin to organize life, to find its predictabilities, and to focus on its regularities rather than on its inconsistencies and unpredictabilities. We can view anxious people as individuals with floundering hope triggered by ambivalent stimuli from life's experiences.

Another example is the even more serious group of conditions we call the schizophrenias. It is a well-known fact that many schizophrenic episodes first appear in the third decade of life when people are moving out of adolescence into adulthood. We do not know precisely why this decade of life often triggers the first signs of schizophrenia. Perhaps it is the stress of adulthood that overwhelms fragile personalities. Perhaps it is the myriad of conflicting and inconsistent stimuli that adulthood invariably brings that pushes people into states of unreality. We do know that hope flounders for those caught in the grip of an acute schizophrenic episode, and recovery often includes the reordering of life so that its experiences will not be so overwhelming in the future.

Hope Waning: The Experience of Loss

At other times the paralytic (we are assuming the sick man of John 5 was a paralytic) must have felt his hope waning away. What was an initial rush of hopefulness could well have deteriorated into a draining of hope from his very being in the face of one loss after another. If we can imagine that friends had brought him to the porticoes faithfully every day for several weeks or even a few months, there undoubtedly were periods of time when he consistently experienced a sense of loss. One chance after another to benefit from the spring disappears. In the competitiveness of the chronically ill for cure, this paralytic was no match for those slightly more nimble, more aggressive or more intimidating. Flagging, sinking, waning hope must surely have been his portion on those days when loss after loss filled his days.

The paralytic may have been experiencing just such a day when Jesus came by. The Lord asked him, "Do you want to be made well?" (Jn 5:6). His presence under the porticoes would indicate that he did want to be made well. But his spirits may well have sagged far below the point of having any hope, at least for that day, that he could make it into the water to find healing. Westcott (1954) suggests that the question of Jesus reveals a downcast spirit in the heart of the paralytic that was probably evident in his facial expression. The question of Jesus then is a prompt, a stimulizing probe to reactivate the hope that had waned in the face of experiential losses.

Hope wanes for all of us at times. It would be hard to imagine human existence without occasional lapses into sad, blue or depressed states of mind. The presence of energizing hope and the presence of depressed feelings probably have an inverse relationship with each other. As one sags, the other increases and vice versa. Thankfully, not all of us experience what can be called clinical depressions, at least not all at the same time! But estimates are that from 10-25 percent of American women and from 5-12 percent of American men experience a clinical depression at some point during their lives (Sue, Sue, & Sue, 1997). Again, these nonclinical depressions as well as those episodes of depression that are diagnosable have a variety of etiological factors: some genetic, some learned behaviors from past experience, and some immediate environmental triggers. A common environmental trigger, however, is loss. Hope frequently wanes for us, as it doubtless did for the paralytic, in the face of repeated experiences of loss.

What is the antidote? The answer is cultivated hope—not just believed hope but enacted hope. The title of Rodman's 1986 book *Keeping Hope Alive: On Becoming a Psychotherapist* describes well the task of helpers, counselors and therapists. Coming alongside those in distress often means that the stronger person of the two has the task of keeping hope alive. Jesus took that role with paralytics, the blind, the diseased, the deaf, the possessed. The apostles Paul and Peter took that role when whey wrote letters to struggling groups of believers facing persecution and suffering. What is needed in the face of losses that slowly corrode the human spirit and cause hope to wane is not necessarily more belief in hope, but more energized and enlivened hope. Only when we can think, decide and act on the basis of our believed hope will we be able to face well the losses that come our way.

Hope Absent: The Experience of Despair

Just as we do not know exactly how long the paralytic had come on a daily basis to the porticoes surrounding the pool, we also do not know if he ever lost all hope to the point of despair. If somehow we were able to extract from a person's current functioning all hope in the future, the person would be left in despair. Hopelessness is a state of mind and attitude that sees nothing positive in the future, only things negative. Often such persons are suicidal or will become suicidal in the future (Stotland, 1969). Suicide is a major problem among both believers and unbelievers. Many of us have had an acquaintance end his or her life. It is a problem that must be taken seriously.

> Every 20 to 30 minutes, someone in the United States takes his or her own life. More than 30,000 persons kill themselves each year. Suicide is among the top ten causes of death in the industrialized parts of the world; it is the second or third leading cause of death among young people. Some evidence shows that the number of actual suicides is probably 25 to 30 percent higher than that recorded. (Sue, Sue, & Sue, 1997)

Academic debates attempt to decide if suicide is always an irrational decision or if on some occasions the decision to kill oneself is a rational decision. From a Christian perspective, suicide is morally wrong because it robs from God himself the prerogative of determining the end of life for those whom he loves. Suicide is always tragic, sometimes understandable, but always avoidable.

Research has consistently shown over the years that depression, hopelessness and suicide are all correlated with each other. Hopelessness—the sense that there is no future or, if there is, it is all bleak and negative—is a better predictor of successful suicide than is depression (Sue, Sue, & Sue, 1997). We also know that in most cases suicide is not a single event but an event preceded by periods of suicidal ideation or actual attempts. We can develop programs to inform and educate people about suicide, so that when someone close to us expresses those wishes or otherwise indicates a state of hopelessness or near-hopelessness, proper action can be taken. Suicidal persons respond well to confident reassurances from friends, whereas nervous, anxious responses from friends are usually unhelpful in preventing the suicide (Stotland, 1969).

The Bible records seven suicides (Samson, Saul, Saul's armor bearer, Ahithophel, Zimri, Abimelech and Judas Iscariot). The cast of biblical suicides includes a general, two kings, a judge, an apostle, and a soldier. The story of Judas is the most tragic of all these accounts. We can read the Gospel accounts involving Judas Iscariot time after time and still be bewildered by the man and his actions. In the space of a few hours at the end of the Passion Week, Judas made the final decision to betray Jesus, to sell his positive identification of Jesus to the nation's officials, and to actually carry out the identification. Then he apparently entered a tailspin in which he flung the blood money back at the high priests (Mt 27) before hanging himself and falling headlong to an ignominious death (Acts 1).

Scripture tells us that Judas was filled with remorse because he had betrayed an innocent man (Mt 27:3-4). Was the suicide of Judas preceded by hopelessness? We do not know. Perhaps his intense remorse led him to believe his situation was hopeless when it really was not. Peter also denied the Lord, but found through repentance and forgiveness that he was not hopeless. Judas never found his hope again; Peter did. That is why Peter could write many years later, "Blessed be the God and Father of our Lord Jesus Christ! By his great mercy he has given us a new birth into a living hope through the resurrection of Jesus Christ from the dead (1 Pet 1:3).

Hope Realized: The Experience of Encountering God's Power

Human nature doesn't change very much. If those first-century residents of Jerusalem were anything like us, the paralyzed, blind and sick people lying under those porticoes likely had to endure more than their share of patronizing stares from gawkers and the curious. And on that feast day, they must have thought the approaching band of men and women from up country was just another group of tourists taking in the ghastly sights of the big city. Indeed, Jesus was looking around. He glanced through the suffering group at all those whose pitiable conditions cried out for relief and healing. The implication of the text is that Jesus fixed his glance on the person with the most serious of the conditions, at least the longest lasting. And Jesus of Nazareth spoke to the man.

All of a sudden, the paralytic entered into hope experienced. His previous roller coaster experience with hope had arrived at the loading port. What had waned, waxed, evaporated and floundered was now experienced. His hoped-for dream, healing of body and spirit, had now arrived. When Jesus received an affirmative answer to his first question— yes, the man indeed wanted healing—Jesus uttered a simple three-part command. "Stand up, take your mat and walk" (Jn 5:8). Could it be that simple? The man was healed by the miraculous power of the Messiah. When he tried to get up and walk, something he no doubt had attempted every day for the past thirty-eight years, he could! Off he went with his mat on his back. In his excitement he forgot to notice exactly who the tourist was who had so touched him. When Jewish officials stopped him and accused him of "working" on the Sabbath, the healed man could not give them the name of the man who had healed him. He had been healed by God, but he did not yet know God.

No human experience is quite as powerful as the wonder of being able to see with our own eyes the fulfillment of a burning hope that wells up from deep inside our souls. Sometimes it is the return of a wayward loved one that stirs the heart (Lk 15). Sometimes it is the conversion of a rebellious child or spouse. And sometimes it is a miraculous healing like that of our nameless friend in John 5. The prophetess Anna and the aged man Simeon both rejoiced because their eyes saw their hopes fulfilled in the baby Jesus (Lk 2:25-38). In each instance, the key to realizing the hope and seeing its fulfillment is encountering in a fresh way the power of God. A distinctive feature of Christianity is the means it affords us of establishing a relationship with God and experiencing his power in our lives.

We have seen how experience comes in all forms to each of us on a daily basis. Our basic personality configuration equips us to respond to those experiences with differing degrees of openness and closedness. We are all different in this regard, just as Jesus and Paul probably varied in slight degrees one from the other. But what all followers of Jesus can experience in common is facing those experiences with hope firmly in place. As our belief in hope, our practice of hope and our conscious awareness of the surety of our hope anchor themselves into our experiential lives, we can encounter the experiences of life in a richer, fuller way. Fresh encounters with the power of God as he touches the hopes of our lives are valuable, sacred interactions that every believer treasures.

Therapists, helpers, counselors, pastors and all who are burdened to help others can profit by remembering these principles. When we deal with those who, like us, struggle with floundering, waning or absent hope, one significant way in which we can help is to reacquaint them with the hope of their Christian faith and what it can do for them. For when they are able to experience a fresh touch of God's power in response to their hopes, their lives can be transformed and energized in new ways.

Hope Anticipated: The Experience of Waiting

We do not know what later happened to this man who was healed by the Master on that feast day long ago. We do know that he went to the temple soon after the healing (Jn 5:14). Entering the temple on his own power and with his own mobility was apparently something he had not been able to do for the past thirty-eight years. Jesus found him there in the temple, and then the healed man knew who it was who had healed him. What became of the healed man? Was he a part of the band of disciples who followed Jesus and praised God for the manifest power of the Messiah? Was he, like the nine lepers who had been healed, a person of marked ingratitude? Or was like the one leper whose heart was thrilled with thanksgiving (Lk 17:11-19)? Was the John 5 healed man among those praising Jesus as he rode into Jerusalem on Palm Sunday (Lk 19)? Or could he have cowered at the trials of Jesus and at the crucifixion as one who could not defend the suffering Christ? We simply do not know.

For the sake of our discussion, let us assume that he became a follower of Jesus and that his spiritual life blossomed to the point where we could identify him as a disciple. In spite of his healing experience that day at the Pool of Bethesda, he would still have in his experiential life the need for hope. One encounter with the power of God does not complete our need for hope. This healed and thankful disciple of Jesus would still yearn for the hope of Israel (Lk 1:52-55); he would still anticipate the time when the throne of David would be established forever (2 Sam 7:13); he would still anticipate and hope for the ultimate fulfillment of promises made to his father Abraham (Gen 15).

As disciples in the great age of the church, we too continue to have hope. Not just hope that God will meet our personal needs, but hope that God will fulfill his master plan of the ages. We all need hope that Jesus will return again (1 Thess 4:13-18), hope that God will raise us all in a glorious resurrection unto new life (1 Cor 15), and hope that evil and sin will be one day contained and brought to an end (Rev 20). This sure hope energizes us, helps us keep the present in divine perspective, gives us reason to rejoice even in the midst of suffering, and equips us to see the future as a time frame in which God will be active and victorious.

> For Christian hope is emphatically more than a doubtful wishing— more even than expectation of good. It is trust in God and love in his family; it is securely anchored in the triumph of Christ's resurrection; it is exhibited in the community in which the Holy Spirit lives and acts. (Moule, 1963, pp. 54-55)

Conclusion

Hope is the experience of individuals, of the church and of nations. We began this chapter with a glimpse of hope in the lives of South Africans in 1989, with the release of Nelson Mandela to come a few months later. We conclude with another look at South African hope just before they were able to see their hope realized as the gradual transfer of political power from the minority to the majority was about to begin. The struggle for freedom and democracy in South Africa is but one more example of how hope lodged and firmly held in the human breast can see fulfillment in spite of all odds. Christians around the world joined with the church in South Africa to pray in hope that God would act and that when he did his name would be praised (Stand for Truth, 1989).

As a group of theological educators, we were deeply privileged to visit the homes of families who lived in Soweto, the famous black township in the southwest portion of Johannesburg. We had been busy and were running very late on the day's schedule. Our van began dropping people off at various homes of Christians who had agreed to host the visiting Americans. My roommates and I were dropped off last, and the Funani family had been waiting a considerable amount of time for us to arrive. This black family, like all other blacks at the time, was almost totally unprotected by the constitution of their country. They had no right of assembly, freedom of speech was restricted, they could not own land, and could not vote. They lived in a township wracked by violence and characterized by poor public services—and they were not allowed to live elsewhere.

The Funani family consisted of Lydia Funani, one unmarried daughter, and two married daughters and their families. They had all gathered that night at the house to give us a warm welcome. As privileged as we felt to stay overnight in their home, they expressed an equal amount of pride that we had come to visit them. "You are the first white people ever to stay in our home." The family fed us, took us to their neighbors to introduce us, and generally treated us like royalty. They freely described their Christian faith and how it had sustained them through unbelievably difficult times. And they also expressed hope that soon their country would stand for justice and freedom.

How can this family sustain hope in the midst of their suffering and in the face of such overwhelming odds? was the nagging thought in our minds as we retired for the night. Clearly God had provided them with sustaining hope; no human source could adequately explain their ability to see positives in their future. If God can sustain his own with hope in such circumstances, he can do the same for me and for all those I seek to help. Then when the experiences of life roll over me, I will be able to greet them with both joy and hope.

Section Two

Conscientiousness

Introduction

Jesus & Our Motivational Life

THE SECOND OF THE BIG FIVE PERSONALITY FACTORS IS CONSCIENTIOUSNESS, and it deals with the motivational side of personality. A major part of this conscientiousness factor consists of what is often called character. High scorers are reliable, low scorers lackadaisical; high scorers are disciplined about working toward goals, while low scorers are less concerned about accomplishing goals. People who score on the higher end of this scale are thought to be more mature psychologically because they display greater degrees of self-control and have the ability to plan, organize and execute the tasks of life.

This determination and drive can result in accomplishing some admirable goals. We have all seen examples of great athletes who arrive at their victories because of the sheer determination they display in training, practice and competition. Musical virtuosos do not achieve recognition because they are lazy; rather, they push and drive themselves until their natural talents are perfected and evident to all. Thus a high level of conscientiousness can have a positive outcome and be a commendable feature of a person's personality.

But high levels of conscientiousness can also have a downside. When high scorers overdo their conscientiousness to the point of workaholism or an excessive sense of responsibility, conscientiousness can become a handicap.

A campus wag once posted on a student bulletin board a placard that

read: "Do not feel totally, personally, irrevocably responsible for everything. That's my job. (Signed) God." We have all known people who take
on a much larger sense of responsibility than is warranted; we may at times
have given in to this excess ourselves. We need the reminder that only God
is responsible for everything.

At first glance we might think that one could never be too conscientious. Obviously conscientiousness is most often an admirable and commendable feature of one's character. But too much of a good thing can kill
you. The risks of workaholism, living life with a sense of undue urgency
and extreme competitiveness (all features of Type A behavior), will almost
certainly raise one's blood level of serum cholesterol and increase the
likelihood of coronary heart disease.

When Friedman and Rosenman were writing their classic *Type A
Behavior and Your Heart* (1974), a reporter came to interview them. This
reporter was a hard-driving, chain-smoking journalist whose life was
racing out of control. He listened to the two physicians as they described
their research into Type A behavior. The next year, when the reporter
returned for a follow-up interview, he was remarkably calmer, less verbally
intrusive—clearly a changed man. He had worked hard to lower his
drivenness, thereby increasing the quality and probably the length of his
life. Conscientiousness is a marvelous human motivation, especially when
it is not excessive and extreme.

Human Motivation

In studying human personality we need to explore human motivation—
what it is and how it works. Not all individuals in the same situation will
behave in the same fashion. We explain this difference by looking for
different motivational factors that may move people in different directions.
In the history of the social sciences, great controversies have raged as to
what are the most basic of human motivations. That people are sometimes
motivated by greed, or selfishness, or hunger, or aggression, or desire for
approval, or desire for achievement, or desire to work out some internal
psychological conflict is not in dispute. The disagreements come when
theorists attempt to determine which are the most basic of all these
possibilities and which are merely caused by other, more foundational
factors.

The options suggested in the past century can be grouped as either biological or psychological determinants. Some argue that our animal-like existence is expressed in the biological factors that determine our behavior, be they instincts, fixed action patterns, modal action patterns or vacuum behavior (Benjamin, Hopkins, & Nation, 1994). Others argue that the most basic of human motivations are more psychological. They may be extrinsic or intrinsic, individual or corporate, but they are psychological in nature (Brehm & Kassin, 1996). To these two options, the Christian must add the spiritual dimension as a major component in human motivation. The spiritual side of motivation is tainted by the effects of the Fall. Many of the operative factors in determining what we do and when we do it are sinful in nature. We are motivated by selfishness and self-seeking desires. However, human behavior is a complex mix of many components and probably cannot be adequately accounted for by any single explanation.

The Big Five theory suggests that in the arena of motivation, humans differ along a continuum from high conscientiousness to a very irresponsible set of motivations toward life. The Big Five theory does not suggest why people are where they are on this continuum, nor does it explain how these various degrees of conscientiousness help determine what a given behavior will be in any certain circumstance. The theory is merely descriptive of the varieties of motivational factors among humans.

Subfacets of Conscientiousness

The first of the six subfacets of conscientiousness is *competence,* the degree to which individuals see themselves as capable and effective, wise and realistic. People will score high on this feature of conscientiousness when they feel fairly well-equipped to live life and face its challenges. Low scorers will be individuals who feel inadequate and ill-prepared for life. The competence subfacet scale of the conscientiousness factor is very highly correlated with measures of self-esteem. High scorers will also score high on internal locus of control scales. In other words, they will feel in charge of and in control of how they behave rather than that external forces or circumstances are governing their lives (Costa & McCrae, 1992c).

A second component of conscientiousness is *order.* High scorers are able to organize things and keep them available for use. The opposite of this trait is the proverbial slob who never seems quite able to find the things that need to be in place. Extremes on either end of this subfacet scale can be devastating to the desire to live life efficiently. *Dutifulness* is the third component—the tendency to behave on the basis of one's moral and ethical convictions. Table 5 shows a conjectured score for Jesus as "very high" on this component, a result we all would have predicted for him.

Conscientiousness Facets	Jesus	Paul
Competence	HIGH	AVERAGE
Order	HIGH	AVERAGE
Dutifulness	VERY HIGH	HIGH
Achievement Striving	HIGH	VERY HIGH
Self-Discipline	HIGH	AVERAGE
Deliberation	VERY HIGH	AVERAGE

Table 5. Jesus and Paul on conscientiousness

The remaining subfacets are *achievement striving* (diligence and purposefulness in working toward goals as opposed to aimless satisfaction with very low levels of achievement), *self-discipline* (the ability to apply oneself to tasks in spite of obstacles such as tedium or distractions) and *deliberation* (the ability to think carefully before acting so as to proceed in life with caution as opposed to reckless haste). Some authors have suggested that the desire to achieve is so central to this personality factor that the entire factor should be named "will to achieve" instead of the more common name, conscientiousness (Digman & Inouye, 1986).

The subfacets are intuitively connected to the idea of conscientiousness. Having confidence in yourself coupled with a capacity to be orderly will help you execute duty and obligation. Likewise, seeking to achieve and having the discipline to do it and the wisdom to think carefully before acting all will help you be a conscientious person. It is interesting to note that high scores on conscientiousness have been positively correlated with physical fitness, good health and length of life (Marshall, et al., 1994). High scores on conscientiousness are excellent predictors of success in the work world (Costa & McCrae, 1992a), and some employers are beginning to use this scale as part of the personnel selection process. Bergeman et al. (1993) found on the basis of a large twin study that conscientiousness shows "moderately high heritability and little evidence of shared rearing environment effects" (p. 171).

Jesus and Conscientiousness

Our conjectured scores for both Paul and Jesus (Table 5) show both of them scoring high on this factor with Jesus outscoring Paul. Jesus led a balanced life in all areas, including this area of conscientiousness. He possessed the right amount, not too much or too little of the trait.

> The mark of his individuality was harmonious completeness: of him alone of men, it may truly said that nothing that is human was alien to him, and that all that is human manifested itself in him in perfect proportion and balance. (Warfield, 1912, p. 86)

Does this fact indicate that our spiritual maturity or standing with God will affect how we score on this factor? Must we strive to develop the exact same score as Jesus had on this personality dimension? Does the high scorer please God more than the low scorer? Is there more sin involved in obtaining a low score than there would be for obtaining a high score? Being a reliable person, especially in our relationship with God, is clearly a commendable trait. A large bulk of the biographical material in the Bible seems designed to teach us this lesson. God commends those who complete their obligations and disciplines those who do not. If, as we have seen before, the ability to be a conscientious person is in part a function of our genetic makeup, then clearly some people will have a more difficult time pleasing God in this regard than others. Yet if someone has a far easier time being a conscientious person, that very same person may have a more difficult time following the commands of God in some other area of life.

Regarding the spiritual implications of conscientiousness, we must exercise some caution lest we glorify traits that we admire and cast more aspersions on those who lack them than the Bible does. I recall one incident during my years at a Christian liberal arts college. I regularly made my bed in the mornings, a habit from childhood and perhaps an expression of some of my conscientiousness trait. But one day I remained in bed for part of the morning, having been ill the night before. As I rushed off to class at the last minute, I neglected to perform that daily duty. Sure enough, Mrs. House Mother inspected our dorm room, found the unmade bed and left a kind but slightly condescending note. The note said, in effect, that cleanliness was next to godliness and an unmade bed was certainly not a sign of cleanliness.

Such linkages between desirable traits (cleanliness) and what pleases God (godliness) need to be made with caution, for in the process we can easily say more than the Bible says. Conscientiousness is a trait that likely pleases God but about which we must be cautious in our attribution of spirituality to it.

We will now examine two behavioral expectations that Jesus has of his followers, ones that express our internal motivation system. We must, in all of our conscientiousness or lack thereof, be committed to displaying *mercy* toward those in need and to the pursuit of *justice* on behalf of those who cannot defend themselves. Since the character of God is so centrally and powerfully motivated by both the display of mercy and the pursuit of justice, our motivational systems must likewise be concerned with these two important motivations.

5

Display Mercy

MERCY IS A CENTRAL FEATURE OF GOD'S CHARACTER AND IS A POWERFUL MOTIVA-
tion in his interactions with the human race that he created. Thus mercy
is also to characterize the motivational life of the believer.

Mercy is the compassionate treatment of others, Scripture's version of
what social scientists describe as altruism and prosocial behavior. Showing
mercy is a cardinal feature of the conscientiousness that the followers of
Jesus must display. More specifically, the desire to show mercy is also a key
component of the attitudes that must flow between a therapist and a client
if psychotherapeutic change is to occur.

We must show mercy to receive mercy. Mercy given and mercy received
are both generous blessings. In *The Merchant of Venice* by William Shakespeare, Portia says,

> The quality of mercy is not strain'd,
> It droppeth as the gentle rain from heaven
> Upon the place beneath: It is twice bless'd;
> It blesseth him that gives and him that takes.

Once we have received mercy from the good hand of God, we should
be motivationally compelled to render it more to others who, like us, stand
in great need of mercy. Every follower of God must show mercy in a

multitude of ways. In this chapter we will focus on how the counselor is to show mercy to clients. The function of showing mercy in the counseling relationship, however, is very similar to how all believers are to show mercy to those they encounter in the course of daily life who are in need.

Mercy as Motivation

The motivational domain of personality ranges from high levels of conscientiousness to irresponsibility. When persons are conscientious, they are motivated to face their responsibilities and opportunities with an appropriate sense of duty and commitment. How does the showing of mercy fit into this personality factor? The followers of God are autonomous human beings but in a way that is distinct from the autonomy of those who are not rightly related to God. Scripture teaches that when women and men come into a restored fellowship with God they take their place in a created order or ranking of existence that is quite different from individualism, independence or absolute personal autonomy. The follower of God is aligned first with God, and second with others. We were created, asserts the Bible, for fellowship with God and for proper relationship with others.

The Bible never affirms the modern concept of humans being motivated by seeking what is good for themselves, what enhances their own personal well-being or what satisfies their own personal preferences. Scripture teaches us that such self-centeredness is sinful and an expression of our fallen state.

The Bible does teach that we fulfill our created intent when we align our motivations with the desires of God and focus these motivations on our relationships with God and others. Showing mercy thus becomes a marvelous motivation for the Christian. It prompts us to action because of the boundless mercy God has displayed toward us, thus giving us constant reminders of our relationship with him. And it also moves us to focus on others who need an incarnational expression of God's mercy directed toward them.

In the parable of the good Samaritan, it was not God's direct display of mercy toward the robbery victim that brought relief. It was instead the merciful actions of God through one human toward another. God works through people. Our motivation to show mercy to others is thus Christianity's answer to the common human problem of self-centeredness. One cannot show mercy to others and be primarily selfish or self-absorbed.

Mercy in Scripture

In both the Old and New Testaments a variety of terms is used to denote the concept of mercy. Hence the study of mercy in Scripture becomes a complicated task, for one word in the original language (for example, *hesed* in Hebrew or *eleos* in Greek) does not always denote mercy. Conversely, English translations will utilize the word *mercy* as the translation for several different Hebrew or Greek words. Consistency of the use of *mercy* also varies from one English translation to another. This chapter does not attempt to deal with the sum total of scriptural teaching regarding mercy, but is a representative summary of a vast quantity of material that is very much worth knowing.

The interaction of mercy with psychotherapy is bi-phasic. First, God has extended mercy to those who call upon him and, in our case, to Christian psychotherapists in particular by remembering his promises to us. The pre-eminent display of God's mercy was the sending of his beloved Son to become a Savior for us. The Christian psychotherapist is thus a recipient of God's mercy, one who stands in debt to its benefits, and is thus constrained to be involved in the second phase of mercy's implications for us: psychotherapists are to demonstrate mercy to others, particularly clients, as a fair and obligatory response to mercy received from God. Jesus was the perfect model of how and in what ways this mercy is to be extended toward others. The concept of mercy for the psychotherapist thus has a clear and central Christological content: Jesus is not only the mediator of God's mercy toward us but he is also the model for how we should in turn display mercy toward others.

An important feature of the biblical concept of mercy is that it is always an inner feeling displayed in outward acts, whether the mercy is displayed by God or by those who faithfully serve God. Never is mercy just an idea or an intent; never does it exist in pure emotional form. Nor does mercy ever truly exist just as an act of charity toward others. It is never purely behavior. Rather mercy is a motivation expressed in behavior (a heartfelt behavior or an enacted motivation).

In the time period immediately following the liberation of Israel from Egypt, God revealed himself to his people in new and instructive ways.

"Because the LORD your God is a merciful God, he will neither abandon you nor destroy you; he will not forget the covenant with your ancestors that he swore to them" (Deut 4:31). His mercy is seen in his forgiveness that is freely offered those who confess and in the gracious faithfulness with which he keeps all of his covenants and promises. The mercy of God is great (2 Sam 24:14); Israel could always turn to God and expect mercy because of the underlying covenants that defined their relationship to him.

These themes are repeated and extended in the New Testament. In the birth narrative we find frequent mention of God's mercy. In the sending of a promised Messiah, God had demonstrated his mercy more extensively than anyone had ever before seen. In the Magnificat Mary said, "His mercy is for those who fear him from generation to generation. . . . He has helped his servant Israel, in remembrance of his mercy, according to the promise he made to our ancestors, to Abraham and to his descendants forever" (Lk 1:50, 54-55). Zechariah prophesied that God "has raised up a mighty savior for us. . . . Thus he has shown the mercy promised to our ancestors, and has remembered his holy covenant," and that the prophet John (his son, the Baptist) was given to Israel "by the tender mercy of our God" (Lk 1:69, 72, 78). Clearly the advent of the Messiah was a vivid expression of the mercy of God toward his own.

Elsewhere in the New Testament this theme is extended. Peter writes, "By his great mercy, he has given us a new birth" (1 Pet 1:3). James writes that "the Lord is compassionate and merciful" (Jas 5:11) and that the wisdom that comes from above is "full of mercy" (Jas 3:17). Paul writes, "But God, who is rich in mercy, out of the great love with which he loved us even when we were dead through our trespasses, made us alive together with Christ—by grace you have been saved" (Eph 2:4-5).

Mercy has as its object the misery of persons and its relief. Indeed Scripture records for us numerous examples of those who have found the full measure of their misery satisfied completely in the mercy of God. The book of Genesis says of Lot and his miserable attachment to the wicked city of Sodom, "But he lingered; so the men seized him and his wife and his two daughters by the hand, the LORD being merciful to him, and they brought him out and left him outside the city" (Gen 19:16).

Paul writes in 1 Timothy 1:13 that, though he was a blasphemer, a persecutor and a man of violence, "I received mercy because I had acted ignorantly in unbelief." Epaphroditus received healing. "He was indeed so ill that he nearly died. But God had mercy on him, and not only on him but on me also, so that I would not have one sorrow after another" (Phil 2:27). Elizabeth was a recipient of God's mercy when she delivered her son in her old age. "Her neighbors and relatives heard that the Lord had shown his great mercy to her, and they rejoiced with her" (Lk 1:58).

The Christian counselor can count himself or herself among this great company of those whose misery has been relieved by the bountiful mercy of God. For, by very definition, the Christian counselor is a child of God, one on whom the good news of the gospel has fallen, one who has responded to God's gracious invitation to accept the sacrifice of the Savior as a gift for our salvation. We have experienced God's mercy chiefly through the manifold blessings that come to us in salvation, even though we are unworthy of such marvels of grace.

Yet our misery and our need for mercy are not fully exhausted in the salvation experience. We are told in Scripture that God is pleased when we continue in an attitude that recognizes our ongoing need for mercy, even though we have been made anew by the precious blood of Christ. We see this theme first in numerous places in the psalter. King David, a chosen vessel for God's work, prayed that God's mercy would fall upon him. "Be merciful to me, LORD, for I am faint; O LORD, heal me, for my bones are in agony" (Ps 6:2 NIV). "I said, 'O LORD, have mercy on me; heal me, for I have sinned against you'" (Ps 41:4 NIV). "Have mercy on me, O God, according to your steadfast love; according to your abundant mercy blot out my transgressions" (Ps 51:1). On many of these occasions David was struggling with his own sinful state, an experience not unknown to the Christian and the Christian counselor.

Jesus left us with three parables that explicitly deal with the issue of mercy. The first of these parables (we will look at the other two later in this chapter) deals with the attitude God expects from his own. In the account of the Pharisee and the tax collector who both went up to the temple to pray at the same time, Jesus draws a sharp contrast between the self-serving attitude of the Pharisee and the humble, contrite attitude of the tax collector (Lk 18:9-14). Luke tells us that Jesus spoke this parable for the benefit of those who were confident of their own righteousness and who felt superior to all others. Those with such an attitude are quite obviously represented in this parable by the Pharisee. Jesus said the Pharisee prayed about himself saying, "God, I thank you that I am not like other people: thieves, rogues, adulterers or even like this tax collector. I fast twice a week; I give a tenth of all my income" (Lk 18:11-12). The Pharisee, who commanded respect from the nation and who enjoyed status, access to power and religious affirmation, was boldly declaring to God, in effect, that he needed nothing from God but had everything to offer to God.

The tax collector, who well represented those on the opposite end of the social ladder, was unable to lift his hands and heart toward God. Instead he looked down and beat on his breast as he prayed, "God, be merciful to me, a sinner" (Lk 18:13). Both were standing before God, one aware of his need (the tax collector) and the other just as needy but oblivious to that neediness (the Pharisee).

As Christian counselors and helpers, we can find ourselves on either side of this self-awareness divide. Perhaps we, like the Pharisee, have achieved some measure of stature within the church and in some circles of our society. We can be proud of our service to God and his church, and we can be just as vulnerable as was the Pharisee to self-deception and self-sufficiency. The powerful lesson of this parable, however, is that we must all cultivate a constant attitude of humility before God and exhibit to him a rightful sense of our own need for ongoing mercy from God's good hand.

In prior centuries of the church's history, each worship service contained a *Kyrie eleison* ("Lord, have mercy"). This feature of early Christian worship was based on the Gospel accounts where needy people cried out for Jesus to have mercy on them. Repeatedly in the Gospels we hear from the lips of miserable people the *Kyrie eleison*. "Have mercy on us, Son of David" (two blind men, Mt 9:27). "Have mercy on me, Lord, Son of David" (the Canaanite woman on behalf of her demon-possessed daughter, Mt 15:22). "Lord, have mercy on my son" (a man on behalf of his epileptic son, Mt 17:15). "Lord, have mercy on us, Son of David" (shouted loudly and repeatedly by two blind men outside Jericho, one of whom was probably Bartimaeus, Mt 20:30 and Mk 10:47). The Gerasene demoniac of Mk 5 was unable to cry out to Jesus on his own behalf for mercy because of his miserable psychotic condition. But Jesus told him, after he had been completely restored, "Go home to your friends, and tell them how much the Lord has done for you, and what mercy he has shown you" (Mk 5:19). These people all knew in a direct, heartfelt manner of their own personal need for mercy from God.

Today most nonliturgical evangelical churches have eliminated the *Kyrie eleison* from their worship services. Have we lost sight of the important lesson of the Luke 18 parable? "I tell you, this man went down to his home justified rather than the other; for all who exalt themselves will be humbled, but all who humble themselves will be exalted" (Lk 18:14). As the author of the book of Hebrews writes, "Let us therefore approach the throne of grace with boldness, so that we may receive mercy and find grace to help in time of need" (Heb 4:16).

Mercy in Early Christian Worship

Believers first met in the houses of believers on a daily basis (Acts 2:46). Later they chose to gather principally on the first day of the week (a day not yet named "Sunday" in Jewish circles), a day on which they celebrated the resurrection every week. The concept of a yearly "Easter" was to come later in the history of the church (Cullmann, 1953). Their services consisted of preaching, prayer, the earliest of which is the *maranatha* ("Come, Lord Jesus"), and the breaking of bread. Confession, benedictions and the liturgical "amen" are also found quite early in the development of Christian worship. In both the East and the West, the ancient Christian church frequently prayed, "Lord, have mercy." The free church tradition in contemporary America has almost totally lost this ancient connection with mercy in regular forms of worship.

For us as evangelicals, what are the consequences of disconnecting ourselves from our need to plead for and experience God's ongoing mercy? We miss a vital opportunity to ground our own expressions of mercy to other people in the mercy we have freshly received from God on a daily basis. When we show mercy to others, then, we do it from an inadequate base. We can lose sight of our frailty, our dependence on God's care and our vulnerability to harm. We can falsely assume that we are safe, secure and barely in need of God's sustaining mercy. Theologically we can be secure in the salvation so freely offered to us, but such positional security does not remove us from our need to experience protection and mercy from God. Perhaps we need to explore ways of reconnecting with ancient worship styles that helped believers realize on a weekly basis just how dependent we are on God. Only then will we be fully prepared to show the amount of mercy to others that faithfully mirrors the amount of mercy that has been shown to us by the Father of Mercies.

The Client and God's Mercy

As recipients of God's mercy, we are commanded to show mercy to others. The fifth beatitude says, "Blessed are the merciful, for they will be shown mercy" (Mt 5:7). The words of Jesus as recorded in Luke 6:36 say, "Be merciful just as your Father is merciful." Thus every believer must make the task of showing mercy to others an important part of life. For the Christian counselor, the most readily available population to whom we can show mercy consists of our clients. Because the counselor has experienced mercy from the hand of God, our clients must also experience mercy from our ministries to them so that they in turn can experience some of the goodness of God's mercy and can learn more about his character.

We first observed that the vertical dimension of our experience with mercy is principally mediated through the work of Jesus Christ. Now as we examine the horizontal aspects of our engagement with mercy we see that it too revolves around the person and work of Jesus during his early ministry. Jesus went about showing God's mercy to others and is the model for us as we are committed to the same task.

The Mercy Ministry of Jesus

Jesus deliberately placed great emphasis on his ministry of showing mercy by choosing to perform a celebrated act of mercy on the sabbath in a manner that would surely come to the attention of the Pharisees. The first of two incidents occurred as Jesus was walking through a field of grain with his hungry disciples. They picked some heads of grain and ate them. To the hair-splitting Pharisees such an act was "harvesting," which in turn was "work" and so could not be performed on the sabbath. So they leveled the charge that Jesus and his disciples were breaking the law. Jesus replied, "If you had known what this means, 'I desire mercy and not sacrifice,' you would not have condemned the guiltless. For the Son of Man is lord of the sabbath" (Mt 12:7-8).

Jesus was quoting from Hosea 6:6, a major text that teaches us how important the showing of mercy is to God. God would rather see his people displaying mercy than offering him a sacrifice in the temple. Jesus also quoted the Hosea text in the account recorded in Matthew 9:13, when Jesus was upbraided by Pharisees for eating with "sinners" and tax collectors, the very people to whom Jesus wanted to show mercy. The Pharisees had succeeded in relegating the showing of mercy to a far lower level of priority, and Jesus chastised them for belittling mercy in that manner.

On the same Sabbath on which Jesus had "harvested" grain, he healed the withered hand of a man who was sitting by their synagogue. Those very same Pharisees had no doubt passed this man by, ignoring his need while they went in to worship on the Sabbath. Jesus showed how important mercy was to him by deliberately engaging the Pharisees in this debate. The Pharisees demonstrated how little importance they placed on the showing of mercy by immediately plotting "how to destroy him" (Mt 12:14). Later Jesus said to the Pharisees,

> You tithe mint, dill, and cummin, and have neglected the weightier matters of the law: justice and mercy and faith. It is these you ought to have practiced without neglecting the others. You blind guides! You strain out a gnat but swallow a camel!" (Mt 23:23-24)

The words of Jesus here echo the famous words of Micah 6:8: "He has showed you, O man, what is good. And what does the LORD require of you? To act justly and to love mercy and to walk humbly with your God" (NIV). Indeed, the acts of Jesus prepared him for his current ministry in heaven on our behalf. "Therefore he had to become like his brothers and sisters in every respect, so that he might be a merciful and faithful high priest in the service of God" (Heb 2:17).

The Mercy Ministry of the Christian Counselor

How does the Christian counselor express mercy to clients? The following set of suggestions is but one approach to linking mercy to the work of the therapist:

1. The counselor acknowledges and is aware of personal benefit obtained from the boundless mercy of God.

2. In response to this blessed state, the counselor determines to obey

the injunctions of Scripture and to show mercy to others by following the example of Jesus.

3. This process of displaying mercy to others begins with compassion for and attention to the misery of others.

4. Empathy forms out of this wellspring of compassion since the counselor is well aware of her or his own misery that has been the object of God's mercy.

5. The client experiences the expression of mercy, now cast in the framework of compassionate empathy, and benefits from it.

6. The Christian counselor explicitly or implicitly give God the glory for this expression of mercy by making its expression a clear component of Christian witness. Thus the Christian counselor faithfully reveals the character of God to those in need.

Such is not the end of the role that mercy can play in undergirding our Christian therapy ministries. The life of Jesus illustrates what happens when the mercy of God is dispensed faithfully. People begin to come looking for this mercy. During the lifetime of Jesus, miserable people recognized the tremendous and rare opportunity they had to receive mercy from one so willing to display it. The same experience comes the way of the Christian counselor who faithfully attempts to show the mercy of God to miserable people. They recognize that such understanding is rare in the world and that they need to come to where it is available. The world has yet to deplete its supply of misery, and the committed Christian psychotherapist has an almost unlimited opportunity to display the mercy that our miserable world so needs and wants.

The Christian counselor's display of mercy is but one expression of the obligation all Christians share, namely to follow the model of the merciful Jesus. Sobrino (1994) likens the task of showing mercy that we all share to what happened to the body of Jesus after his death on the cross. Joseph of Arimathea, a rich man who was a disciple of Jesus, went to the official courts of Pilate and requested the corpse of Jesus. Pilate ordered that the body be given to Joseph. "So Joseph took the body and wrapped it in a clean linen cloth and laid it in his own new tomb, which he had hewn in the rock" (Mt 27:59-60). Our acts of mercy are, in effect, similar to this act of Joseph's, according to Sobrino, whose book is entitled *The Principle of Mercy: Taking the Crucified People from the Cross.* Bearing the burden of others is the doing of mercy (Storms, 1991).

The therapist occupies a natural and logical arena for the display of mercy: the relationship the therapist builds between self and client.

> Man's mercy . . . is understood in the context of a relationship; and the human relationship thus becomes part of the relationship to God. To truly love God, one must also love one's neighbor. Mercy given to man was homage rendered to the Lord. (Achtemeier, 1962, p. 353)

Whether a follower of Jesus has been granted a special spiritual gift of showing mercy (see Rom 12:8) or not, the obligation to be merciful as our heavenly Father is merciful is incumbent on all followers of Jesus.

The second of Jesus' parables on mercy is widely known as the parable of the unmerciful servant (Mt 18:21-35). Here the emphasis is on a poor example of what it means to show mercy to others. A servant owed a great deal of money to the king. Because the servant was unable to pay the debt (as all of us are unable to pay for the salvation we have been given), the servant pleaded for mercy, a plea the king kindly heard and granted (salvation comes to us as a free gift). The king's decision was a reprieve of what otherwise would have happened to the debtor. The king had ordered him "to be sold, together with his wife and children and all his possessions, and payment to be made" (Mt 18:25). Instead, he totally forgave the man's debt.

The debtor who had thus been shown the king's generous mercy later encountered a colleague who owed him a far smaller amount than his own debt to the king, now canceled, had been. The debtor to whom mercy had been shown immediately demanded payment of the lesser debt. When his colleague pleaded for mercy, none was granted. Instead, the now unmerciful debtor had his friend thrown in jail.

The king later exploded in rage at the lack of mercy displayed by the debtor, who should have known better. The king reinstated the forgiven debt and ordered the first debtor tortured until the total sum was repaid! Of the king's behavior, Jesus said, "So my heavenly Father will also do to every one of you, if you do not forgive your brother or sister from your heart" (Mt 18:35). Sobering words from the otherwise merciful Jesus. The consequences are severe to the person who has been shown mercy but who refuses to grant it to others. As James writes, "So speak and so act as those who are to be judged by the law of liberty. For judgment will be without mercy to anyone who has shown no mercy; mercy triumphs over judgment" (Jas 2:12-13).

The third parable Jesus told dealing with the subject of mercy is much more familiar: the parable of the good Samaritan (Lk 10:25-37). This parable again highlights the central place held by the requirement to display mercy in the economy of God's kingdom. Jesus told this parable in response to the query of a legal expert, "And who is my neighbor?" (Lk 10:29). The question was a legitimate one; if the second greatest commandment is to love one's neighbor as oneself, we do need to know just who is a neighbor. The answer found in the parable of the Good Samaritan is that a neighbor is anyone we encounter in need.

The Christian counselor again finds himself or herself in a natural context for this display of mercy. The population served by Christian therapists, is, by definition, in need. We do not have to travel a lonely, treacherous stretch of highway from Jerusalem to Jericho to encounter needy people. They fill our caseloads and waiting rooms.

Again, Jesus sharply contrasts what the non-display of mercy looks like with what true merciful acts look like. When people do not display mercy, as was the case with the religiously qualified but heartless priest and the hypocritical Levite, needs go unmet, and the miserable and dying people of this world do not receive an expression of God's mercy. But the despised Samaritan, who had endured painful racism and rejection from the very people who passed by the wounded traveler, himself stopped to administer mercy. His act as memorialized in this well-known parable has forever changed the reputation of Samaritans. Now we almost automatically think of them as "good" because of this one example of giving mercy. At the end of the parable Jesus asked which of these three people had been a neighbor to the robbed man. The answer given by the expert in the law was correct: "The one who showed him mercy." "Go and do likewise," replied Jesus (Lk 10:37).

Specific Applications

Showing mercy versus giving empathy. We have seen how the process of displaying mercy (its internal affective state and its praxis, both of which are necessary for the full display of mercy) is encompassed by the parallel process of compassion and empathy. Every counselor must be skilled in the application of empathy and compassion to the problems of clients. This basic skill forms the bedrock of the profession, and no therapist can survive without knowing how to offer empathy in an effective manner to hurting clients. If the expression of compassion and empathy is thus so common among therapists, Christian and non-Christian alike, why should we seek to link it to the display of mercy? Is not it sufficient that Christian counselors are empathetic? Should that not suffice?

The answer is no. It is very possible for us to be empathetic with needy people just because that is what good counselors do. We have extensive training in the "niceness" of our profession: the giving of respect, genuine caring and unconditional positive regard. Christian therapists can offer these approaches to clients with a vague sense that such respect is surely Christian and is consistent with our faith. But if the Christian counselor does not envision the expression of these qualities to clients as a direct extension of our Christian obligation to show mercy, he or she will neglect giving due consideration to this most important scriptural duty.

Counseling is a ministry. It is a ministry not because we do it with Christians or in connection with the general ministries of the church but because it gives us the opportunity to obey Christ, to follow his example, and to honor God by being merciful even as God has been merciful to us.

Resistance and non-compliance. Both resistance and non-compliance from a client provide a perfect yet challenging arena in which the therapist can display mercy. In this age of quick therapies, one might be tempted to think that the issue of non-cooperation with treatment, both conscious and unconscious, will soon be only a feature of the therapeutic landscape of the past. But upon reflection we must admit that everywhere, in all modalities of treatment and in any of the varying lengths of therapy, clients will at times express resistance to the direction of intervention selected by the therapist or show noncompliance with what the therapist indicates as best (Blackstone, 1991; Kottler & Blau, 1989). Observers of the therapeutic scene are uniform in their assessment of the difficulty of handling both resistance and non-compliance in a way that facilitates process and serves the best interests of the client (Mahoney, 1991).

The burned-out therapist and the careless counselor or the therapist locked in some convoluted countertransference trap, be they Christian or non-Christian, can easily respond to these difficulties in treatment with behavior in kind. We are skilled at applying none-too-flattering labels to such people; we can downgrade their diagnoses to one of the lower ranges of pathology; we can harbor feelings of resentment and dislike for the uncooperative client. Therapists all know better than to succumb to these temptations, but, imperfect as we are, we surely do fail some of the time.

For the Christian therapist who is consciously aware of the continual obligation we have to search for opportunities to display mercy, a client's resistance or noncompliance gives us the perfect occasion to offer mercy. True mercy does not condemn, coddle, hamper, or patronize clients. It does offer second chances, additional understanding and compassion, reflection and renewed effort. Resistant clients are silently but intensely crying out, "Please have mercy on us, for we are thoroughly confused and stuck in our misery."

Therapists must be aware of justice issues in the execution of their responsibilities to clients and to society. Mercy and justice are both themes that demand the attention of every therapist; they also require us to implement our Christian convictions in difficult situations. Shakespeare wrote on mercy with keen insight as he penned for Portia lines in *The Merchant of Venice* (IV), "It is enthroned in the heart of kings, it is an attribute to God himself; and earthly power doth then show likest God's when mercy seasons justice." Murphy writes that mercy "flows from a certain kind of character—a character disposed to perform merciful acts from love or compassion while not losing sight of the importance of justice" (Murphy, 1988, p. 166). Clients who resist or exercise non-compliance force us as therapists to wrestle with the issues of both justice and mercy. We will address justice issues more specifically in the next chapter.

Apathy and chronicity. Some clients do not resist or fight progress in the therapeutic enterprise—they just do not seem to work hard at the process. Our ethical obligation in these situations has been clearly delineated in recent editions of ethical codes. When clients are not making progress or when the therapy is no longer beneficial to them, we must take steps to refer them to others or in other ways take action to facilitate their progress and improvement.

But the ethical standards in this regard do not remove from our practices all evidence of therapeutic languor and apparent indifference. These client characteristics may sometimes be only temporary in nature, but they are always frustrating and annoying to the therapist. The apathy of a client who continues to need care and treatment but who does not seem energized enough to pursue it effectively can trigger any number of reactions on the part of the therapist. Christian or non-Christian counselors alike can react to a client's indifference as if it were an assault on the competence and self-worth of the therapist. After all, are not we well trained? Should not people be grateful for the insightful help we can provide? Are not our skills so effective that we assist people in the ideal amount of time? Why do not these clients whose needs seem chronic get better and move on from our caseloads?

Again, mercy is the Christian grace we need to learn to apply in such frustrating situations. The matchless patience and longsuffering of God on our behalf, the gentle prompting of the Spirit that nudges us periodically toward greater zeal for God, and the example of the patience of Jesus with his often apathetic disciples give us challenging examples to follow. Our display of mercy to the apathetic client can serve as a powerful lesson to the client regarding the rich, full and constant mercy of God toward all of us.

Fee for service and the granting of mercy. Critics of Christian counseling, especially its private-practice expressions, have consistently argued that the Christian counselor is participating in an endeavor that is fundamentally flawed in its conception. How can you charge for your services if, at the same time, you seek to maintain that your work is a ministry and an expression of mercy toward the miserable? Are you not making money, and exorbitant levels of income at that, from the suffering and unhappiness of people? If you say that most mental illness is not the result of personal irresponsibility, how can you charge money from these people in exchange for helping them with problems they did not create? Is not this practice a modern form of simony? These questions are honest and deserve honest answers. And they raise some fundamental issues with which we must struggle. The entire mental health field struggles to know how best to deal with fees (Tulipan, 1986).

Our response to these questions of integrity revolves around several facts. First, showing mercy is not the only engagement we are making with our clients. We are also providing them with professional care that our society has come to expect in certain painful circumstances of life.

Second, we are committed to devoting our total energy to this cause and thus do not have the opportunity to support ourselves via other means of income. An alternative to this arrangement would be for all therapists to function bivocationally but to use the nontherapeutic job as the only source of income. While not impossible, such an arrangement would present a host of difficulties. Another option would be for churches to support a counselor so that no direct fees would have to be charged to the client. Most churches, however, have been very reluctant—or simply unable—to subsidize such ministries to the degree that would be necessary.

Third, the issue of client motivation is involved in sorting out this issue. Our culture values what is costly, not what is provided free of charge. Critics might counter that we cannot design our ethics around the fallen preferences of our post-Christian culture, but the reality remains: many people in our society are willing and, most of the time, able to pay for what they receive in terms of professional help with their problems. Of course, delivering counseling services to people whose income levels are too low to pay is a substantial problem. They literally cannot afford such care.

Fourth, Christian therapists of good conscience strive to make their services available to those who cannot afford them or who are in dire financial straits. Never can or should the giving of mercy be contingent on financial capability. Nor should our acts of mercy exploit, manipulate or otherwise demean those who are languishing in their misery. Instead, we must constantly strive to make our expressions of mercy charitable, kind, compassionate, always offering mercy to people in the name of Jesus Christ and for the glory of God. We have no greater opportunity by which to express the human motivation of conscientiousness.

6

Pursue Justice

THE HUMAN PERSONALITY CONTAINS A MOTIVATIONAL DOMAIN THAT IS CENTRAL to our functioning. Totally unmotivated persons are essentially vegetablelike in that they accomplish nothing; they are inert, completely inactive. Activity and accomplishment are predicated upon some type of underlying motivational system that prompts and fuels the person to act. The Big Five factor theory of personality suggests that this motivational domain varies in its qualities: some people's motivational lives are characterized by intense levels of conscientiousness and some by minimal levels of responsibility.

We have seen how God requires that his followers have responsible levels of conscientiousness in order to please him. In order to be faithful, to obey with regularity the commands of God and to be consistent disciples, we must display a fair amount of conscientiousness. Persons who score very low on conscientiousness measures thus may have to employ specific spiritual correctives in their obedience to the Lord.

Pursuing justice is, surprisingly, a controversial subject among evangelical Christians. Shouldn't it be obvious that Christians should be at the forefront of the pursuit of justice? Isn't this teaching so clear and obvious in the Bible that no one could dispute it? The fact is that when evangelical believers talk about justice, the discussion almost immediately gets entangled in a host of related controversies and unsettled issues. Evangelicals in the United States have succeeded in subordinating justice to just about everything else.

Why are we so deathly afraid of the topic of justice? Here are four contributing factors.

1. We are descendants of the fundamentalist battles earlier in this century against theological liberalism. A key element in those battles was the attendant social and sociological issues that complicated the matter. Theological liberals were committed to the pursuit of social justice, often, as the conservatives alleged, at the expense of evangelism or the preaching of the gospel. Our fundamentalist forebears strove diligently to forge back into the central mission of the church the clear preaching of the saving gospel of Jesus Christ. Social justice had to take a back seat in that struggle, and evangelicals have been distrustful of the pursuit of justice ever since.

2. Pursuing justice, as we shall see, can be a very unsettling and disruptive process. By definition, pursuing justice occurs in arenas where injustice reigns and where change must occur if the situation is to be remedied according to God's standards. The pursuit of justice requires change and reform, both of which can be threatening to the comfortable status quo.

3. Persons who live in the shadow of justice, who are able to attain their goals, who do not regularly suffer the indignity of injustice can easily insulate themselves from situations where justice is not the common experience of people. If I benefit consistently from just treatment that is fair, and that gives me freedom and opportunity, I may assume it's the same for everyone. Basking in the benefits of justice makes it difficult for us to realize that such is not the experience of all people.

4. Evangelicals have consistently spiritualized justice, righteousness and the just to refer only to personal, internal conditions of one's relationship to God. This spiritualizing of the concept is surprising given the typical abhorrence that evangelicals have for spiritualizing hermeneutics. Restricting the concept of justice or righteousness only to its spiritual connotations results in a dismissal of all other features of the concept of justice, some of which we will discuss in this chapter.

As a result, the pursuit of justice can sometimes suffer from benign neglect among evangelicals. We often like to focus on other topics that are not so complicated and personally costly. During the nuclear arms struggles of the 1980s, politically and religiously liberal groups worked hard on "peace and justice" issues. Peace and justice became their hallmarks. When evangelicals sought to address these serious and threatening human problems, they devised a "peace and freedom" campaign. Peace and freedom were themes far more comfortable than the unnerving requirements of pursuing justice (Beck, 1988).

What Is Justice?

Justice is a normative principle "for evaluating and harmonizing conflicting claims of rights, duties, and responsibilities" (Rhoades, 1990, p. 1189). Justice is obviously far simpler for God to execute than it is for humans to administer. God knows everything, can weigh all the factors involved in a situation with the greatest of fairness and accuracy, and has the power to enforce justice wherever and whenever it is needed. Humans are not so blessed. We often cannot determine inner motivations and hidden factors that impact an unjust event. We cannot know all the factors that influence injustice, and we are often powerless to act effectively in circumstances where we might wish to impose justice.

The pursuit of justice is made necessary by the presence of sin in human affairs. If it were not for the presence of sin in the world, we would not have to worry about justice. Our sinful bents propel us to treat persons unequally, to overestimate or underestimate what is right, and to indulge in excessive retribution or lenient vindication. It is even true that the just side of God's character is revealed only in the presence of rebellion, sin and defiance on the part of humans or angels.

A classical approach to the theory of justice (Aristotelian) discusses two main types of justice: universal and particular. Nash (1983) argues that the Aristotelian concept of universal justice, in a Christian context, refers to the personal righteousness that the gospel bestows on those who believe in it. Particular justice is divided into three types: (a) commercial justice (fairness with regard to economic exchanges, just weights and so on), (b) remedial justice (fairness in the legal sense, equal application of the law to all persons), and (c) distributive justice (sometimes called social justice, equal opportunities afforded to all persons). Even further distinctions can be made. For example, in the legal sense one can favor three different

approaches to crime: retribution, justice (fairness to victims and perpetra-
tors alike) or therapy (rehabilitation, retraining) (Murphy, 1979).

In the Bible, two Greek words are used to convey justice. First, *dikaios*
is an adjective translated "upright," "just" or "righteous." Justice and
righteousness are highly related concepts in Scripture. In fact, "the original
Hebrew and Greek words [for justice] are the same as those rendered
"righteousness" (Rall, 1955, p. 1781). Translators must use the context to
determine whether to use "justice" or "righteousness" as the English
translation for these words.

In a legal sense, godly people can be described as "just" when they
conform to the laws of God and humans and live in accordance with them.
Thus Joseph (Mt 1:19), a good bishop (Tit 1:8) and one who does right (1
Jn 3:7) are all described as just persons. Regarding adherence to the laws
of God in a meritorious sense, the standards are much higher. Romans 3:10
says, "There is no one righteous *[dikaios]*, not even one." The meaning
here is that no one can be fair enough, just enough or righteous enough
to earn merit toward salvation with God. Only through the substitutionary
death of Christ can a person earn righteousness in a meritorious sense. A
second word *(krisis)* is used in the New Testament specifically of justice.

Justice is related to mercy. In a legal sense, if God applied absolute
justice to us without any of the amelioration that mercy brings, we would
sustain the wrath of God in our lives and experience. Refusing God's mercy
leaves us no hope but to face God's justice and judgment. "Let us hope for
her mercy. For judgment is mercy rejected" (McCaslin, 1994, p.1). The
application of justice to those suffering from injustice is merciful and a
generous display of God's mercy. So in many ways justice and mercy are
intermingled. Together they serve as magnificent motivations for the
believer. When we can allow these motivations to characterize our lives
we will become more Christlike and better imitators of the character of
God himself.

Pursuing Justice as a Human Motivation

The study of justice in the secular world of scholarship is characterized by
widespread disagreement. "Indeed, the exploration is complicated at the
outset because there is precious little agreement as to how the arena justice
is to be characterized and defined" (Lebacqz, 1986, p. 10). Over the

centuries several different approaches have emerged, including the utilitarian view of John Stuart Mill. In this century alone, the approaches to justice have varied greatly. John Rawls advocates a contract approach; Robert Nozick speaks of entitlement as the basis of justice. The National Conference of Catholic Bishops in the United States advocates a corporate approach to the topic over against a purely individualistic perspective. Reinhold Niebuhr stresses the role of sin and takes a dialectical approach to justice and love. Liberation theology seeks to expose how institutions perpetuate injustice; it advocates changing these institutional systems as a means of pursuing justice. All of this variation, mainly in the arena of distributive justice, makes the study of justice complex.

Lerner (1980) argues that most people carry with them an implicit belief in a just world (BJW) that is fundamental in our society. The belief is that people get what they deserve, and a corollary is the conviction that I have what I have because I deserve it. Obviously, this BJW theory is mainly the province of those who live with the benefit of justice and prosperity working for and with them as opposed to against them.

The two "bases for entitlement or deserving," among those who hold to the BJW theory, are one's behavior and one's attributes. In other words, people have what they have because they have earned it by their behavior, or they deserve it because of their attributes. Lerner argues that we defend our belief in a just world against all contradictory evidence by using rational or nonrational defenses. Rationally we apply social services to the alleviation of distress without any attempt to address more underlying causes of the injustice; we also seek to accept our own limitations that prevent us from dealing with all the injustice of the world.

Nonrationally, we defend our belief in a just world against contradictory evidence by denial of or withdrawal from examples of injustice.

> This is a primitive device, but it works. All it requires is an intelligent selection of the information to which one is exposed. And it has the added advantage of requiring no direct distortion of reality. If you have any sense, you arrange not to see what is happening in the ghettoes, in the poverty-stricken areas of the country or the world. You don't make a practice of hanging around emergency rooms, mental hospitals, or homes for the mentally "disadvantaged." If you

do, by some mischance, see a crime or a terrible accident, or meet someone who is blind or crippled, then get . . . out of there. Leave the scene physically, and hopefully, with the help of other diversions, the event will leave your mind. (Lerner, 1980, p. 20)

Another nonrational defense we can use to maintain our belief that the world really is a just place if we simply live right and do the right things is to reinterpret the data so that the outcome of "injustice" is seen as a good rather than a bad outcome, or to reinterpret the cause of the injustices ("They brought it on themselves"), or to cast aspersions on the character of the victims so as to make them appear deserving of the injustice.

By and large, in the long run, for people like us, it is a just world. We can, for the most part, with our share of "the breaks," get what we want, what we are willing to work for, what we deserve. Of course, we recognize that the world of victims exists, and that something can and will be done about it, but we can't let that interfere with how we live our own lives and what we can do for our families. (Lerner, 1980, p. 26)

Psychological experiments have confirmed some aspects of this theory. Subjects in laboratory experiments have shown tendencies to prefer that good things happen to attractive people and less good things happen to less attractive people; if the outcome if different from our preferences, we are upset. Normal people will try to intervene when an injustice occurs, but if they fail to be effective in the intervention, they will then resort to a condemnation of the victim. All of these cognitions appear to be efforts to buttress our underlying belief in a just world. We do not want to give up that belief.

Justice in Scripture
Research in the social sciences is not as helpful to our discussion, however, as a survey of what Scripture teaches us about justice. As we have already seen with mercy, justice is a central concern of God and has characterized his interactions with his people from the very beginning. In Exodus 2 we read how Jehovah heard the groaning and saw the suffering of his people in the land of Egypt. "I have heard their cry on account of their taskmasters. Indeed, I know their sufferings, and I have come down to deliver them

from the Egyptians, and to bring them up out of that land to a good and broad land, a land flowing with milk and honey" (Ex 3:7-8).

God's response to the injustice his people were suffering was a grand and glorious rescue intervention. The Bible has always thus been good news for the poor and the suffering, because it reveals the character of God, who

> loves justice (Is 61:8); is a stronghold to the poor and needy (Is 25:4; Ps 9:9); hears the desire of the meek, strengthens their hearts, and does justice to the orphan and the oppressed (Ps 10:17-18); hears the groans of the prisoners and sets free those who are doomed to die (Ps 102:20); hears the cry of the hungry (Ps 107:4-6); raises the poor from the dust and lifts the needy from the ash heap (Ps 113:7); . . . maintains the cause of the afflicted and executes justice for the needy (Ps 140:12). (Nelson, 1980, p. 184)

The laws God gave the ancient nation of Israel reflect his standards regarding righteousness and justice. Weights and measures were to be accurate (Lev 19:35-36). Justice was to prevail in the courts of the land so that rich, poor, citizen and alien were all treated alike. To be obedient to the law, God's people had to actively seek to establish justice where none existed. Later the prophets were to preach their thunderous message that when the leaders of the nation failed to establish justice for the disadvantaged within their borders they had violated a central feature of the law. The prophets would speak against the injustice of people who in many other ways appeared very religious (Gallardo, 1983).

> I hate, I despise your festivals,
> and I take no delight in your solemn assemblies.
> Even though you offer me your burnt offerings and grain offerings,
> I will not accept them;
> and the offerings of well-being of your fatted animals
> I will not look upon.
> Take away from me the noise of your songs;
> I will not listen to the melody of your harps.
> But let justice roll down like waters,
> and righteousness like an ever-flowing stream. (Amos 5:21-24)

God loves justice and does justice because he cares so deeply for the victims of injustice, for even the one out of a hundred (Wolterstorff, 1986). He is a God who

> executes justice for the oppressed;
> who gives food to the hungry.
> The LORD sets the prisoners free;
> the LORD opens the eyes of the blind.
> The LORD lifts up those who are bowed down;
> the LORD loves the righteous.
> The LORD watches over the strangers;
> he upholds the orphan and the widow,
> but the way of the wicked he brings to ruin. (Ps 146:7-9)

These themes are repeated many times in Scripture. "Father of orphans and protector of widows is God in his holy habitation" (Ps 68:5). The test of whether or not a society is just and is interested in the justice that moves the heart of God is how its defenseless citizens are treated. "The test is not whether the economically powerful have enough to eat—they almost always do; but whether the economically power*less* have enough" (Wolterstorff, 1986, p. 10). This long tradition in the nation of Israel is repeated in instructions to the New Testament church when its leaders are constantly challenged to provide for widows and others in need, especially those of the household of faith (Gal 6:10).

These themes continue in the New Testament. "The way of the gospel and the way of justice cannot be separated" (Zorilla, 1988, p. 79). Jesus taught that when the Son of Man comes at the end of the age, He will mete out judgment (retributive justice) on the basis of how people pursued or did not pursue distributive justice. Those whom he will sort to his right (the sheep) are those who gave the thirsty something to drink and the stranger some shelter; those whom he will sort to his left (the goats) are those who did not clothe those who needed clothes or look after those who were sick and in prison (Mt 25:31-46). "A passion for Jesus leads his followers to have a passion for justice" (Bruland & Mott, 1983, p. 8). The Bible then describes in extensive detail the love of God for justice, based on his deep caring and concern for the victims of injustice. "The sheer volume of biblical material that pertains to questions of hunger, justice, and the poor is astonishing" (Sider, 1980, p. 3). Again we must ask, how can it be that the pursuit of justice so often gets overlooked and downplayed in evangelical circles?

Sometimes we are tempted to dodge the demands of pursuing justice by relegating the Old Testaments commands to do justice to the economy of the Old Covenant. We say that what applied to Israel is different from what applies to the church. Or that the emphasis of the New Testament has shifted to the spiritual aspects of righteousness and justice, and that God's concerns for justice are now fulfilled in his desire that no one would perish but that all would come to faith in Christ (2 Pet 3:9).

While it is true that the New Testament reveals more to us about the spiritual dimensions of righteousness and justice, that in no way cancels out the extensive revelation in the Old Testament about God's heartbeat for justice; it simply expands on it. We have seen how Jesus clearly taught that God's concerns are still focused on how we treat the poor, the prisoner, the naked and the alien (Mt 25). And again James is clear when he writes, "Religion that is pure and undefiled before God, the Father, is this: to care for orphans and widows in their distress, and to keep oneself unstained by the world" (Jas 1:27). No amount of dodging, theological or otherwise, will help us escape the powerful example of justice given to us by the life of Christ himself, a subject we shall now address.

Jesus and Justice

In our discussion of mercy, we examined the Matthew 12 account of Jesus healing the man with a shriveled hand on the Sabbath. Immediately following that passage is a comment by Matthew that the healing work of Jesus at that point in his ministry was a fulfillment of the prophecies of Isaiah 42:1-4. Notice how justice is a prominent feature of the promised Messiah.

> Here is my servant, whom I have chosen,
> my beloved, with whom my soul is well pleased.
> I will put my Spirit upon him,
> and he will proclaim justice to the Gentiles.
> He will not wrangle or cry aloud,

> nor will anyone hear his voice in the streets.
> He will not break a bruised reed
> or quench a smoldering wick
> until he brings justice to victory.
> And in his name the Gentiles will hope. (Mt 12:18-21)

A major feature of the work of Jesus the Messiah is the proclamation of justice.

We have seen that one of the two words used in the New Testament for justice is *krisis*. The most frequent meaning of the word *krisis* in the New Testament is judgment. Judgment, of course, is closely related to justice because when God makes judgments for or against people, he is using his standard of justice as the guide or standard on which to base his decisions. The Gospel of John contains many of the occurrences of *krisis* when it is used in the sense of judgment. In a discourse of Jesus recorded only in John 5, the word occurs several times. "The Father judges no one but has given all judgment to the Son, so that all may honor the Son just as they honor the Father" (Jn 5:22-23). Jesus continued by discussing with his hearers how in the last days judgments will be given to all—either to life or to condemnation. "I can do nothing on my own. As I hear, I judge; and my judgment is just, because I seek to do not my own will but the will of him who sent me" (Jn 5:30). Clearly Jesus is involved both now and in the future in the administration of God's justice.

In John 12:31 Jesus says, "Now is the judgment *[krisis]* of this world; now the ruler of this world will be driven out." In John 16:8, 11 Jesus reveals that when the Holy Spirit comes in the absence of Jesus, "he will prove the world wrong about sin and righteousness and judgment *[krisis]* . . . about judgment *[krisis],* because the ruler of this world has been condemned." We learn here that the upcoming substitutionary death of Jesus with his accompanying resurrection from the dead is a vital component in the administration of God's judgment and justice in the world. By this act of sacrifice all other acts will be judged. By this display of God's vindication will all other innocence be determined. By this display of God's mighty power will the evil Satan be ultimately condemned.

These verses describe a scene in which God the Father, Jesus the Messiah, the Holy Spirit, and the prince of this world all come together in a massive struggle with a clear and decisive outcome: God's justice reigns supreme. Lexical scholars feel that when *krisis* is used in John 12 and 16, both the meaning of judgment and of justice are probably involved (Arndt & Gingrich, 1952). The life and ministry of Jesus were intimately involved with the presentation and execution of justice in this world. Followers of Jesus must likewise be deeply concerned with the application of justice to the problems of this world as we seek to emulate the life and behavior of the Savior. More specifically, we will now examine how justice played a role in the mission, the teaching and the death of Jesus as described in Luke's Gospel.

Justice and his mission. If the promised Messiah was to be concerned with justice, just how was this aspect of his mission to be executed? What would it look like? We can find a marvelous description of this phase of the Messiah's mission in Luke 4. Jesus had started his ministry of healing and preaching in the area around his home village of Nazareth. But he had yet to "come home" in his new role as a prophet. People in Nazareth still knew him as Joseph's son, as a carpenter not a Messiah.

Luke records for us that Jesus returned to Galilee early in his public ministry in the power of the Spirit (Lk 4:14). Just as the Holy Spirit had sustained him during the wilderness temptation (Lk 4:1) and just as the Holy Spirit would fill Peter when he preached his great Pentecost sermon (Acts 2), so now does the Spirit enable Jesus to do what was very difficult: to return to his home district. No one was surprised when Jesus attended the sabbath service that particular day because it had been his custom to worship there in Nazareth (Lk 4:16). But everyone was no doubt interested in what Jesus would say and do since he had now started his popular teaching and healing ministry in the surrounding areas (Lk 4:14-15).

Synagogue worship services at this time consisted of three parts: prayer, readings from the Law and Prophets, and a teaching session from local leaders or from a visiting rabbi (Barclay, 1975). When it came time to read from the prophets, the synagogue attendant handed Jesus the Isaiah scroll. Jesus unrolled it to Isaiah 61:1-2 and stood to read.

> The Spirit of the LORD is upon me,
>   because he has anointed me
>   to bring good news to the poor.

He has sent me to proclaim release to the captives
   and recovery of sight to the blind,
      to let the oppressed go free,
   to proclaim the year of the Lord's favor. (Lk 4:18-19)

Then he sat down to teach. "The eyes of all in the synagogue were fixed on him" (Lk 4:20). "Today this Scripture has been fulfilled in your hearing" (Lk 4:21). Jesus had announced to those who knew him best that he was the promised Messiah.

Jewish leaders had always regarded Isaiah 61 as a messianic prophecy— a prophecy that described the mission of the promised Messiah. The Messiah would address his ministry to those who were the victims of injustice: the poor, the prisoners, the blind and the oppressed. Justice would finally arrive among God's people. It is one thing for us and for these Jewish leaders to be in favor of such justice in principle; it is quite another thing to know that such rectification of past wrongs is about to happen immediately. The chaos, the radical nature of such reversals, and the challenge that it would bring to the establishment were unnerving.

The residents of Nazareth knew only too well what had happened in nearby Sepphoris in A.D. 6. A messianic revolt in that town just four miles away from Nazareth brought down the wrath of Rome; the Roman army destroyed the village for its audacity (Keener, 1993). Messianic talk could be costly, and the leaders in Nazareth knew it.

This liberating theme of the Messiah's work was in the tradition of the Year of Jubilee (Lev 25). The most recent year of Jubilee, A.D. 26-27, was fresh in their minds (Marshall, 1978). The Messiah's work would be "the year of the Lord's favor" (Lk 4:19).

To the dismay of the leaders, Jesus added yet another solemn pronouncement. The good news that this Messiah would preach would be given to and received by people in areas other than Nazareth and by people other than Jews. God had blessed non-Jews through the ministry of Elijah to the non-Jewish widow of Zarephath in Sidon and through the work of Elisha when he brought healing to Naaman, a Syrian. The standard Jewish interpretation in first- century Palestine of the Messiah's coming work was that the Messiah would richly bless Israel and would ravish the Gentiles (Evans, 1990). Now Jesus is pronouncing quite a different mission for the

Messiah. The combination of these two shocking lessons from the lips of Jesus (that Jesus was naming himself as a liberating Messiah and that his mission would not be exclusively to the Jews of Nazareth or even Galilee) threw the leaders of the synagogue into a rage. They drove him out of town in an impulsive attempt to execute him; only at the last minute did Jesus walk through their midst to safety (Lk 4:28-30).

The synagogue reading that day clearly signaled, to all who were interested in knowing, that the promised Messiah had arrived and that, just as the prophets had prophesied, he would be deeply concerned with reversing the tragic effects of injustice by the powerful application of God's justice to the wrongs of this world.

Justice and his teaching. One day Jesus went to the home of a Pharisee to eat (Lk 11:37-54). What might have been an ordinary lunch turned into a stinging rebuke of the Pharisees, presumably including the meal's host. Jesus began to eat without first washing his hands in the ritualistic manner of the Pharisees. The cleansing ritual practiced by the Pharisees before eating was not required by the law of Moses but was an effort by the Pharisees to gain extra righteousness by exceeding the standards of law.

> First the water must be poured over the hands beginning at the tips of the fingers and running right up to the wrist. Then the palm of each hand must be cleansed by rubbing the fist of the other into it. Finally, water must again be poured over the hand, this time beginning at the wrist and running down to the fingertips. To the Pharisee, to omit the slightest detail of this was to sin. (Barclay, 1975, p. 155)

Jesus knew the law well, and he chose to obey it but not to obey the accretions that had been added to it. The Pharisees were surprised that Jesus would be that bold.

Jesus then began to confront the Pharisees about their concern for the appearance of righteousness and their unconcern for actual, inner cleanliness before God (Lk 11:39-41). Jesus pronounced a series of five woes on the Pharisees that had to do with their religious practices: their tithing, their love of display in public, their lack of transparency, their failure to respond to God's message to them through the prophets of God, and the damage they did to the faith of others by blocking them from true knowledge. This set of lunchtime rebukes significantly escalated their hatred for Jesus. "When Jesus left there, the Pharisees and the teachers of the law began to oppose him fiercely and to besiege him with questions, waiting to catch him in something he might say" (Lk 11:53-54 NIV).

Our interest is in the first woe that Jesus pronounced here against the Pharisees, the woe about their habits of tithing (Lk 11:42). The Old Testament did not require the tithing of herbs specifically. The law did require a tithe of grain, fruit, all herds and flocks, and even some processed products such as new wine and oil (Lev 27:30-33; Deut 14:22-29). But because garden herbs were used to season food, the Pharisees practiced tithing of such small seasonings as mint and rue. (Matthew also includes in a similar passage the tithing of dill and cummin.) Imagine counting mint leaves, setting aside one out of every ten, and taking them to the Temple. Rue, a strongly scented herb with yellow flowers and bitter tasting leaves used in ancient medicinal concoctions, would have been even more difficult to sort into piles, and was specifically exempted from tithing requirements by the Talmud (Plummer, 1906). Yet these Pharisees were amazingly anxious to prove that they not only obeyed the law, they also went far beyond it into levels of super-righteousness.

Why was Jesus upset by what might be harmless religious scrupulosity? Because in the process of abiding by such elaborate nonessential rules for righteousness, they had neglected the central requirements of the law: justice and love. This passage is central to the considerations of this chapter because it shows the importance Jesus attached to the doing of justice. Pursuing justice and loving God are uttered in the same breath and given the same importance. Clearly the teaching of Jesus stressed how important it was for the followers of God to be concerned with the pursuit of justice.

Justice and his death. The Gospel of Matthew gives us a glimpse into the household of Pilate that is not found in the other Gospel accounts of the trials of Jesus. "While Pilate was sitting on the judge's seat, his wife sent him this message: 'Have nothing to do with that innocent *[dikaios]* man, for today I have suffered a great deal because of a dream about him' " (Mt 27:19). A similar comment is made by a Roman centurion who was present, apparently in an official capacity, at the crucifixion of Jesus. He said, "Certainly this man was innocent" (Lk 23:47).

Versions vary as to how they translate these two occurrences of *dikaios*.

Even commentators disagree on what would be the best translation. Keener (1993) and Marshall (1978) both favor "innocent" while Evans (1990) and Geldenhuys (1966) prefer "righteous." The Greek word in question broadly means "just and righteous." Only in a narrow and restricted sense does it mean "innocent." Jesus was certainly both innocent and righteous or just. Both translations would fit the context. In the case of Pilate's wife, the translation "innocent" makes good sense since she is not likely to have been a woman who understood the terminology of the Old Testament and its understanding of justice. But in the case of the centurion, "just" or "righteous" may be a better translation than "innocent," given Luke's interest in presenting the death of Jesus as an example of injustice. Luke's theme of justice is powerful and is found throughout the book.

> Jesus' ministry of calling sinners to righteous ways of life—for example, almsgiving—is denounced by religious leaders who appear to be righteous. Jesus is *the* righteous one, who, obedient to God's will and plan, reveals and embodies that plan. He reveals a God who is just to the poor and afflicted. He unjustly meets with opposition from the religious leaders, stereotypes of unrighteous conduct. Embattled, Jesus is the suffering righteous one. In him God is on trial. God vindicates himself and his plan for creation in exalting the crucified righteous one, Jesus. When the centurion sees the mighty deed of God's fidelity to Jesus and Jesus' fidelity to his Father, this pagan confesses that Jesus is indeed God's righteous one. Pagans who should have no eyes see and those who have eyes are blind. (Karris, 1986, p. 71)

Justice then is a theme pervasive in the mission, teaching and death of Jesus. Those who would follow him have a special obligation to include within their internal system of motivations a keen desire to pursue justice in all areas where injustice now reigns.

Obstacles to the Pursuit of Justice
We thus face a dilemma. On the one hand, Scripture compels us to be motivated by what motivates the heart of God: the pursuit of justice. On the other hand, many of us practice our faith in a wing of the church that

has displayed significant apathy toward and suspiciousness of the pursuit of justice. How are we to resolve this dilemma? A first step is for us to face honestly the obstacles that impede our pursuit of justice.

Overwhelming need. We are surrounded by needs of great magnitude. Great numbers of people suffer injustice of every kind. Plagues, disease and illness rage in some parts of the world due to lack of medicines. Violent storms ravage masses of people in Bangladesh who have no other place to live than the low-lying delta lands of East Bengal. Earthquakes kill thousands in the mountains of Turkey because residents there cannot afford to build homes sturdy enough to withstand the violent shaking of the earth. Children are malnourished because of tragic civil wars fought for ethnic or religious reasons. Negligence, lying, corruption and deceit characterize governments that should be protecting their citizens rather than tyrannizing them. War leaves scars on the earth, on entire generations of children and youth, and on societies that require decades if not centuries to heal. And just when we think we have a sense of the needs of the world, we learn of new evidences of human injustice to other humans.

> Women and men who take seriously the humane sensibilities of Jesus the Christ have trouble accommodating the international arms trade. Certain moral concerns chafe. There is profiteering that benefits a few and there is enormous destruction—by weapons directly, or economic neglect indirectly—of the poor (predominantly women, children, and the elderly) in weapons-buying countries of the "two-thirds world." (Rankin, 1994, p. 90)

This issue alone almost overwhelms us with its sheer magnitude and complexity, particularly once we learn that the United States sells 70 percent of the world's arms every year.

No one can deny that the problem of injustice on the planet is very serious. But we must remember that Jesus too could have been overwhelmed with needs and instances of injustice. Like the prophets before him (Lk 4:24-27), he did not heal everyone who needed healing; he did not cure all the paralytics of the nation; he did not restore vision to all the blind, nor did he raise from the dead all who died during the years of his public ministry. Instead, he relied on the Spirit's leading to direct him to those people and situations where God wished him to intervene in a special way. Likewise, we must rely on the Holy Spirit's leading in our lives to determine when and how we should speak for God's standards of justice in the face of overwhelming injustice. Never can we allow the size of the problem to cower us into inactivity and passivity regarding injustice.

Complexity of issues. How can we be sure that a particular situation represents an opportunity God is providing us? How can we get reliable information? Issues in our world are indeed complex and difficult to sort out. One recent example will illustrate this frustration.

When the Republic of South Africa was still governed by a white minority government, the American Christian public was bombarded with contradictory information. On the one hand, Christian groups decried apartheid and urged Christians everywhere to join in efforts to impose an embargo on the RSA as one way of bringing an end to apartheid and minority rule. Other Christian groups disseminated very different information. They claimed that apartheid was not evil, that the press was inventing problems that did not exist, that majority rule in that country was simply not possible, that the white minority rulers were genuine Christians who deserved support from Christians everywhere, and that the whole furor over South Africa was caused by communists who would likely take over the country if the white government was toppled.

This array of contradictory information is not an isolated example. It is hard for the Christian public to ferret out the truth. Most people are simply befuddled by the confusion.

One way around this obstacle is to watch for trustworthy sources of information so that we can capitalize on the expertise of people we have confidence in. Organizations, newsletters, books and magazines that have a proven track record are helpful in this quest for good information. Organizations and individuals that predicted a bloody civil war if the white government of South Africa ever left power must now be judged by history; they were wrong and their information was misleading.

We learn, to cite another example, that since Guatemala's civil war began over thirty years ago, "47,000 people have 'disappeared,' 150,000 have been killed, and one million have been displaced" (Johnson & Gallegos, 1995, p. 14). Was this an issue of rampant injustice that needed U.S. intervention, or should we have stayed above the fray and allowed the politics of the region to continue to battle it out? An American lawyer,

Jennifer Harbury, insisted that the governments of Guatemala and the United States knew something about the death of her husband, Efrain Bamaca Velasquez. The Guatemalan government insisted that he was killed in battle. Only after her two hunger fasts did the American government reveal that her husband had been murdered by a Guatemalan intelligence officer who was on the payroll of the CIA (Johnson & Gallegos, 1995). We do not want to learn information like this about our own government, but closing our eyes to injustice wherever it is found contradicts what Jesus would have us do. Complexity does not give us permission to indulge in passivity.

Why not just wait? We know the outcome of human history. God will intervene to right all wrongs, to end all suffering, to execute justice on all those who have defied God's love, and to bring an end to all injustice. Only God in his infinite wisdom with his infinite power and his limitless presence is capable of rectifying injustice. Why not wait for God to do it in the end rather than work for justice now? In addition, many Bible teachers tell us that we don't need to be worried about these earthly instances of injustice. They belong to God's sphere of activity. We should not get bogged down, they say, with tasks that will divert us from our true and central purpose as the body of Christ here on earth: preaching the gospel.

We have already examined some of the theology that supports this "waiting for justice rather than working for justice" approach. Its main weakness is that it overlooks the central place that justice and its pursuit took in the life and ministry of Jesus. We are commanded to pattern our lives after his. And it overlooks the fact that the heart of God is grieved constantly over those he loves intensely, the victims of injustice. God spoke through his prophets clearly and consistently, giving us clarity about God's attitudes toward those who ignore injustice (Amos 5:21-24), who wait for God to correct all wrongs (Mic 6:8) and who busy themselves with less central concerns (Lk 11:42).

What Can We Do?

God honors those who seek out ways to pursue justice as a central motivation of their lives. We have almost limitless opportunities to add the pursuit of justice to the other ways by which we seek to serve and honor God. As we seek to make the pursuit of justice an important part of our lives, we must remember seven important principles.

With God's blessing, one person can accomplish a great deal. Even though the problems around us are massive, we can never forget that God can use one person to accomplish much. We should never give space to the idea that one person is ineffective is triggering change.

On December 1, 1955, one woman changed the course of American civil rights history by refusing to give up her seat to a white man. Rosa Parks says, "I was not in the front of the bus trying to challenge racial segregation. I was seated in the 'colored' section. When one white male passenger got on the bus, the driver saw fit to have the four of us—the man who shared the seat with me and the two women across the aisle—stand up so this white man could have a seat" (Golphin, 1995, p. 11). Having one whole row to himself would then allow him the "comfort" of not having to sit next to or near an African-American.

She was the only one of the four who refused to move, and her act of conviction sparked a long-needed revolution. "She knows, perhaps better than most, that it is the sacrifice of the one that can shape the destiny of the many" (Golphin, 1995, p. 10).

Or consider the story of Wheeling Gaunt, an ex-slave who died in 1894. In his will he provided a bequest that to this day funds an annual gift of flour and sugar to all the widows of Yellow Springs, Ohio. He wanted to have a small part in alleviating the poverty of widows, black or white, old or young, with children or without. His effort to relieve the pressures of the injustices of life continues over a hundred years after his death. One person can accomplish much.

One person cannot do it all. Everyone realizes that the efforts of a single person, no matter how effective, cannot eliminate all injustice. God does not ask us to do that. That is his task. He merely expects us to be concerned and involved—committed to the things to which he himself is committed. Because one person cannot do it all, we need to join with others who share the same convictions. Doing justice is best done by communities of faith (Wallis, 1992). The amazing success of the Truth and Reconciliation Commission in the new South Africa gives us a challenging example of what committed groups of people can accomplish in the pursuit of justice (Storey, 1997).

We need to re-evaluate our lifestyle on a regular basis. Does our personal use of time, energy, money and other resources contribute to what matters most to us? Are there changes we can make in our priorities that would help us obey the commands of Jesus better? Can we make adjustments that would free up time to help with an important project that needs assistance? To what new and challenging tasks is God calling us? Only by this type of re-evaluation will we ever make room in our busy lives for the pursuit of justice. Otherwise everyone is too busy to care about what God cares about.

We need to expand our horizons. Wendell Primus (1996) suggests an interesting experiment for us all. Imagine you are to be born a second time in the United States, only this time you do not know if you will be born male or female, African-American, white, Asian-American or Hispanic, whether you will be intelligent, average or otherwise, whether you will be born to a teenage mother (you have a 1:8 chance), whether your parents will be married when you are born (you have a 1:3 chance they will not be married), whether you will spend much of your childhood years living in a single-parent household (you have a 1:2 chance), whether your family will live below the poverty level (1 out of 3 males will earn under $15,000 per year), or if one of your parents will be mentally disabled, alcoholic or addicted to drugs. If it were your plight to grow up in an underprivileged situation or if you were part of a group that systematically receives unjust treatment, how would it feel? How would your life be different? Would you be more interested in pursuing justice than you currently are?

We need to study, learn and listen to new perspectives. There are many types of social analysis that can help us understand better the conditions of injustice, how they are perpetuated and what can be done to alleviate the suffering they cause (Holland & Henriot, 1983). Do we know, for example, that poverty is not as much caused by scarcity as it is by poor distribution and systems of power and control that provide for inequality? (Jeune, 1983). Do we know that affirmative action may mean significantly different things to a believer who is a minority person than it does to a believer who is white? (Rosado, 1995). Are we willing to listen to new perspectives from people who are different from us? Are we willing to try new avenues of intervention? Perhaps you have been disillusioned with politics. Congressman Paul B. Henry says, "Involvement in the political process is one of many ways in which the Christian community can be faithful to the redemptive power of the gospel. Political involvement means seeking justice in and through the public, institutional structures" (Henry, 1988, p. 13).

Pursuing justice is lonely, sometimes risky work for God. No doubt you will be lonely in your struggle to pursue justice, because many Christians around you may not understand or care. Thus it is helpful to gather around you friends of like mind. A group of people interested in justice issues, even a small group, can do a great deal to encourage each other in the task. They can share information and pool their vision for action.

Pursuing justice can be costly. John Perkins relates a powerful story from the early years of his ministry in Mendenhall, Mississippi. He boldly made visits to the ministers of white churches in Mendenhall to present the ministry he planned to begin among the poor blacks of that Mississippi town.

Perkins talked with one white pastor to present his plans for a new ministry to the poor: " 'How do you feel,' I went on, 'when you think about your elaborate church building with its beautiful chandeliers, when you realize that your denomination is supporting missionaries in Africa and all the time right here in Mendenhall are people who have never really heard the gospel of Jesus Christ?' " (Perkins, 1982, p. 29).

The boldness of John Perkins shocked the white minister. But he thought about it, and then he began to preach sermons challenging his congregation to join in the pursuit of justice right in their own backyards. Sadly, the congregation turned against the preacher, and tragedy ensued when the minister later committed suicide, apparently in part from the stress his newfound commitments had introduced to his life. Justice work is difficult, lonely and often misunderstood. But when God calls us to it and is for us, who can be against us?

To God belongs the ultimate victory in all cases of injustice. Jesus acted against the formidable powers of evil and injustice only in the power of the Holy Spirit. We can afford to do no less. But with God's help and enablement, we can work for justice in the knowledge that God will be victorious in the struggle, that the battle is his, and that we are merely trying to serve God, not save the world. Pursuing justice is ministry that pleases God. Justice shall prevail. Terry Mattingly's syndicated religion column for May 14, 1997, carried the tragic story of strife in southern Sudan. The conflict there has been largely ignored by the world press, yet a relentless assault against Christians has been going on for years. Yet God will prevail. Not a single church building is left standing in southern Sudan, but the church is still there, meeting under trees and worshiping Christ as a persecuted body of believers (Mattingly, 1997). God has the ultimate victory.

Conclusion
We have been deeply affected in recent years by the film *Schindler's List*. The story of what one person did in the face of massive injustice is amazing. Those people on Schindler's list were rescued from injustice and given the opportunity to live in just societies because of the actions of one person. Does Jesus have a list? (Olson, 1994). Who is on that list? Who is Jesus calling to help fight injustice for those people? Maybe it is I. Or you and I.

Section Three

Extraversion

Introduction

Jesus & Our Interpersonal Life

PARTIES ARE A LOT MORE FUN WHEN PEOPLE ATTEND WHO HAVE A LOT OF IT. YOU know if a stranger has it after only a few minutes of conversation. If you have two children, one of them may have a lot of it. People who have quite bit of it are usually fun to be around. What is it? *Extraversion.*

Extraversion and its counterpart, introversion, are two of the most well-known personality descriptors. A broad band of people understand what these two traits are and can correctly identify where other people are on this continuum. Research has found that the degree to which an individual is outgoing, sociable, friendly, adventuresome and fun-loving is known to those around that individual, and different raters describing the same person are likely to agree with each other about the person's extraversion (Brehm & Kassin, 1996).

Whereas some persons will score very high on extraversion and a few will score very low on the scale, most people fall in the middle ranges. Not only do other people tend to know us accurately regarding our relative place on this personality factor, but also we tend to know ourselves quite well with regard to extraversion. Of the five factors in the Big Five constellation, extraversion is the most easily understood and the most familiar to the general public.

Prior to the emergence of the Big Five factor approach, a major trait theory was Hans Eysenck's three-factor model. One of the three main factors for Eysenck was extraversion, a factor he defined quite closely to how the Big Five theory describes it. Carl Jung also wrote a great deal about extraversion as a basic feature of human personality. When Myers and Briggs put Jungian theory into a psychological measurement (the Myers-Briggs Type Indicator), extraversion-introversion was one of the four main dimensions. Some technical differences exist between how Myers-Briggs describe extraversion and how the Big Five approach describes it. Nonetheless, they are very similar to each other.

People who score high on the extraversion factor are friendly and sociable. They like people and groups, even big groups. They are assertive, talkative and active. Most often they are optimistic. They like adventure and excitement. The stereotype of the extravert in our culture is the salesperson who sometimes possesses an uncanny ability to make people feel at ease and a friendliness that just makes you want to buy things! Costa and McCrae (1992c) warn us against viewing the introvert as the opposite of the extravert. The fact that extraverts are friendly, outgoing and optimistic does not mean that introverts are hostile, shy and pessimistic. Introverts are reserved rather than unfriendly; they are less outgoing; they are not necessarily unhappy.

Subfacets of Extraversion

On Table 6 the conjectured results for both Jesus and Paul list the six subfacets of the extraversion factor. The first is *warmth*. Extraverts are warm, affectionate and friendly. They like people, and it is easy for them to build relationships with others. Low scorers on this subfacet tend to be reserved, formal and somewhat distant.

Gregariousness is another subfacet. High scorers genuinely enjoy the company of others, as opposed to low scorers, who may be less comfortable in groups or at least do not seek out social encounters.

On the subfacet of *assertiveness,* low scorers prefer to stay in the background and let others take leadership. High scorers quickly become leaders in a group and can be dominant and forceful.

Regarding *activity,* high scorers move quickly through life and exude a sense of energy and busyness. Low scorers are more leisurely about life, although they are not lazy.

Extraversion Facets	Jesus	Paul
Warmth	AVERAGE	AVERAGE
Gregariousness	AVERAGE	HIGH
Assertiveness	HIGH	AVERAGE
Activity	AVERAGE	HIGH
Excitement Seeking	LOW	AVERAGE
Positive Emotions	HIGH	AVERAGE

Table 6. Jesus and Paul on extraversion

The subfacet of *excitement-seeking* is one which is clearly obvious to most friends of those who score high. Stimulation, excitement, noise, bright colors—all are enjoyable for them. By contrast, low scorers on this subfacet enjoy quiet and calm, the very things that to the high scorer seem boring.

Finally and most important, positive emotions are a critical component of what it means to be an extravert. High scorers laugh easily and frequently and report many positive emotions such as joy, happiness, love, excitement. Optimism normally accompanies these features. Low scorers are less exuberant and less emotionally animated.

Correlates of Extraversion

Research on extraversion has uncovered some interesting characteristics for high scorers. First, extraversion is positively correlated with happiness. In other words, when people are evaluated for the degree of well-being they experience, for how much and how frequently they feel happy, and for how much they experience positive affect, these characteristics are found far more frequently among extraverts than among introverts. Quite simply, extraverts are happier people. They feel better about life and about themselves. This correlation is stable and persists over time so that we know it is not related to mood or to passing circumstance. Extraverts report higher levels of satisfaction with life. "There is a robust positive relationship between extraversion and subjective well-being, a relationship that is stable over time and generalizable to diverse populations" (Pavot, Diener, & Fujita, 1990, p. 1299). We are all familiar with the expression "Blonds have more fun." It might be more accurate to say, "Extraverts have more fun."

Second, extraverts experience more positive life events, and persons scoring high on neuroticism (see section five) experience more negative life events. Examples of positive life events are promotions, raises, marriage, engagement, the receipt of an award. Examples of negative life events are weight gain, personal injury or illness, divorce, loss of job, suicide attempt (Magnus, Diener, Fujita, & Pavot, 1993). It seems that extraversion, the desire to be with people and the genuine liking of people, predisposes those who score high on this factor to experience more positive events in life than do their neurotic friends. Theorists have attempted to understand this phenomenon. Perhaps the extraverts seek out positive experiences and receive from others positive responses because of their likeableness. As a result they tend to have more positive experiences in life.

Extraversion, like others of the Big Five factors, is heavily influenced by genetic factors. Mothers will report differences in this trait among their children very early in life. One has to wonder then if some persons are genetically programmed to have a more positive encounter with life than are others. In any event, we do know that we differ among ourselves on how we approach the interpersonal side of life. If we seek to reach out to others, actively and assertively, we are likely extraverts. If we are more reserved and cautious in our interpersonal relationships, we are likely introverts. Both interpersonal styles can serve God well; both can be used mightily by God.

When our New Testament scholars attempted to rate Jesus and Paul, some interesting differences emerged. They pictured Paul as more gregarious than Jesus. People came to Jesus; Paul went to people. The high assertiveness score for Jesus no doubt is based on his almost fearless attack on the powerful, entrenched leaders of the nation. Paul could sometimes hesitate in confronting problems, as illustrated in the Corinthian letters where he would confront people but only in a very cautious manner. Paul exceeds Jesus on activity levels. One does get the impression from reading the book of Acts that Paul is dauntless and at times very active on his missionary journeys.

The Gospel accounts give us several instances of Jesus taking proper time to rest, which probably influences his score here. Jesus may have had less interest in excitement than Paul, but the positive emotional level for

Jesus was undoubtedly higher. What is most interesting of these conjectured test results is that both Paul and Jesus received an overall rating of average on the extraversion factor. But by examining the subfacets we can see that their averages were made up of very different ratings on the composing elements of the factor. Each person is unique, and each person's personality configuration will be different.

Jesus calls all of us to two major interpersonal tasks: to love others and to be trustworthy. This divine calling for our interpersonal lives applies to extravert and introvert alike. The command to love people could be harder for the introvert, just as the command to be trustworthy and reliable might be more difficult for the extravert. Yet we all are called to pursue these two interpersonal virtues with all our strength and might.

7
Show Love

THE TEACHINGS OF JESUS REQUIRE OF EXTRAVERTS AND INTROVERTS ALIKE TWO major interpersonal behaviors: to show love and to be trustworthy. Both of these interpersonal callings are to be expressions of our love for God, are to reflect God's love and trustworthiness toward us, and are to be central to our lives as followers of Jesus. These two are not totally unique to Christianity, nor are they totally absent values in the secular world around us. But the love and trustworthiness that Jesus taught are distinctive enough that when the world observes our conformity to these demands of Jesus, the world will know we are Christians.

The Many Splendors of Love

God has created us as individuals who must participate in relationships. It is quite literally impossible to be a human and to be totally detached and unconnected to other human beings. "An isolated man is a denaturalized man" (Chauchard, 1968, p. 76). The dependency of the infant is just the first of many requisite relationships. Granted, some individuals can manage to live in relative isolation; but even the most detached person will have some relationships somewhere with some other human being. We have already seen that a basic personality factor (extraversion and its accompanying introversion) is also characteristic of all of us and that we each vary in how much of these qualities we possess. But even the most introverted of persons will have the obligation to show love and to be trustworthy in relationships. No one is exempt from these interpersonal demands of Jesus. In this chapter we will consider the teaching of Jesus regarding love and how it must characterize in an ongoing way the interpersonal life of the believer.

Definitions of love. The first hazard we face in attempting to understand the subject of love is a definitional problem. The word *love* in English, as in most other languages, has spread across many domains and is used to describe and denote a large variety of very different entities. We can speak, for example, of how plants love water, of how to score a tennis match, of how patriotic citizens love their country's flag, and of how someone loves country-western music or chocolate ice cream. And at the same time the very same word, *love,* is used for the most intimate of human contacts, for the basic attitude of God toward the human race, and for the response we are commanded to give to God. The word covers terrain, quite literally, from the ridiculous to the sublime. It can describe fondness, preference, altruism or ultimate self-sacrifice. By way of contrast, the opposite word, *hate,* is quite straightforward and has only a very few dictionary meanings. Perhaps we should be glad that there is more variety to love than there is to hate.

The religions of the world speak of love in its loftier, more spiritual senses. The following quotations are representative of three major world religions.

When all the people in the world love each other, then the strong will not overpower the weak. — Mo Tzu (Confucianism)

When he [Bodhisattva] exerts himself for the good of others, he should be filled with love and love alone without any admixture of self-interest. — Arycuna (Buddhism)

Those who desire to transcend all limitations and bondages must accept supreme love as the highest goal. — Narada (Hinduism) (Mohler, 1975, pp. 1, 24, 38)

Yet in spite of these themes of love in many of the world's religions, love has become a defining characteristic of Christianity. The teachings of

Christ elevated love to the level of the supreme ethic, a central place for love not present in other religions. The followers of Jesus were commanded to love both God and neighbor. But in our day Christians may not continue to have the reputation they earned at great price in the first centuries. "To unbelievers Christians are the most divided of all groups, with evidence of the animosity of one Christian group to another being a regular item on our newscasts" (Conway, 1992, p. 7). If love is to be the defining characteristic of Christians, we have before us a major challenge: to restore the reputation of the church to its earlier state when believers were known for their love for each other.

Hierarchies of love. Over the centuries countless scholars have attempted to reduce the confusion about what love means. Any analysis of love, however, tends to sterilize or demystify a thing of wonder. For example, we all know that the heart is not the organ with which we love others; the brain is where we love or not love. But can you imagine how ridiculous Valentine's Day cards would look decorated with pictures of the human brain? Or when we seek to define love scientifically, we reduce it to a unedifying level.

Love is "an attitudinal-behavioral configuration" (Greenfield, 1973, p. 37). Does this definition stir you? Probably not. We do know that love is inherently altruistic, that hate is inherently selfish, and that genuine love (especially as defined by the New Testament) is the sacrificing of self. Love gives us life, beautifies life and makes life good. But can we describe the various kinds of love beyond these categories? Scholars disagree as to whether love is an instinct or a behavior. The widespread existence of love among humans suggests that it is an instinct or at least a very basic human need (Karmel, 1973). Yet others argue that love must be learned and that a person must want to learn to love before it will happen. "Anthropologists have described entire societies in which love is absent, and there are certainly many individuals in our own love-oriented society who have never loved" (Casler, 1973, p. 2).

The discipline of arranging the various types of love into hierarchies or categories has a long history going back to the Scholastics of the Middle Ages (Brunner, 1956). A contemporary attempt is represented in the work of Sorokin (1972), who suggests that we can rate the characteristics and qualities of love on five dimensions: (1) intensity of love, from its absence to its maximal levels; (2) extensity, from love of self only to love of all creatures on the planet; (3) duration, from the briefest encounter to lifelong relationships; (4) purity, from love extensively contaminated with mixed motives to the most genuine and unadulterated love; and (5) adequacy. Sorokin defines inadequate love as either an objective love expressed through acts but without any accompanying emotion or a highly subjective and affectional love that has no counterpart in behavior or action. Adequate love is composed of both subjective feelings and objective acts. This attempt to organize all the various shades of meaning reminds us that love is a complicated feature of human functioning that we cannot easily analyze or describe.

Eros Versus Agape Love

One of the most well-known facts about the love of New Testament Christianity is that it is expressed in a specific Greek word, *agape,* that is quite distinct from another Greek word for love, *eros.* We are well acquainted with *eros* because of the English word *erotic,* a derivative of the earlier Greek word. *Erotic* is connected with human sexuality and its role in serving as an attraction or connection between one human being with another. The word *erotic* also has acquired a significant number of negative connotations, since we can easily link the erotic with lust, promiscuity and other forms of sexual excess. But in the history of human thought, *eros* signified a great deal more than just the sexual.

In the *Symposium* Plato described *eros* through a dialogue. *Eros* was a type of love which filled up or completed something that was lacking in the person. Someone who is experiencing *eros* love has a soul that "is attracted to something that it lacks" (Brunner, 1956, p. 63). The deficiency is filled once connection with the attraction is completed, much as a vacuum is filled once it is unsealed. Thus *eros* love includes the sexual longings that are part of human experience, but much more than just that. Even platonic love, a phrase we now use to refer to love that is not expressed through sex, is *eros* love to the extent that it completes or fulfills in one person what is lacking or deficient. The *Symposium* went on to describe *eros* love in lofty and almost mystical terms.

Hence *eros* love pulls a person toward another. We are attracted by being pulled, by the yearning we have for wholeness. St. Augustine said *eros* was the force that pulls us to God since we all seek to fill a vacuum in our life that only God can fill. *Eros* is "the power in us yearning for wholeness, the drive to give meaning and pattern to our variegation, form to our otherwise impoverishing formlessness, integration to counter our disintegrative trends" (May, 1969, p. 78).

The word is occasionally used in the Septuagint (the Greek translation of the Hebrew Old Testament) and in the Jewish writer Philo. "In view of this, it becomes truly significant that the New Testament never employs *eros*" (Moffatt, 1929, p. 38). The writers of the New Testament, under the inspiration of the Holy Spirit, appear determined not to describe God's love for us or the love we should have for God and others by using the very commonly used Greek word *eros*. Instead they chose *agape*.

The reason for this dramatic shift was apparently that they wanted to make sure everyone knew that God's love (and what it does for us and others) is radically different in composition and character from *eros* love. *Agape* love is not contingent on the character or the worthwhileness of the object of that love. It is a seeking love, a love that reaches out toward others. Rather than being pulled by *eros* love toward someone who can fill a lack we have, *agape* love enables us to reach out to replenish the emptiness that the other person may have. God reaches out to us with *agape* love, and we are to reach out to others with this same giving attitude.

Agape love "is a love that does not seek to fill my own soul, but to fill you; to replenish your emptiness and not my own" (Brunner, 1956, p. 64). The motivation for loving with this type of selflessness cannot come from within the human spirit. Hence the Greeks knew nothing about this kind of love as described by the authors of the New Testament. Its origin is from God himself. He loved us with *agape* love even when we were very unlovable rebels. Through the miracle of redemption and salvation, we are then equipped by the power of God to display this type of love to others. To understand the nature of *agape* love, then, we must understand the nature of God's love.

The Bible says that God is love (*agape,* 1 Jn 4:8, 16). The statement is a mystery we cannot fully understand. But it does indicate to us that a core characteristic of God's person is *agape* love. "There is no other book of religion in which God is called love" (Brunner, 1956, p. 66). God is not a remote, detached deity whom people must implore before he acts. Instead he reaches out to us with the good news of his provisions for us. So powerful was the impulse of *agape* love that he gave his only begotten Son to the world. The excruciating suffering of the Savior on the Cross caused God to turn his back in anguish, an indication of the extent and nature of his *agape* love for us. "Yet this was not the end of love. For in the resurrection, the glory of God's love became an invincible power for all ages. It will remain alive despite human unfaithfulness and egoism" (De Jong, 1974, p. 62). The love of John 3:16 is clearly *agape* love.

Jesus loved the Father with *agape* love, and the Father loved the Son with *agape* love. Jesus prayed in John 17:26, "I made your name known to them, and I will make it known, so that the love *[agape]* with which you have loved me may be in them, and I in them." And earlier that evening Jesus said to his disciples, "If you keep my commandments, you will abide in my love *[agape]*, just as I have kept my Father's commandments and abide in his love *[agape]*" (Jn 15:10). The apostle Paul writes, "He has rescued us from the power of darkness and transferred us into the kingdom of his beloved *[agape]* Son, in whom we have redemption, the forgiveness of sins" (Col 1:13-14). Both creation and redemption display for us the great love God has for the world and those in it (Chauchard, 1968). This *agape* love that characterized the Godhead before the incarnation, during the incarnation and after the incarnation is the moral basis on which God's people are commanded to love God and others with *agape* love.

The Commands to Love
Against this impressive and almost indescribable background of God's love for us, we now turn to a discussion of how we are to respond. In many ways it is easier to study God's love for us—its extent, its comprehensiveness, its limitlessness. But the task of learning about how we should love him in return is quite different. Here we put ourselves under some obligation to re-examine how we ought to love, with the strong possibility that our feeble love responses to God may not yet match what our loving of God should be.

The Greatest Commandment
Jesus often faced questions that came from an array of questionable motives, including the hope to trap him in his own words (Mt 22:15). On one such

occasion Jesus had answered a question from the Sadducees about the resurrection. His answer had foiled their attempts to trap him to the point where the crowd listening in on the inquisition was astonished at his teaching (Mt 22:29-33). The Pharisees then tried their best to trap Jesus by sending one of their best, a legal expert, to ask Jesus about the greatest commandment in the law (Mt 22:34-40; Mk 12:28-31; Lk 10:25-29). "The wrong answer—i.e., other than that given by Jesus, which could be construed as including within it all the other commandments—could have proved useful to the Pharisees in their attempt to get rid of Jesus" (Hagner, 1995, p. 646).

Matthew tells us that the answer Jesus gave was apparently sufficient to impress the Pharisees. Their subsequent conversation did not escalate. But Jesus actually engaged them in a conversation in which he asked *them* a question about the Messiah. It was a somewhat rare exchange of rather calm demeanor between Jesus and his enemies. Mark gives us some additional details. He tells us that the expert they had selected to pose the question said of Jesus' answer, "You are right, Teacher" (Mk 12:32). "When Jesus saw that he [the expert in the law] answered wisely, he said to him, 'You are not far from the kingdom of God.' After that no one dared to ask him any question" (Mk 12:34). Luke tells us the additional fact that the lawyer then asked Jesus, "And who is my neighbor?" (Lk 10:29). We will discuss this question below. The answer Jesus gave not only mollified the crowd, it silenced them and gave at least one person some very sobering issues about which to think.

The question these Pharisees asked, "Of all the commandments, which is the most important?" (Mk 12:28 NIV), was a strategic question to all adherents of the Old Testament law. Various other rabbis had attempted to summarize the 613 commandments found in the Mosaic law into a somewhat shorter summary list. Hillel summarized the entire law into a negative form of what we now know as the Golden Rule, a rule for life expressed by Jesus in positive terms (Mt 7:12).

In the Sermon on the Mount Jesus taught that the Golden Rule summarized the law and the prophets. Are Matthew 7 and Matthew 22 then in conflict because Jesus give a different summary of the law in the latter passage? No, in Matthew 22 Jesus elaborates on the Golden Rule to cite two specific commandments from the Old Testament that epitomize how the Golden Rule operates in our lives. Rabbi Simlai found several summaries of the law in other Old Testament passages. He taught, for example, that David summarized the entire law into eleven commandments that are listed in Psalm 15. The list of six commandments in Isaiah 33:15-16, according to Simlai, is Isaiah's summary of the entire law. Other summaries are listed by Micah in Micah 6:8, by Isaiah again in Isaiah 56:1, by Amos in Amos 5:4 and by Habakkuk in Habakkuk 2:4 (Hagner, 1995). So when the legal expert asked Jesus what was the greatest commandment, he was merely collecting another Rabbi's opinion.

The first and greatest command, said Jesus, was the command found in Deuteronomy 6:4-5 in the context of the famous *shema:* "Hear, O Israel: The LORD is our God, the LORD alone. You shall love the LORD your God with all your heart, and with all your soul, and with all your might."

The greatest command is to love God without limit. Even the Pharisees could not dispute Jesus on this point. The questioner said, "You are right . . . [it] is much more important than all whole burnt offerings and sacrifices" (Mk 12:32-33). The answer of Jesus obligates his followers to achieve levels of *agape* love that require a response with one's whole being; loving God is not an incidental, minor or small requirement. Human efforts to love God this completely fall short of what we owe God. We can never love God as completely as we should.

What enables us to love God is the love God has first shown us. In Deuteronomy Moses said that the love command was built upon the promises of God that he had given them (Deut 6:3). And the New Testament repeats that the basis of our love (*agape*) for God is the love displayed so extensively and completely by God toward us (Rom 5:8). Bernard of Clairvaux said that the reason for loving God is God himself (Mohler, 1975). Jesus gave us the greatest commandment of all with an important accompanying standard: We are to love God extensively, comprehensively and limitlessly. We are to love with our entire being.

Many people have understood these descriptions of comprehensiveness as an inspired revelation of how the human personality is structured. The list of components of the human self (heart, soul and mind, according to Matthew) do seem to be a helpful explanation of the different parts of the human personality. However, we soon encounter a difficulty when we compare the listed terms from the Deuteronomy passage with the three parallel passages in Matthew, Mark and Luke. Table 7 lists the terms as they appear, along with a transliterated listing of the Hebrew or Greek word used. The best conclusion based on this comparative data is that the listing of human personality terms in these five locations is designed to demonstrate the comprehensiveness of the command to love God rather than to give us a divinely inspired revelation of human personality structure.

Terms	Deut 6 Moses	Mt 22 Jesus	Mk 12:30 Jesus	Mk 12:33 Lawyer	Lk 10 Jesus
Heart (H: *lebab*)	X				
Heart (G: *kardia*)		X	X	X	X
Mind (G: *dianoia*)		X	X		X
Soul (H: *nephesh*)	X				
Soul (G: *psyche*)		X	X		X
Strength (H: *meod*)	X				
Strength (G: *ischuos*)			X	X	X
Understanding (G: *suneseos*)				X	

Table 7. **Human personality terms associated with the greatest commandment**

The Second-Greatest Commandment

To our first and greatest responsibility to love God in return for his love to us), Jesus then adds a second expectation: the law of neighbor love. Both Matthew and Mark tell us the lawyer only asked for one commandment; Jesus volunteers the second-greatest commandment as well. "Love your neighbor as yourself" is a quotation from Leviticus 19:18.

We have seen how a reader of the Old Testament might readily spot the greatest commandment in its original context as a command of great importance. But it is more difficult to spot the second-greatest commandment as we read through Leviticus 19. Depending how one counts, the chapter contains more than thirty-five commands. At the beginning of this section Moses lists again many of the commands of the Decalogue followed by some less familiar laws: do not hold back the wages of a hired man overnight (v. 13); do not curse the deaf or put a stumbling block in front of the blind (v. 14). The next section treats neighbor laws, one of which is quoted by Jesus as the second-greatest commandment. Followers of God were not to show partiality to the poor or favoritism to the rich, were not to slander a neighbor or do anything that would endanger a neighbor's life.

neighbor's life. They were not to hate their brothers and sisters but to rebuke their neighbors honestly. The final section of the chapter deals with miscellaneous laws regarding the planting of crops, sexual offenses and hair cutting, among other topics. Out of this wide variety of commands, Jesus lifts part of a verse and declares that it is the second-greatest commandment.

The command contains a built-in self-check: We are to love our neighbors *as we love ourselves.* Not only does the second-greatest commandment prevent egoism, it also prevents excessive altruism by the inclusion of this self-check standard (Chauchard, 1968). We will deal with this intriguing qualifying phrase in the chapter on self-acceptance. Our concern here is with the *agape* love we are to show to neighbors. Again, the enemies of Jesus did not contest his selection of this command as the second greatest. The lawyer, as recorded by Mark, agrees with Jesus and states that keeping the greatest and the second-greatest commands is more important than the entire Jewish sacrificial system (Mk 12:32-33).

The New Testament, however, takes this second-greatest commandment and highlights it with two major treatments. First, the New Testament reverses the relative obscurity of the command as it was originally embedded in the Pentateuch and highlights it with a series of statements that quite literally transforms the attention we need to give to the command. Note the comments added to the second-greatest commandment not only in the Gospels but in the balance of the New Testament.

On these two commandments hang all the law and the prophets. (Mt 22:40)

There is no other commandment greater than these. (Mk 12:31)

This is much more important than all whole burnt offerings and sacrifices. (Mk 12:33)

Do this, and you will live. (Lk 10:28)

[The commandments] . . . are summed up in this word, "Love your neighbor as yourself." (Rom 13:9)

For the whole law is summed up in a single commandment: "You shall love you neighbor as yourself." (Gal 5:14)

You do well if you really fulfill the royal law according to the scripture, "You shall love your neighbor as yourself." (Jas 2:8)

The New Testament clearly lifts this law from obscurity to noticeable prominence. The second change is that Jesus takes two terms from the command, "love" (*agape*) and "neighbor," and explodes their meanings. For example, Jews regularly interpreted "neighbor" to mean those within the nation and aliens within the nation. Leviticus 19, the chapter where the second-greatest command is embedded, also deals with how the nation is to treat aliens: "When an alien resides with you in your land, you shall not oppress the alien. The alien who resides with you shall be to you as the citizen among you; you shall love the alien as yourself, for you were aliens in the land of Egypt; I am the LORD your God" (Lev 19:33-34). It was a stretch for the Hebrew people, with their strong national loyalties, even to reach out to the aliens among them. And now Jesus stretched them further. When the lawyer asked, "And who is my neighbor?" Jesus' parable of the good Samaritan was a clear and expanding definition: A neighbor is anyone around you who is in need.

If the command was difficult to obey in its Old Testament form, it is now even more challenging. Needy people are all around us. But that is not the end of the expansion. The resurrected Jesus leaves a new commission with his disciples just before he ascends into heaven. They are to take the gospel into all the nations. Neighbors whom we are to love now include every person (Carter & Thompson, 1990). Jesus expanded "neighbor" to its largest possible meaning.

The second expansion of terms has to do with love. However the lawyer may have understood *agape* love, Jesus clearly taught that it now meant love even for enemies. These two changes were major and important. "For Jesus had extended the term 'neighbor' till it included anyone near and in need, and he had also widened the term 'love' till it embraced personal duty toward an opponent" (Moffatt, 1929, p. 32). We now turn our attention to this important interpersonal command Jesus has given to us.

Matthew's Presentation of Enemy Love

The teaching of Jesus regarding *agape* love for enemies occurs in three

Gospel passages. In one of them, Matthew's recording of the Sermon on the Mount, Jesus presents six antitheses, each of which compares the religious teaching of the day and a contrasting approach that Jesus taught. The antitheses deal with murder-anger, adultery-lust, divorce, oaths, violence-nonviolence and love for enemies.

> You have heard that is was said, "You shall love your neighbor and hate your enemy." But I say to you, Love your enemies and pray for those who persecute you, so that you may be children of your Father in heaven; for he makes his sun rise on the evil and on the good, and sends rain on the righteous and on the unrighteous. For if you love those who love you, what reward do you have? Do not even the tax collectors do the same? And if you greet only your brothers and sisters, what more are you doing than others? Do not even the Gentiles do the same? Be perfect, therefore, as your heavenly Father is perfect. (Mt 5:43-48)

The Old Testament did not command hatred for one's enemies. Where then did this teaching originate? Jewish leaders of the day interpreted several Old Testament passages in ways that, according to them, gave them sanction to hate an enemy. Parts of Psalm 139 are well-known; its passage about the unborn is used frequently in abortion debates, its comments about the omnipresence of Jehovah are among the clearest in the Bible, and its last two verses imploring "Search me, O God" are widely used. But the psalm also speaks about hatred. David writes: "Do I not hate those who hate you, O LORD, and do I not loathe those who rise up against you? I hate them with perfect hatred; I count them my enemies" (vv. 21-22). In Psalm 26:5 David similarly says, "I hate the company of evildoers, and will not sit with the wicked." But the behavior of David with regard to enemies falls short of providing us with a command that should be obeyed. In Deuteronomy Jehovah was very clear about how the invading Israelites were to deal with the Canaanites who lived there.

> When the LORD your God brings you into the land that you are about to enter and occupy, and he clears away many nations before you—the Hittites, the Girgashites, the Amorites, the Canaanites, the Perizzites, the Hivites, and the Jebusites, seven nations mightier and

more numerous than you—and when the LORD your God gives them over to you and you defeat them, then you must utterly destroy them. (Deut 7:1-2)

And in Deuteronomy 30:7 Moses said in his final address to the nation, "The LORD your God will put all these curses on your enemies and on the adversaries who took advantage of you." We would not interpret this Old Testament data as constituting a divine standard that we should hate our enemies, but Jewish leaders in the first century did. We know that the Essenes at Qumran did teach that faithful Jews were to hate their enemies (Hagner, 1993). Enemies to the first-century Jew were Gentiles, seen as synonymous with persecutors; neighbors were fellow Jews (Geldenhuys, 1966). In spite of what the religion of the day advocated, Jesus said the actual obligation of God's people was that they love their enemies with *agape* love. He did not just correct the false teaching of the day, he required of his followers that they actually reach out to their enemies, that they seek the best for their enemies, and that they love them with the highest form of love.

The New Testament does speak in other places of enemies. Zechariah sang of the day when the promised Messiah would provide the nation with salvation from their enemies and safety from their threats (Lk 1:71, 74). When the seventy-two returned to Jesus from their mission of evangelism, Jesus said he had given them power over their enemies (Lk 10:19). But nothing in the Old Testament or the Talmud paralleled the teaching of Jesus in Matthew 5:43: The disciples of Jesus are to love their enemies (Hagner, 1993; McNeile, 1961). This standard is not a minor or unimportant part of God's economy. Jesus said we are to love our enemies and to pray for them so "that you may be children of your Father in heaven" (Mt 5:45). As God provides good things for the good and wicked alike (v. 45), so are we to love with *agape* love both friend and enemy.

Luke's Presentation of Enemy Love

Luke records this command of Jesus as part of his Sermon on the Plain, so named because of Luke 6:17: "He came down with them and stood on a level place." This sermon expands upon the Isaiah text Jesus read at the synagogue in Nazareth as recorded by Luke in chapter four. The Sermon on the Plain calls for a living out of the ideals that the Messiah proclaimed were the essence of his mission (Evans, 1990). In this sermon, Jesus used teaching materials arranged in an order different from that of the Sermon on the Mount. The new standard of *agape* love for enemies appears to open a major section of the sermon. Loving one's enemies consists of doing good to them, blessing them and praying for them (Lk 6:27-28). All of these verbs are in the present imperative form, indicating that we are to habitually perform these acts toward those who are against us (Plummer, 1906). Enemies include not only those whom we hate but those who hate us; we cannot maintain personal vendettas, nurse along bitterness and resentment toward others or harbor ill-will (Moffatt, 1929). Instead we are to love our enemies.

In the verses that follow, Jesus elaborates on enemy love to discuss several important themes (Lk 6:29-36). When we are targets of violence, Jesus calls us to turn the other cheek (v. 29). When people steal from us, we are not to stop them, and we are to give of what we have to those who need it (vv. 29-30). In other words, "Do to others as you would have them do to you," the famous Golden Rule (v. 31). What Jesus is demanding of us is radical and beyond the limits of what godless people do or would want to do. Loving the loving, doing good to the good, lending to the credit-worthy are all behaviors that even "sinners" do, said Jesus (vv. 32-34). But what Jesus is asking from his followers is that they love their enemies by doing good to them and even by lending to them (vv. 35). "Your reward will be great, and you will be children of the Most High; for he is kind to the ungrateful and the wicked. Be merciful, just as your Father is merciful" (Lk 6:35-36). Because God loves all people equally, both good and bad, we are prompted to forgive and love all people as God does (Mohler, 1975).

This new ethical standard places heavy interpersonal expectations on all believers. In effect, we will never fulfill it perfectly or completely, and it will require our constant attention as we seek to implement it in our lives. We strive toward attainment even though we know that its extensive demands can never be fully met.

Does this mean we are to labor and strive in continual defeat? No, it means that we are to love, and love some more, and continue growing in love. We are not just to enjoy the love that God has displayed toward us, but to manifest that love to others so that they also may know of God's great love for them. The indwelling Spirit grants strength to grow in the practice of the love ethic of Jesus.

It is striking that Jesus gives us no guarantee that loving our enemies will change them. Should that be the outcome, one would naturally rejoice. But the focus and intent of our love for enemies is not that they would change. This hope is peculiarly attractive to North American Christians who are obsessed with outcomes and with what works. But we are to love enemies because God does and because doing so will change *us*. It will bring the disciples of Jesus closer to their Master. It will add a cubit to your "own moral stature" (Moffatt, 1929, p. 116). It will help wash away from our interpersonal lives the resentments that can so easily characterize our attitudes toward others.

The nature of enemy love. Just what is *agape* love for enemies? It is clearly love for people not because of what they are but in spite of their "being just that" (Brunner, 1956, p. 65).

> Such love cannot be exactly the same as the love of personal affection which knits people closely in special ties; it is generalized into a goodwill of active interest, for which the best definition is 'devotion to the ends of God in human personality.' . . . Neither is it possible to 'love' our enemies in the sense that we can pretend to care for them as we do for the like-minded. (Moffatt, 1929, pp. 43-44)

Love of one's enemies is not love in the stead of love for family and friends but in addition to it. We cannot love enemies in exactly the same way we love a spouse or a close family member, but we can seek the highest good for our enemy just as we would for spouse or family (Barclay, 1975). Sometimes we seek to soften this command by making a distinction between liking someone and loving someone. We say, sometimes rather tritely, that while we do have to love everyone, we don't have to like everyone. Such distinctions may help us feel we can obey the law of enemy love, but they probably were not at all in the mind of Jesus when he first laid down for us this new standard. "Let me say very clearly and simply that loving without liking is not loving at all. . . . Please deliver me from the love of people who do not like me" (Kelsey, 1981, p. 155).

The example of Jesus. When we think of examples of Jesus' love for us we recall the graciousness of his washing the disciples' feet (Jn 13), his generous invitation to all to come to him (Mt 11:28-30), and especially his death on the cross. Jesus loved everyone he encountered with *agape* love, but we are surprised that on only one occasion do the Gospel records explicitly state that Jesus loved a specific individual.

We know that Jesus loved Lazarus, but the Greek work used there is *phileo* (Jn 11:3). John describes himself as the disciple Jesus loved (*agape*, Jn 13:23; 19:26; 21:7, 20), but these statements reflect John's experience and are not a direct statement of Jesus. The only direct reference to the *agape* love of Jesus for an individual comes in Mark 10:21: "Jesus, looking at him, loved him." We learn a great deal about this rich young man in Mark's account. Both Matthew and Luke who also record the story omit the reference to the love of Jesus for this young man. The young man approached Jesus in a very worshipful manner and asked Jesus what he should do to inherit eternal life (v. 17). Jesus told him to obey the commandments. "He said to him, 'Teacher, I have kept all these since my youth'" (v. 20). He apparently had been reared in a pious Jewish home. At that point in Mark's account, we learn that Jesus loved this young man. The account ends on a sad note, however, when Jesus challenges the young man to give up his wealth and share it with the poor. "When he heard this, he was shocked and went away grieving, for he had many possessions" (v. 22).

We can see the love of Jesus for his enemies when he prays for them from the cross: "Father, forgive them; for they do not know what they are doing" (Lk 23:34). The best account we have of the love of Jesus for a specific enemy is his treatment of an official who represented the high priest at one phase of the trial of Jesus. "One of the police standing nearby struck Jesus on the face, saying, 'Is that how you answer the high priest?' " (Jn 18:22).

The *agape* love of Jesus for this official who hit him prompted a response that was aimed at seeking God's best for the man. Jesus firmly confronted the man with his offense and did not cower or shrink from the confrontation. "Jesus answered, 'If I have spoken wrongly, testify to the wrong. But if I have spoken rightly, why do you strike me?' " (Jn 18:23). We wonder how long this question of Jesus rang in the ears and the heart of this man. Did he later come to realize his offense against the Son of Man? Or did he go to his grave never having responded to this instance of *agape* love from the Savior? An *agape* love response to an enemy may not always look exactly like the response Jesus gave this religious official, but it will always seek God's best for the enemy, no matter who he or she may be.

The Practice of Enemy Love

Strategies to help us implement this interpersonal standard Jesus has given to us must necessarily consist of generalizations and broad principles. In each specific case, we must rely on the leading of the Holy Spirit to direct us in what we do for enemies and how we love them (Mt 10:17-20). Nonetheless, we can learn some strategies which will put us on the correct trajectory toward learning what it means to love our enemies with *agape* love. The three imperatives that follow the command to love our enemies in Luke's Gospel will serve as our outline. The entire process of loving one's enemies, however, is predicated on first admitting that we do have enemies, that people do hate or dislike us, and that we are capable of exceedingly sinful attitudes of malice, retribution and revenge. If we attempt to maintain that we love everyone, that everyone loves us and that we have no ill will toward anyone, we are not prepared to begin obeying Christ's command to love our enemies. Jesus had enemies; so do we. Only after we have made a fair and complete analysis of our own imperfections are we ready to start on the quest to "Be perfect, therefore, as your heavenly Father is perfect" (Mt 5:48).

Do good to your enemies. How shall we shape our behaviors toward those from whom we feel dislike or hostility, or those toward whom we feel ill will or bitterness? Obviously we must first stop all bad behaviors toward them: plotting revenge in our imagination, withholding normal interactions with them, avoiding them, retreating from opportunities to have relationships with them. Taking punitive action, seeking to get even, or sabotaging those we hate may all be temptations to the very hurt or angry person, but these behaviors never honor God. A major bad behavior toward enemies that we must stop is the powerful impulse we have to gossip about those with whom we have some type of grudge. Passing along information that does not belong to others, that unfairly puts people in a bad light or that exaggerates or falsifies the truth is often the most damaging behavior we can display regarding our enemies. And just because it is unknown to the person does not ameliorate its tragic damage.

Eventually, taking positive actions that will benefit the enemy may become possible. In the case of Jesus at his trial, it was the positive action of firmly confronting the police officer with his offense. But the positive actions the Spirit may lead us to will vary from individual to individual and from situation to situation. Watching for opportunities to be kind is an important beginning step. Finding redeeming qualities in our enemies can also be a positive act, though a private one.

A challenging example of doing good toward enemies in the most difficult circumstances comes from the life of St. Perpetua.

> St. Perpetua was martyred by wild beasts in North Africa in the first part of the second century. When she was asked why she did not curse the informers, the judge, those who were about to put her into the arena and those gathered to watch, she replied, "They already suffer from the attack of the evil one. I would not want to add to their burden with my curses." (Kelsey, 1981, p. 162)

Bless your enemies. Curiously, we can bless our enemies by learning about ourselves in the process of learning to love them. When we react with hurt and anger as a result of an interpersonal conflict, the conflict may reveal more about ourselves than it does about the other party of the conflict itself. Have we ever stopped to ask ourselves why we so often take offense or get angry or react negatively in certain situations? Do these repeated conflicts, in fact, tell us important things about ourselves? "Frequently others are clever enough to hit upon our Achilles heel and reveal to us something we should know about ourselves but never would have discovered without their help" (Michael & Norrisey, 1981, p. 145). The best way to learn about these inner flaws in ourselves that continually get provoked by other people is to spend time in a relationship with a trusted friend who can help us identify these personal weaknesses.

We bless our enemies when we conduct an attitude check. How do we treat those who oppose us, those with whom we have marked disagreements both within and outside the church? It is a common human temptation to allow our negative attitudes to snowball and take on a life of their own. When our enemies then look at the impact of our lives, they are hardly able to see what should be the hallmark of the

Christian: that we love as Christ loved. Snowballing negative attitudes can consume us even when we are engaged in working for goals that please God.

> In the culture wars of the first century, there was a group of activists who came down on the right side of all the values questions. They rejected relativism and secularism. They were unwavering adherents of ethical absolutism. They were committed to the Judeo-Christian values of monogamy in marriage and chastity outside it. They promoted monotheism against polytheistic Roman paganism. Clearly the Pharisees were considered the Religious Right of Israel. (Ortberg, 1997, p. 25)

But the Pharisees were unable to love their enemies because of their entrenchment in and commitment to being theologically correct. Only frequent attitude checks regarding our interactions with our enemies will prevent spiritual hardness and disobedience to Christ's command to love our enemies.

Pray for your enemies. This last command of Jesus regarding love for enemies is surely the hardest to obey. Praying for enemies requires great spiritual discipline and strength. If we cannot find a place to start, Kelsey (1981) suggests praying the Lord's Prayer for them. "Our Father in heaven, hallowed be your name in the life of my enemy; may your kingdom come to his life; may your will be done in her life." Praying thus will change us and enable us to do more loving of enemies than we have done in the past. Morton Kelsey gives us another practical suggestion: don't list your enemies on your prayer list under the topic *Enemies!* (Kelsey scatters names throughout his prayer list so no wandering eyes could ever reconstruct his own private enemy list.) We need to see our enemies as God sees them. He loves them; so should we. He grants them common grace and blessing; so should we. He has a purpose for their lives, and we should be praying that such divine purposes will be accomplished in them. Praying for our enemies can help create this sensitivity to how God views our enemies.

Conclusion
The interpersonal factor in human personality equips us with an approach

to others that is extraverted or introverted, warm or cool, gregarious or isolating, assertive or retreating, active or inactive, excitement-seeking or excitement-avoiding, and positive or negative. As believers we are to add to this repertoire loving even our enemies. Loving our enemies is a lifelong growth process for us all.

Someone asked me once what happens when we have dealt with all the enemies in our lives. I replied that we need not worry. God loves us so much and is so interested in our growth that in his infinite mercy and love he will always provide us with a few more! (Kelsey, 1981, p. 168)

8

Be Trustworthy

INTEGRITY. TRUSTWORTHINESS. HONESTY. THESE ARE FAMILIAR THEMES THAT challenge and stretch all of us. Mark O. Hatfield, former senator from Oregon, has lived a consistent witness to these character traits during his entire career of public service. His display of Christian integrity is an example for every follower of Jesus.

In 1966, for example, as governor of Oregon, Hatfield was adamantly opposed to the Vietnam War, a position that drew opposition and even hostility from many quarters. At the same time, President Lyndon Johnson, himself under criticism, was seeking the endorsement of continued American involvement in Southeast Asia from leaders across the country. Thus, when the governors of every state held a conference in Los Angeles that July, Johnson asked that they go on record as approving his policy. The nation was deeply divided over the Vietnam conflict, and many political leaders felt such a showing of unity with the president would help heal the rift. Influential politicians told Hatfield, "Don't rat on America." If he wasn't willing to vote in favor of Johnson's policy, they asked him to at least be conveniently out of the meeting room when the poll of governors was taken. At the appointed time, the roll call began, and each governor cast his vote under the harsh glare of the television lights. One by one they said yes to the president's policy, until at last there were 49 affirmative votes. But when Hatfield's turn came, knowing his political career might be at risk, he nonetheless quietly voted no—the lone dissenting vote. (Integrity under pressure, 1988, p. 128)

The second interpersonal requirement of Jesus' followers is that they be *trustworthy*—persons of simple but powerful integrity like Senator Hatfield. We have seen how Jesus' asking us to show love is a difficult interpersonal expectation because it is so extensive and comprehensive. We can spend an entire lifetime working at our commitment to love even enemies and never fully fulfill that commandment of Jesus. Being trustworthy is quite a different thing. We can attain a standard of trustworthiness and a deserved reputation for integrity by consistently following the precepts of Jesus. We can establish trustworthiness as a habit of holiness, especially when we begin that pattern early in life. Parenting is crucial to building this trait into our lives. Yet even for those who had inadequate parenting, it is never too late to develop patterns of trustworthiness. The Holy Spirit is ready to help us incorporate this quality into our lives, and God is pleased when we pursue it with vigor.

Why does Jesus make interpersonal demands of his followers that exceed the interpersonal traits of humans in general? Why is it so essential that the followers of Jesus be known as persons who show love and are trustworthy? The answer revolves around the character of God. Because he is love and because he is absolutely trustworthy, his children must mirror these traits. Loving persons of integrity thus become winsome witnesses to the character and care of God—something the world desperately needs to see and know about.

Could we live in a world where integrity and trustworthiness were totally absent? Life would be exceedingly difficult.

Imagine a society, no matter how ideal in other respects, where word and gesture could never be counted upon. Questions asked, answers given, information exchanged—all would be worthless. Were all statements randomly truthful or deceptive, action and choice would be undermined from the outset. There must be a minimal degree of trust in communication for language and action to be more than a stab in the dark. This is why some level of truthfulness has always been seen as essential to human society, no matter how deficient the observance of other moral principles. (Bok, 1978, p. 18)

We depend on trustworthiness in those around us. Simple tasks such as shopping for groceries require that we trust not only the packaging and labeling information on the products we purchase but also the computer's calculation of our total amount due for these purchases. If we were convinced that everyone around us was untrustworthy, we would never present our money to the grocery clerk until the clerk had laid out for us within easy reach the precise amount of change due us. And if the grocery clerk considered all customers absolutely untrustworthy, the clerk would never bother to tally up the total cost until we had proven that we had sufficient funds with us to complete the transaction. Trust is a must if society is to function smoothly.

The trustworthiness that Jesus expects from us, however, is above and beyond these normal, societal levels of integrity. Jesus challenges us to be as trustworthy as he was during his earthly life and as trustworthy as his Father is. His followers are to witness to the world of their faith in the living God not just by word alone but by the consistency of both word and deed, the hallmark of integrity.

What Is Honesty?

In spite of society's dependence upon trustworthiness, and in spite of widespread trust that allows commerce and important forms of interpersonal interactions to proceed rather smoothly, people remain concerned that integrity in our society as a whole and in the lives of individuals is eroding at an alarming rate. We have become increasingly skeptical of politicians and their promises because pre-election words and post-election deeds often do not match well. We have learned to avoid most informal business interactions with people we do not know because financial irresponsibility is so common. We have learned to be skeptical of marketing slogans and promotional hype because we have seen normal words stretched and forced to take on new meanings in order to sell merchandise and trinkets.

Some people handle these problems by refusing to vote, by never lending money to anyone under any circumstances, or by poking fun at how the commercial promotion of products stretches and alters the truth. One observer wrote that "exclusive" on a product label can sometimes mean "imported," "all new" may mean that parts are not interchangeable with the previous design, "maintenance-free" means that the product is impossible to repair, and "aerospace technology" may mean that a technician in their plant had been laid off by a defense contractor before being hired by them. Humor does help, but it does not solve the problem. The insidious growth of untrustworthiness in our culture breeds skepticism, cynicism and interpersonal distance. All the more reason for us to follow the commands of Jesus, who calls us to higher levels of trustworthiness and integrity than are found among those who do not follow the teachings of Jesus.

Trying to decide the meaning of honesty appears simple on the surface. Honesty is telling the truth and nothing but the truth. The command of the Old Testament not to bear false witness is clear: only the truth will please God. We must never lie. Augustine ruled out all lies and wrote that all are sinful, though admittedly some lies are more sinful than others. He constructed an eight-fold hierarchy of deceit from the greatest sin of lying (using lies in the teaching of religion) to the least sinful lies (lies which harm no one and which save people from defilement).

An example of this latter type of sin would occur during a time of war when soldiers bent on rape and pillage break into a civilian home and demand to know if women are present. When the Christian homeowner replies "No, no women are here," when in fact they are hiding in the closets, Augustine would say that the statement is a lie and therefore is sinful but is the least sinful of all lies. Such a lie protects and spares people from harm and can be forgiven by God. Augustine's position is distinct from situational ethics, which would say that because the statement helps and does not harm, it is not a lie to be confessed and is not sinful.

An important part of the definition of a lie resides at the level of intention. Clearly intended lies are "the most sharply etched forms of duplicity" (Bok, 1978, p. 242). When someone intends to mislead and deliberately does so, the nature of the statement is clear: it is a lie. When someone deceives or misleads another person without the intention to do so, the statement is still a lie but with different import. Integrity is discerning what is right and wrong, acting in accordance with that discernment even if at great personal cost, and affirming openly that you are acting on what you think is right and wrong (Carter, 1996b).

We can participate in untruthfulness in a multitude of ways. "Whether to lie, equivocate, be silent, or tell the truth in any given situation is often a hard decision. Hard because duplicity can take so many forms, be present to such different degrees, and have such different purposes and results" (Bok, 1978, p. xvi). For example, we can be dishonest by not representing the full and complete truth with a statement we make, by communicating material that is slanderous, by misrepresenting or compromising standards, by cheating or by remaining silent. We can be evasive or exaggerate. We can use a euphemism to describe an act or object indirectly, to avoid being truthfully descriptive. We can change the subject rather artfully so as avoid a certain topic. Doctors do not always share with their patients the full and unvarnished truth about their illnesses. We can disguise material so its true identity is difficult to discern. All of these forms of deceit and untruthfulness make the issue of determining what is a lie and what is not a lie somewhat difficult.

"White lies," lies about trivial matters that have no harmful intent, are common. In the normal exchanges of polite social conversation we often allow convention to determine our answers, rather than absolute truthfulness. "How do you like my new jacket?" "Nice! It looks great on you!" Saying "Frankly, it makes you look dumpy" just isn't polite.

At times the actual truth is not a part of anyone's concern. When doctors give patients a placebo medication without informing the patient, the intent is positive, the effects may be positive—but the nature of the interaction is dishonest. When we write letters of reference as part of job applications or school admission procedures, are we always totally honest? Do we sometimes omit material that could be important to the process? Is it fair to the applicant for us to pursue brutal honesty in these circumstances? When a phone call awakens me from sleep, I am sure my groggy voice and muddled orientation make it obvious to the caller that I was asleep when the call came. But it is personally difficult for me in that situation to be truthful. "Oh, I'm sorry—did I wake you?" "No, I wasn't asleep . . ."

Facing these forms of dishonesty is necessary yet difficult. The Bible calls us to integrity in our business dealings with other people. The standards are clear and the implications many.

> You shall not have in your bag two kinds of weights, large and small. You shall not have in your house two kinds of measures, large and small. You shall have only a full and honest weight; you shall have only a full and honest measure, so that your days may be long in the land that the LORD your God is giving you. (Deut 25:13-16)

Our interpersonal dealings are to be characterized by honesty and integrity.

> Interpersonal functioning is extensive and embraces a multitude of relationships: how we conduct ourselves in friendship, in intimacy, in commerce, in politics, in civic life, and in church life. Perhaps the most challenging arena of all is in the church.
>
> Conflict, misrepresentation, gossip, and false pride chip away at the church. Congregations split. Friendships collapse. Effectiveness sinks. The church's testimony in the community suffers. And it all happens because we have not learned to apply basic principles of honesty in the body of Christ. (White, 1979, p. 145)

Applying standards of honesty in the church may be so difficult for us because it is the one place in our lives where we would like to believe all people are honest and above deceit. Yet we are all fallen sinners. How we interpret the Bible, how we witness to our faith, how we construct our theologies, are also important expressions of honesty that God calls for in our interpersonal dealings within the church (Sell, 1990). Stephen L. Carter relates a line sometimes attributed to Sam Goldwyn of Hollywood fame: "The most important thing in acting is honesty; once you learn to fake that, you're in" (Carter, 1996a, p. 74).

How often does that ethic apply to church, church membership, church leadership and church participation?

Jesus and Trustworthiness

Trustworthiness involves the reliability of a person's word. When someone makes a promise, does the person intend to keep the promise and have the ability to keep the promise, and can others count on the fulfillment of the promise? The reason these issues are so important for interpersonal functioning is obvious: If agreements between people are so uncertain as to be essentially worthless, how can people live together in the necessary relationships of life? We have learned that all humans share a basic propensity to deal with interpersonal matters with either a great deal of extraversion, a great deal of introversion, or some gradation of the two. But the gospel calls God's people to additional interpersonal responsibilities, one of which is to the solidity and reliability of a word that others can count on.

Jesus addressed this problem among the religious leaders of his day. The Gospel of Matthew records for us two different occasions on which Jesus dealt with this problem. Both of these events appear only in Matthew and not in Mark, Luke or John. We wonder if Matthew had a special interest in the topic of integrity. Could his background as a tax collector have made him sensitive to issues of honesty and trustworthiness? The reputation for tax collectors was not good, and Matthew may have carried with him a lifelong interest in this problem. We will first examine the account that comes chronologically late in the public ministry of Jesus and conclude with the second major account that we find in the Sermon on the Mount.

The Third Woe

In the last section of his Gospel, Matthew draws together material that summarizes and epitomizes the opposition Jesus the Messiah experienced as he preached the good news of the kingdom to the people of God. Matthew 23 contains some of the sharpest language we have recorded from the lips of Jesus. In Matthew 23 Jesus first addresses the crowds and his own disciples. He urges them to continue obeying the words of the scribes and the Pharisees since they were the religious leaders of the day, but Jesus warned the crowds not to follow their deeds, "for they do not practice what they preach" (Mt 23:3). The religious leaders of the nation were guilty of adding to the burdens of the people (Mt 23:4), an indictment made all the worse when Jesus charges that the leaders did not even care about the plight of those who tried to follow their leadership. The behavior of the Pharisees was in sharp contrast to that of Jesus who told his followers, "Come to me, all you that are weary and are carrying burdens, and I will give you rest. Take my yoke upon you, and learn from me; for I am gentle and humble in heart, and you will find rest for your souls. For my yoke is easy, and my burden is light" (Mt 11:28-30).

After warning the crowds and his disciples about the hypocrisy of the Pharisees, Jesus begins to pronounce a series of seven woes on the scribes and Pharisees. The third woe deals with oaths and is the subject of our interest here. The giving of oaths was common practice when people wished to impress upon their business partners the fact that they could be trusted to keep their word. But the practice had developed to ludicrous levels that totally bypassed the central issue: If people lived interpersonal lives that were centrally characterized by trustworthiness, all the oath-taking in the world would not be necessary.

> Woe to you, blind guides, who say, "Whoever swears by the sanctuary is bound by nothing, but whoever swears by the gold of the sanctuary is bound by the oath." You blind fools! For which is greater, the gold or the sanctuary that has made the gold sacred? And you say, "Whoever swears by the altar is bound by nothing, but whoever swears by the gift that is on the altar is bound by the oath." How blind you are! For which is greater, the gift or the altar that makes the gift sacred? So whoever swears by the altar, swears by it and by everything on it; and whoever swears by the sanctuary, swears by it and by the one who dwells in it; and whoever swears by heaven swears by the throne of God and by the one who is seated upon it. (Mt 23:16-22)

Jewish society developed over a period of several centuries an elaborate system of oath-taking. The practice began with God himself in the Old Testament. God entered into an important covenant with Abram (Gen 12) when he lived in the land of Ur, a covenant that was renewed with Abraham once he arrived in the Promised Land (Gen 15) and on the occasion of Abraham's willingness to sacrifice Isaac (Gen 22).

Later in the Old Testament, writers refer back to the Abrahamic covenant as an oath that God took to certify the surety and sanctity of his promises to Abraham and his descendants (Ex 33:1; see also Ex 13:11; Deut 6:18). When the people of Israel entered into a renewal of the covenant at the end of the life of Moses, God again sealed the covenant with an oath (Deut 29:12). God fulfilled his oath to his people because he loved them (Deut 7:8). God swore this oath by using his own name, the ultimate guarantee of fulfillment. This same language is employed to describe the covenant God made with David as recorded in 1 Chronicles 17 and 2 Samuel 7. "The LORD swore to David a sure oath from which he will not turn back: 'One of the sons of your body I will set on your throne' " (Ps 132:11).

Not all the oaths God swore were pleasant ones for the people of Israel. "For forty years I loathed that generation and said, 'They are a people whose hearts go astray, and they do not regard my ways.' Therefore in my anger I swore, 'They shall not enter my rest' " (Ps 95:10-11).

The Mosaic law provided for oath taking. "When a man makes a vow to the LORD or swears an oath to bind himself by a pledge, he shall not break his word; he shall do according to all that proceeds out of his mouth" (Num 30:2). An example of such an oath is referred to in Psalm 119:106: "I have sworn an oath and confirmed it, to observe your righteous ordinances."

So the Jewish habit of oath taking had a valid foundation; it rested on the behavior of God toward his people, and it was allowed in the Old Testament. The only provision that the law made was that when a person made an oath, it must be kept. However, various additions and accretions gradually added themselves to the simple command of Numbers 30:2 so that by the days of Jesus, the religious leaders of the nation had developed an elaborate schema for determining the worth of various types of oaths. It is these elaborations that Jesus attacks in the third woe of Matthew 23 (vv. 16-22).

Oaths between human individuals were needed to counter the expectation of deceit and untrustworthiness. If every person were honest and committed to keeping his or her word, no oaths would be necessary. But because of human depravity and frailty, the giving and taking of oaths facilitated human interaction. By the first century, Jewish tradition forbade faithful Jews from uttering the name of the Most High (Keener, 1993). Thus pious Jews sought to find sacred and important items on which to swear an oath that would be important but less important than the name of God himself. The items listed in this third woe, the temple, the altar, and heaven itself, were examples of the various bases for oaths in use at that time.

In this passage Jesus is not objecting to the giving and taking of oaths as much as he scorns the gradations of importance that Pharisaical law had determined for these items. The Pharisees had resolved that if someone swore by the temple the oath was not binding unless one swore by the gold of the temple. Swearing by the altar was not binding, but swearing by the gift on the altar was. Jesus said that these distinctions were foolish. The gold of the temple was only sacred because it was located in the temple. The offering on the altar was only sacred because it was on the altar. Ultimately, no valid distinction can be made. All oaths are binding because all oaths are made in the presence of God himself. "The conclusion is again clear: the implied distinctions are unjustified, and thus all oaths must be honored. Oath taking is always in effect an agreement in God's presence" (Hagner, 1995, p. 670). The gradations of binding and non-binding oaths must have applied to the oath taking of a Jew with a pagan, since all faithful Jews would presumably know which oaths were the good ones and which oaths were the worthless ones!

The guideline that Jesus gives us here for trustworthiness is clear: We must honor our word and be persons of reliability because we consistently and faithfully keep our word. To punctuate this truth even more sharply, Jesus changes his style of address when speaking to the Pharisees from calling them "hypocrites" (as he does in each of the other six woes, Mt 23:13, 15, 23, 25, 27, 29) to calling them "blind guides" three different times (Mt 23:16-17, 19) in the third woe. Jesus had used this appellation for Pharisees on one earlier occasion (Mt 15:14). The spectacle of a blind person serving as a guide for another blind person is ludicrous, even humorous. No doubt the Pharisees, however, were not amused by this disparaging label Jesus attached to them.

The Fourth Antithesis
Matthew was fond of giving his readers lists of memorable material from the lips of Jesus. Whereas the Matthew 23 material regarding oaths was tucked into a list of seven woes, the Matthew 5 recording of the Sermon on the Mount gives us six antitheses in the form of "You have heard that it was said . . . but I say unto you" (Mt 5:21, 27, 31, 33, 38, 43). The antithesis concerned with oaths is the fourth.

Again, you have heard that it was said to those of ancient times, "You shall not swear falsely, but carry out the vows you have made to the Lord." But I say to you, Do not swear at all, either by heaven, for it is the throne of God, or by the earth, for it is his footstool, or by Jerusalem, for it is the city of the great King. And do not swear by your head, for you cannot make one hair white or black. Let your word be "Yes, Yes" or "No, No"; anything more than this comes from the evil one. (Mt 5:33-37)

Here the teaching of Jesus regarding oaths is more extensive. He not only questions the elaborate system of swearing oaths by different levels of sacred and honored parts of God's world, he adds a ban on oaths altogether. While the religious leaders of the day were negotiating the minute parts of the various types of oaths, Jesus was telling the people to be persons of integrity, people whose word and deed are congruent.

Jesus began by affirming the Old Testament's approach to oaths: the people of God must keep all the oaths they make. "And you shall not swear falsely by my name, profaning the name of your God: I am the LORD" (Lev 19:12). As we have seen before, the very necessity of a law to govern the giving and taking of oaths was because of the untruthfulness that pervades the human race. Jesus calls his followers to such a high ethic so that they will be known by those around them as persons whose word can be trusted.

Instead of fretting about the relative value of this oath versus that oath, Jesus says let your word mean what it says. Be known as people who when they say yes mean yes and who when they say no mean no. This teaching of Jesus is repeated in the book of James. "Above all, my beloved, do not swear, either by heaven or by earth or by any other oath, but let your "Yes" be yes and your "No" be no, so that you may not fall under condemnation" (Jas 5:12). To those who wished to use an oath that would not obligate them but would allow them appear trustworthy, Jesus and James say, "No!"

Various Anabaptist groups and the Quakers have understood the words of Jesus here as an absolute ban on swearing an oath just as they have understood the words of Jesus earlier in Matthew as a mandate for pacifism. Refusing to take oaths has made life difficult for them in many ways, and they have endured persecution because of it. Many of the

Anabaptist groups also understood these important words of Jesus as a ban on signing a promissory note at bank. To do so would be to violate their dignity and to assume that their word of promise was not trustworthy.

> [People] who so believe insist that the integrity of life transcends any and all oaths. Furthermore, being called on to swear an oath is itself a violation of that integrity. Such a position is difficult for others to understand. Time and again, when attempting to explain my reluctance to swear an oath, I have been told: "What difference does it make? Go ahead and take it." And I must reply: "That is exactly the point. If it makes no difference why do it? And wouldn't taking it hypocritically debase its coinage?" (Kermit Eby in Hess, 1978, p. 15)

Other followers of Jesus argue that these words of Jesus do not represent an absolute ban on swearing an oath; rather Jesus is calling us to lives of integrity that will not have to depend on the swearing of oaths for our reputation of trustworthiness. Our word should be valuable and trusted by others because we have lived lives of integrity and trustworthiness. Elsewhere in the New Testament we have indications that oaths continued to be used, although not in the style and manner of their use by the Pharisees.

At the trial of Jesus before Caiaphas, Jesus is put under oath. He does not refuse to participate in the oath but responds to it. "The high priest said to him, 'I charge you under oath by the living God, tell us if you are the Messiah, the Son of God" (Mt 26:63). Although Jesus had previously remained silent, he answered under the oath (Mt 26:64).

In 1 Corinthians 15:31 Paul appears to give his readers an oath just as he appears to do in 1 Thessalonians 5:27. In Hebrews 6:13-17 the author of that book uses oaths made by one individual to another as a point of illustration regarding the certainty of God's promises. The author would hardly have used oaths for this illustration if the ban of Jesus on oaths had been absolute. What is clear is that in no way are oaths to be used extensively, casually or deceitfully. Instead our word is to mean what it says.

The Hard Part

Interpreting these various passages of the teaching of Jesus regarding integrity is the easy part. Putting them into practice is the hard task facing us. We are to be known by those around us as people of integrity. Our interpersonal relationships must be trustworthy. Integrity can only come from the discipline of consistent application of the intent to be truthful and to keep our word. Eusebius Hieronymus Sophrojius, whom we know as St. Jerome, wrote about the integrity needed by the clergy.

> Your deeds must not belie your words, lest, when you are speaking in church, someone may say to himself, "Why do you not practice what you preach?" A teacher fond of good living may fill his own stomach and the discourse on the benefits of fasting; even a robber can possibly accuse others of greed; but in a priest of Christ mind and mouth should be in harmony. (Jerome, 1992, p. 60)

Keeping mind and mouth in harmony is the path to interpersonal integrity. Anyone who has been deceived by a person who reneges on a promise or who simply does not carry through on responsibilities knows how devastating that disappointment can be. We want to trust others, but sometimes that trust is violated. And when it is, the hurt, harm and long-term consequences are many and extensive. Integrity is normally at the heart of a good person's reputation. A story is told about Abraham Lincoln as a young man, working as a postmaster in New Salem, Illinois. When the Post Office was closed, Lincoln lost his job. It wasn't until several years later that a federal auditor was able to come to Illinois to settle up accounts with the former postmaster, now attorney Lincoln. When the auditor determined that Lincoln owed the government $17, Lincoln went to a trunk, pulled out a bundle in which was tied $17, and paid the amount due (Engstrom, 1990).

While some tales of integrity regarding the great people of our heritage take on mythological proportions (e.g., George Washington and the cherry tree), the very fact that we cherish and nurture these stories is evidence of how important are the matters of honesty and personal integrity in human affairs.

The apostle Paul experienced several frustrating encounters with the church in Corinth, misunderstandings that at times had to be settled through correspondence. We read of some of these exchanges in the two Corinthian letters in the New Testament. In 2 Corinthians 1, the apostle contends that he has dealt with the Corinthian believers "with frankness and godly sincerity" (v. 12). God's grace characterized his dealings with this struggling group of believers (v. 12); Paul was convinced that his letters to them had been written with clarity that they understood partially but would someday understand completely (v. 13, 14). One contentious matter concerned his planned visit to Corinth.

> Since I was sure of this, I wanted to come to you first, so that you might have a double favor; I wanted to visit you on my way to Macedonia, and to come back to you from Macedonia and have you send me on to Judea. Was I vacillating when I wanted to do this? Do I make my plans according to ordinary human standards, ready to say "Yes, yes" and "No, no" at the same time? (2 Cor 1:15-17)

This passage reminds us of Matthew 5. Paul is asserting that he did not make his plans lightly or indecisively as would someone "in a worldly manner" (v. 17 NIV). Paul's interpersonal skills included trustworthiness that is so frequently missing among those who do not follow God. He was deeply distressed, however, that the Corinthians did not seem to recognize his trustworthiness and were interpreting facts in such a way as to question the reliability of Paul and his word. He goes on to remind the Corinthian believers that the gospel message he has preached to them is not a mixed message with good and bad news. "For the Son of God, Jesus Christ, whom we proclaimed among you, Silvanus and Timothy and I, was not 'Yes and No'; but in him it is always 'Yes' " (2 Cor 1:19). The passage is a forceful reminder that our word and its reputation is a vital component of our Christian witness. As Jesus has commanded us, we must diligently work to ensure that our word is reliable and that we carry a reputation for trustworthiness to all who know us.

The Devil Made Me Do It

Stand-up comedian Flip Wilson could evoke tremendous laughter from his audiences with the excuse "The devil made me do it." He had the knack of attributing his behavior to the devil at the most incongruous of times— and with impeccable timing. At first glance we may recoil from such attempts to evade responsibility for action by invoking an external, satanic influence. But in the passage we have been considering, the presence of the devil is not far away. When Jesus taught that we should avoid oaths and let our simple, unvarnished word stand for reliability and trustworthiness, he concluded that section of his sermon with the statement, "Anything more than this comes from the evil one" (Mt 5:37).

Matthew refers to the "evil one" more than any other book in the New Testament with the exception of 1 John. When Jesus taught his disciples to pray, he included the petition "And do not bring us to the time of trial, but rescue us from the evil one" (Mt 6:13). The evil one is featured in the parable of the sower as snatching away sown seed (Mt 13:19) and as the father of weeds and tares that hinder the growth of the Word of God in otherwise fertile soil (Mt 13:38).

"And the enemy who sowed them is the devil" (Mt 13:39). In John's Gospel we learn that Jesus prayed that his disciples would be protected from the evil one (Jn 17:15). How then is the devil connected to the issue of trustworthiness and to the necessity of avoiding oaths? Because lies and liars are part of his kingdom and sphere of influence.

> You are from you father the devil, and you choose to do your father's desires. He was a murderer from the beginning and does not stand in the truth, because there is no truth in him. When he lies, he speaks according to his own nature, for he is a liar and the father of lies. (Jn 8:44)

The connection is simple. God is a God of truth; Satan exists because of and thrives on deceit. Lies come from him; he breeds liars. And while we might be tempted to think that this attribution is too simple, too elementary, we must remember that it is an attribution made by the Lord himself. Truth comes from God and has no other source; lies come from the evil one. This connection then helps us understand why the language of Jesus regarding oaths in both Matthew 23 and Matthew 5 is so strong. Our word and its veracity are powerful and effective witnesses to our connection with the living God. Lies, untrustworthiness, unreliability, equivocation and undependability reveal our connection to the evil one and not to the Lord.

Contemporary Examples

We are always most surprised by dishonesty and lack of integrity when it occurs in a population of people who have a reputation for sterling character and unvarnished honesty. If cheating occurs at West Point, if the Federal Bureau of Investigation is caught in a lack of candor, if the President of the United States lies, if a pastor swindles his congregation, or if a prominent Christian is discovered to be dishonest, we take note. At times we decry the media's interest in such bad news among Christians. But God would probably have it no other way. To hush up deceit when it is found among the people of God would be contrary to what the light of truth does: it exposes and reveals so that we can correct the situation. People who serve the God of truth ought not to be lying and cheating others; if so, they serve the devil, and bringing this tragedy into the light of day is the best thing that could happen.

Internal character is the best and most important determiner of integrity. If all is well on the inside of a person, trustworthiness should be the result.

The story is told of a little boy who walked down the beach. As he did, he spied a rather matronly looking lady sitting under a beach umbrella on the sand. He walked up to her and asked, "Are you a Christian?"

"Yes."

"Do you read your Bible every day?" She nodded her head yes.

"Do you pray often?"

Again she answered, "Yes."

With that he asked his final question: "Will you hold my quarter while I go swimming?"

By way of contrast, Senator Sam Ervin of Watergate fame was asked for his opinions about a recently released book by a convicted Watergate participant. He replied, "A man that would commit perjury under oath might possibly be tempted to commit it when he is not under oath. . . . I would say that before I would accept his book as credible, I would want it corroborated by all the apostles, except Judas" (*Dallas Times Herald,* 1978).

Yet, given the powerful and determining role of inner character, we also wonder about the role of the environment, external forces, and even the devil himself. Jesus indicated that the devil was not far away from problems of deceit.

Why are people untrustworthy? Recently federal agents exposed a cheating ring that helped applicants for graduate school pass their entrance examinations. Employees of the ringleader would take the examination on the east coast of the United States, telephone the questions to the west coast where a group of people would then take the examination with prior knowledge of the questions. The ringleader provided every student who paid $6,000 for his services a pencil with answers carefully encoded on the side of the pencil that enabled these students to achieve impressive scores. By the time the scam was uncovered, many students had falsely earned admission to prestigious graduate schools, had graduated, and landed jobs with prominent firms. (Rogers, 1996).

A few years earlier a major cheating scandal broke forth at the Naval Academy in Annapolis, Maryland. Again, everyone knew that the cheating was indeed cheating because of the well-defined codes of behavior that prevailed at the academy. What was uncertain to the public and the press was how much blame should be attached to the individuals involved and how much to the academic system at the school.

Pressure is indeed high. "Midshipmen combine traditional college courses with military instruction and compulsory athletics, often taking in excess of 20 credit hours a semester" (Glick & Turque, 1993, p. 44). "Midshipmen are intentionally overwhelmed with class work and drill, some of it demeaning and trivial. . . .The idea is to strengthen character in adversity. The effect, however, is to make many midshipmen deeply cynical" (Caplan, 1994, p. 33). As a result, say some analysts, students cheat in order to survive the system.

A recent survey found that 67 percent of college students admit to cheating while in school. The survey included students at the most selective colleges and universities in the nation (Kibler, 1992). But even experts in the secular arena are now arguing that we have placed too much value on the role of the environment in creating the current crisis in campus trustworthiness. Campuses must now establish training courses that "should also include education in moral development, to help students understand the relationship between moral reasoning and behavior" (Kibler, 1992, p. 32).

One professor advocates that campus cheaters be required to complete successfully a non-credit course on academic integrity. "The course would teach how to perform research, how to properly document sources, how to make full and accurate use of library and computer resources, and explain why integrity is vital in academic life" (Fishbein, 1993, p. 52). But what would prevent such dishonest students from hiring someone else to write their papers? Abigail Witherspoon, a pseudonym, describes her life writing papers for students as the life of an academic call girl. Underground paper writing industries thrive in many parts of the country (Witherspoon, 1995).

The environment does have a role to play in promoting untrustworthiness or shoring up trustworthiness. In every case, however, the person is responsible for all behaviors that have to do with a lack of integrity, and the person's inner character is likely the more powerful influence on what behaviors are displayed. Whether one's lack of integrity is wholly caused by inner forces or partially caused by the environment, the devil is involved. Flip Wilson was right, because the devil is a liar and the father of all lies.

Conclusion

A marvelous story, perhaps apocryphal, circulates about honesty and how our environment influences us.

> In the eighteenth century, Frederick II, then king of Prussia, toured a Berlin prison. The moment he set foot inside the prison, he was besieged by prisoners telling him of their unjust punishment. "I'm innocent, I'm innocent," was the cry he heard repeatedly. Finally his attention was drawn to the only man in the room who was not attempting to catch his eye. "Why are you here?" the king addressed the solitary man. "Armed robbery, Your Majesty." "Were you guilty?" the king asked. "Oh, yes, indeed, Your Majesty. I'm here because I deserve to be here." At that reply, Frederick II called to the jailer. "Release that guilty man at once. I will not have him kept in prison where he will contaminate all these fine innocent men who now occupy it." (Engstrom, 1990, p. 37)

The call of Jesus upon our lives is that we pursue our interpersonal relationships with high levels of trustworthiness and integrity, levels of character supported by inner strength and outer community support. Only then will our yes be yes and our no be no.

Section Four

Agreeableness

Introduction

Jesus & Our Attitudinal Life

AGREEABLENESS IS A PERSONALITY FACTOR THAT MEETS WITH ALMOST UNIVERSAL approval. Except for extremely Pollyannalike individuals, we tend to like agreeable people and think that they are pleasant to be around. After all, high scorers on this personality factor are sympathetic toward others and willing to reach out to help them. The agreeable person tends to feel that others will be equally helpful in return. Low scorers on agreeableness are antagonistic, far less trusting of the motives of other people, and competitive rather than cooperative. So we can see why agreeable persons are liked and why disagreeable persons are less popular.

However, disagreeableness can have its advantages. For example, in certain legal procedures in a courtroom one would not be best represented by an attorney whose primary attitude was agreeableness. Sometimes good old-fashioned bulldog tenacity is needed to prosecute a case or defend an accused person. Likewise, a law enforcement officer who could display only agreeable attitudes might have a very difficult time arresting people or enforcing traffic laws. Military officers and other soldiers must also carry out orders that call for fairly high levels of disagreeableness. Still, the preferred score on this attitudinal scale would be on the agreeable end of the continuum.

Characteristics of Agreeableness

Researchers have attached to this personality factor names such as conformity, likability, friendliness and friendly compliance (Bergeman et al., 1993). The major genetic study conducted by Bergeman and his associates detected the least amount of genetic influence on agreeableness when compared to the other four factors in the Big Five system. Research on this question is not yet conclusive. It remains possible that parenting has a significant impact on how a child develops regarding agreeableness versus disagreeableness.

Agreeableness is apparently an important component of the personality configuration of physically healthy people. Health research has worked for many years toward the identification of those personality factors that seem to characterize healthy versus unhealthy people.

> The notion that personality characteristics might influence vulnerability to illness and illness progression continues to attract widespread attention. The vigorous pace of health-related personality research offers the promise of achieving important insights into the potential role of personality in health maintenance and promotion. (Marshall, et al., 1994, p. 278)

Recent results in this field of health research suggest that two personality qualities are important in maintaining personal health:

☐ optimism, hope, a sense of internal control and the capacity to find meaning in life, a factor sometimes called *optimistic control*.

☐ rational rather than emotional expression of anger, a factor called *anger expression*.

In other words, people who have a sense of optimistic control over their lives and who express anger rationally tend to be healthier physically and tend to maintain their health better than other individuals. Both of these factors seem to have significant relationship to agreeableness. Persons with high scores in the area of optimistic control are also likely to be high scorers on agreeableness, and persons who display large amounts of anger are likely to be low scorers on agreeableness. Agreeableness seems to be an important component of what it means to be a physically healthy person.

Facets of Agreeableness

The six facets of agreeableness, like those of the other Big Five factors, demonstrate how each of the Big Five are actually composites of related traits and how a person's score on the factor can be constituted in any number of ways. The first facet is *trust,* the tendency to believe that other people are honest and well-intentioned versus believing in a cynical or skeptical manner that they are dishonest or dangerous. High scorers believe in people; low scorers are not so sure. The second facet is called *straightforwardness,* the characteristic of frank and sincere interactions with people as opposed to indirect, crafty or manipulative techniques. Straightforwardness is valued in some societies more than in others.

Altruism is the third facet of agreeableness, and it has to do with concern for the welfare of others, showing itself in generosity and willingness to assist. Low scorers are more detached from the problems of others. Facet four is *compliance.* "The high scorer tends to defer to others, to inhibit aggression, and to forgive and forget" (Costa & McCrae, 1992c, p. 18). Low scorers prefer to compete rather than to cooperate and will express anger freely when needed. The final two facets are *modesty* (humble and self-effacing rather than arrogant and conceited) and *tendermindedness* (high levels of concern for others, unlike "realists" who use only cold logic to make their decisions).

Jesus and Paul on Agreeableness

The scores that we have conjectured for Jesus and Paul (see table 8) give us a few surprises on the factor of agreeableness. Jesus scores as average, Paul as low on the factor as a whole. These results are colored by the fact that

Agreeableness Facets	Jesus	Paul
Trust	VERY LOW	VERY LOW
Straightforwardness	VERY HIGH	AVERAGE
Altruism	AVERAGE	LOW
Compliance	LOW	LOW
Modesty	LOW	AVERAGE
Tender-Mindedness	VERY HIGH	HIGH

Table 8. Jesus and Paul on agreeableness

they both experienced strong opposition to their ministries. Much of what we know about the personality of Jesus comes from accounts of his interactions with Pharisees, and we learn of Paul mainly from his exchanges with those who opposed his leadership, especially in Corinth.

Thus both Jesus and Paul score very low on trust, the tendency to take people at face value and to believe that their intentions and motivations were pure. Both routinely had to question the motives of their opponents in order to continue defending their work against strong resistance. That Jesus was straightforward and that Paul and Jesus were both high on tendermindedness are conjectures on which few would disagree.

The agreeableness factor contains a strong component of sympathy, empathy and care for others. We have seen these features in the scale as a whole and in the facets of altruism and tendermindedness. High scorers are quite simply compassionate people. In spite of the "average" score for Jesus on this factor, he was known for his compassion.

> The emotion which we should naturally expect to find most frequently attributed to that Jesus whose whole life was a mission of mercy, and whose ministry . . . was summed up in the memory of his followers as a going through the land "doing good" (Acts xi.38), is no doubt "compassion." In point of fact, this is the emotion which is most frequently attributed to him. (Warfield, 1912, p. 40)

In at least nine different places in the Gospels we learn that Jesus experienced the emotion of compassion for others. The emotion came from his internal nature as well as from his encounter with the misery and intense needs of others. We have one record in the Gospels where Jesus describes in his own words his feelings of compassion for the needs of others: "I have compassion for the crowd, because they have been with me now for these three days and have nothing to eat. If I send them away hungry to their homes, they will faint on the way—and some of them have come from a great distance" (Mk 8:2-3).

The tears of Jesus when he observed the sadness of Mary who brought to Jesus news of the death of Lazarus were tears of grief and sympathy. He wept over the unbelief of Jerusalem (Lk 19:41-42), and he uttered deep, wrenching sighs at the unbelief of the Pharisees (Mk 8:12). Clearly Jesus was a compassionate Messiah.

Humans then have as an important component of their personality makeup a range of possibilities in attitude from very agreeable to very disagreeable. What attitudes does Jesus teach should be part of our lives as his disciples? In the next two chapters we will examine two: peace of mind and self-acceptance.

9

Enjoy Peace

GOD HAS CREATED US WITH A PERSONALITY DIMENSION ON WHICH OUR ATTITUDES range from highly agreeable to highly disagreeable. These attitudes toward life in general and specific events in particular will differ from individual to individual. To this common, human attitudinal factor Jesus calls his followers to two additional attitudes. We who give allegiance to Jesus will bear the distinctive marks of peace of mind and calm self-acceptance.

Many people despair of ever enjoying peace of mind. In the heady, optimistic years after World War II, many people in North America saw a bright future to come once the political affairs of Europe had settled into peace and America's economy recovered from the war. Yet individual peace of mind remained elusive. An old Jewish rabbi lamented this state of affairs: "Talent and beauty He gives to many. Wealth is commonplace, fame not rare. But peace of mind—that is His final guerdon of approval, the fondest sign of His love. He bestows it charily. Most men are never blessed with it; others wait all their lives—yes, far into advanced age—for this gift to descend upon them" (Liebman, 1946, p. 4).

People continue to search for the peace of mind that eluded Rabbi Liebman. The promise of material prosperity, the lure of personal fulfillment through psychotherapy, and the easy demands of secularism have all failed to deliver on their pledge to provide people today with personal peace.

Yet the call of Jesus to his followers is still characterized by the promise of peace of mind, that state of calmness so many people desire. We will see that peace of mind is basically an attitude. Peace of mind is not some divinely-imposed anesthesia that numbs us to life, creating the illusion of peacefulness when reality is chaotic. Rather it is an attitude that equips us to reflect on past events, to react to present events and to anticipate future events with a confidence that God is sovereign and that we can rely on his care for us. Zechariah, the father of John the Baptist, prayed in the temple under the filling of the Holy Spirit. He knew that his child would be a forerunner of the coming Messiah.

> And you, child, will be called the prophet of the Most High;
>   for you will go before the Lord to prepare his ways,
> to give knowledge of salvation to his people
>   by the forgiveness of their sins.
> By the tender mercy of our God,
>   the dawn from on high will break upon us,
> to give light to those who sit in darkness and in the shadow of death,
>   to guide our feet into the way of peace. (Lk 1:76-79)

The promised Messiah did come, and he does guide our feet into the path of peace. In this chapter we will explore how Jesus wishes to bring peace into our lives and how we can enter into that attitude of peace in ever-increasing experience.

Greetings of Peace

The Bible is a seamless document of revelation that lays before us the full plan of God for his people. In the progress of revelation, God's design for the peace of those who follow him falls into three main divisions. In the Old Testament, we learn of the *shalom* of God that he bestows on his children. *Shalom* peace is rich and wonderful, and it forms the basis for what we later learn regarding peace in the New Testament. *Shalom* is both interpersonal and attitudinal, both situational and eschatological, both individual and corporate. When the Messiah arrives and begins his teaching as recorded for us in the New Testament, we find new material revealed to us in two revelatory forms. First, Jesus teaches his disciples a great deal about peace in the upper room discourse (Jn 13—17); second, Jesus teaches us about peace in the stylized commands and greetings that dot the Gospels. The third major component of the Bible's teaching about peace comes in the epistles of the New Testament, particularly the book of Philippians.

Varieties of Teaching About Peace

Some authors build on the Old Testament's *shalom* themes by emphasizing the Bible's emphasis on rest (Hinthorn, 1996; Stanley, 1993). Jehovah promised the people of Israel plenty and even superabundance when they entered the Promised Land. Water (Deut 8:7), food (Deut 8:8), bread (Deut 8:9), milk and honey (Deut 11:9) would all be plenteous. They would enjoy superabundance (Deut 28:11) from the hand of God. In the New Testament, some of these themes reappear in the discussion of rest in the book of Hebrews (Heb 3:19; 4:1; 4:3) and in the superabundance of spiritual fruit that the Holy Spirit desires to produce in the lives of believers—love (1 Thess 3:12), joy (2 Cor 7:4), hope (Rom 15:13) and so on.

When writers discuss peace based on the practice of Jesus during his earthly life, they emphasize places of refuge and quiet retreat (Skoglund, 1986) or Christian meditation using the Jesus prayer (DeBlassie, 1985). If the writer is building on the New Testament Epistles, the teaching about peace is likely to emphasize 1 Peter 5:7 ("Cast all your anxiety on him, because he cares for you") and the letter to the Philippians (Hull, 1987).

Of all these elements of biblical teaching about peace, the one least examined is the stylized commands and greetings of Jesus. Perhaps we miss some key elements of the Bible's teaching regarding peace when we overlook these greetings. They consist of two salutations, two commands and one farewell greeting. Table 9 lists the topics we will address in this chapter. These stylized comments of Jesus address the major enemies of

Enemy of Peace	Corresponding Role of Jesus	Passage
Satan, demons	Jesus the Omnipotent	Luke 4
Sin	Jesus the Savior of the World	Luke 7
Danger	Jesus the Lord of Creation	Luke 8
Illness	Jesus the Great Physician	Luke 8
Fear	Jesus the Resurrected Lord	Luke 24

Table 9. Peace and the greetings of Jesus

peace (Satan, sin, danger, illness and fear) by teaching us that when we encounter Jesus in each of these areas, we will enjoy peace. Before we look at these five areas, however, we need to determine if the content of such greetings and stylized comments is, in fact, meaningful, or if they are so routine as to be void of important content and information.

Stylized Greetings

Greetings, salutations and stylized commands are important in the Gospel narratives as well as in the Epistles of the New Testament. I personally am very aware of this issue when I compose or receive a letter. The advent of electronic forms of mail has introduced new protocols for what is appropriate and inappropriate for communication, but if we set these new standards aside for the sake of our discussion here, we are all quite familiar with the levels of meaning attached to greetings and salutations that are part of our postal correspondence.

For example, we will open and close a letter to a loved one (perhaps using "Dearest" or "With all my love") far differently than we would a letter addressed to someone we did not know ("Dear Sir or Madam" or "Sincerely"). Even though these unwritten rules are quite stylized, they are still meaningful and important. We realize their importance when we sit down to write or to read an important letter. The same is true of the social encounters we have with other people. The social rituals we use in initiating and terminating contact with others ("Hi, how are you?" and "It was good to see you—goodbye") are also very important to the social fabric of our interactions.

In the 1960s it was stylish for social critics to minimize the value of such "small talk." What was really important was not "superficial chatter" but deep, meaningful conversation. The attempt to dispense with stylized initiating and terminating verbal exchanges was, of course, a total failure because they serve very strategic functions. Likewise, the greetings and stylized commands that Jesus used are also purposeful and important to our understanding and application of the biblical view of peace.

Commissioning of the Missionaries

Jesus regarded greetings and stylized salutations as very important. The clear proof of his interest in greetings is found in two major events recorded in the Synoptic Gospels: the commissioning of the Twelve and the commissioning of the seventy. The two commissionings contain many parallel elements. When Matthew writes about the sending of the Twelve, he includes a general mission statement for their work (Mt 10:1), a list of the twelve apostles (Mt 10:2-4), specific instructions on what to do, what to take and where to stay (Mt 10:5-13) and procedures to use if their message is not well received (Mt 10:13-16). These very same elements are found in Luke's account of the commissioning of the seventy, with the exception of a listing of their names.

The missionaries received specific packing instructions. Instead of the normal preparations one would make for a first-century journey through the countryside of Palestine, these bearers of good news were to pack lightly, were not to take money with them and were not to pack extra clothing or food. The lists of what to take and what not to take are not exactly the same, but the message is clear: the missionaries are to be efficient, mobile and single-minded as they carry their urgent kingdom message to those who need to hear it. The restrictions regarding what they carry seem to be temporary, since Luke 22:36 suggests they can carry items that previously they had to leave home (Hagner, 1993). Even so, various ascetic groups throughout the history of the church have taken these instructions as personal callings on their own lives (McNeile, 1961).

The message of the missionaries was clear: they were to preach that the kingdom of God was at hand (Mt 10:7; Lk 9:2; 10:9). They were to display the power of the kingdom by healing the sick, cleansing lepers, casting out demons and raising the dead. The harvest was ready; only laborers to work in the harvest were needed.

One common component of both commissioning events is the very detailed set of instructions Jesus gave to these missionaries regarding the salutations and the farewell greetings they were to use. To whom and under what circumstances one should give greetings were very important components of first-century social protocol (Keener, 1993). These greeting and departure instructions are key elements in the commissionings, and they give us insight into how Jesus viewed them.

The missionaries were to enter a community and immediately seek out "worthy" persons who could offer them hospitality and receive them well. Hospitality was important in Jewish society, and the missionaries were given explicit instructions about how they were to utilize that hospitality so that they could proclaim the good news of the kingdom. Writers of later New Testament epistles repeatedly urge Christians who may not have been accustomed to the Jewish practice to take up the tradition of generous hospitality, now a Christian grace, so that God's work in the world can continue unimpeded (Rom 12:13; Heb 13:2; 1 Pet 4:9). Once they had located a suitable host, they were not to move around, perhaps to look for better accommodations (Mt 10:13). In spite of this command, we know from the *Didache* that in the late first century certain Christian prophets were sponging off of generous hosts (Barclay, 1975).

Once the missionaries found a worthy host, they were to pronounce a salutation of peace on the household. Peace was a customary oriental greeting (Geldenhuys, 1966) that was also heavily Jewish. To wish *shalom* on a household was intended to convey peace in its fullest sense and was not a mere stylized greeting. "This *eirene* "peace" is a benediction or blessing . . . which cannot ultimately be separated from the deeper sense of well-being associated with the gospel and its reception" (Hagner, 1993, p. 272).

If the reception they received in a household or in a village was not positive, the missionaries were to take back the initial blessing of peace (Mt 10:13; Lk 10:6) and replace it with a departing curse. "But whenever you enter a town and they do not welcome you, go out into its streets and say, 'Even the dust of your town that clings to our feet, we wipe off in protest against you. Yet know this: the kingdom of God has come near' " (Lk 10:10-11). Thus the blessing of God would descend upon the household if its members were worthy and would be removed if they were unworthy. The disciples "control the coming and going of peace, i.e., of divine blessing" (Geldenhuys, 1966, p. 189). In this way, God's word as spoken by the missionaries would not be revoked and his word would not return empty (Is 45:23; 55:11). Blessed would be those who received the missionaries well because they would then participate in the peace that only the Messiah can provide: messianic *shalom*. The commissioning accounts thus give us a glimpse of how seriously Jesus regarded the blessings, greetings and farewells that conveyed the peace of God to other people.

Greetings of Peace in New Testament Epistles

The importance on peace blessings continues in the balance of the New

Testament. The majority of the Epistles open with a blessing of peace upon the readers. Normally Greek letter writers would wish their readers "grace" in the opening sentences. Now, under the inspiration of the Holy Spirit, New Testament writers added the Hebrew shalom to convey a salutation of grace and peace to readers (Rom 1:7; 1 Cor 1:3; 2 Cor 1:2; Gal 1:3; Eph 1:2; Phil 1:2; Col 1:2; 1 Thess 1:1; 2 Thess 1:2; Tit 1:4; Philem 3). A few epistles convey a triple blessing (grace, peace and mercy) on their readers (1 Tim 1:2; 2 Tim 1:2; 2 Jn 3). Jude (2) blesses his readers with mercy, peace and love, and Peter uses "grace and peace be yours in abundance" at the beginning of his letters (1 Pet 1:2; 2 Pet 1:2).

Peace is used as part of the benediction or farewell in five of the Epistles (Gal 6:16; Eph 6:23; 2 Thess 3:16; 1 Pet 5:14; 3 Jn 15). All of these greetings or farewell benedictions are meaningful with important content, just as are all of the peace greetings, farewells and stylized commands Jesus used during his earthly ministry, a topic to which we now turn.

Peace as Bestowed by Jesus
Table 9 designates the five Gospel events that include a peace salutation, farewell or stylized command. These words of Jesus attack the main enemies of peace in our lives, and they give us instruction as to how our relationship with Jesus gives us peace of mind.

Jesus the Omnipotent God
Both Mark and Luke write that the first miracle performed by Jesus during his earthly ministry was an exorcism on a Sabbath day in the synagogue at Capernaum (or City of Nahum, perhaps named for the Old Testament prophet of that name).

> He went down to Capernaum, a city in Galilee, and was teaching them on the sabbath. They were astounded at his teaching, because he spoke with authority. In the synagogue there was a man who had the spirit of an unclean demon, and he cried out with a loud voice, "Let us alone! What have you to do with us, Jesus of Nazareth? Have you come to destroy us? I know who you are, the Holy One of God." But Jesus rebuked him, saying, "Be silent, and come out of him!" When the demon had thrown him down before them, he came out

of him without having done him any harm. They were all amazed
and kept saying to one another, "What kind of utterance is this? For
with authority and power he commands the unclean spirits, and out
they come!" (Lk 4:31-36)

In the King James Version the command of Jesus to the demon is
translated with the words "Hold thy peace!" The word used in the original
specifically means "Be quiet!' and most modern versions have switched to
that rendering. Holding (keeping) one's peace, in older English, means to
be quiet. The connection between peace and quiet is familiar to everyone.
Peace is not noisy or raucous. It is quiet. And when Jesus exorcised the
demon who had been inhabiting that Jewish worshiper, peace came to that
troubled man with deafening silence. Whereas Jesus had previously been
rejected in his home town synagogue of Nazareth, he now was seen as the
Omnipotent God who can bring peace even when Satan and his demons
seek to destroy the peace.

The devil—or the Evil One, as the Gospels often describe him—has
extensive spiritual power. Satan has spiritual power that is extensive. And
although he was totally defeated by the death and resurrection of Jesus, his
ultimate restraint and imprisonment is yet future. In this age the father of all
lies "prowls around, looking for someone to devour" (1 Pet 5:8) and accusing
believers day and night before God (Rev 12:10). Both the devil's roaring and
his accusing are not peaceable, quiet activities but just the opposite. And
although his power is always less than that of God, his power is still greater
and stronger than that of humans. Thus Satan is a great disturber of the peace
that God wishes us all to have in our attitudinal lives.

Luke the Gospel writer records twenty-one miracles of Jesus, although
we know that the Savior performed many more miracles than have been
recorded for us (Jn 20:30-31). The miracles Luke includes for us consist
of healings (13), resuscitations (2), nature miracles (3), and exorcisms (3).
This Luke 4 account of exorcism comes at the front end of his account
because Luke wishes his readers to realize early on that Jesus demonstrated
power that overruled even that of the archenemy of God, Satan, and his
demons. Other first-century exorcisms were odd and very different from
the method of Jesus. They consisted of incantations, charms and supersti-
tious ceremony. Records indicate that at times the exorcists would stick a

smelly root up the nose of the possessed person hoping that the demon could not stand it (Keener, 1993). Or another example:

> An exorcist would put a ring under the afflicted person's nose; he would recite a long spell; and then all of a sudden there would be a splash in a basin of water which he had put near to hand—and the demon was out! . . . What a difference between all this hysterical paraphernalia and the calm single word of command of Jesus! (Barclay, 1975, p. 51)

The demon claimed to know who Jesus was. At times this strategy was used in the first century by magicians to gain power over people by invoking their names (Keener, 1993); if so, the demon failed miserably. The demon was not the only one that day who found out that Jesus was a person of unusual authority. When Jesus taught, the people were amazed "because he spoke with authority" (Lk 4:32). He did not use the favorite style of other teaching rabbis, an almost endless citing of other authorities, but instead spoke simply and directly, just as he did with the demon. Jesus had just recently announced that he was the anointed one of God upon whom the Spirit had come. Now he demonstrated these characteristics of the omnipotent God by a stellar teaching style that arrested the attention of all the synagogue worshipers that Sabbath and by exorcising this noisy demon by commanding peace. Jesus came to destroy the works of the devil (1 Jn 3:8); redemption would never have been complete until it could demonstrate a clear and decisive victory over Satan (Geldenhuys, 1966). This miracle was the first step toward that redemptive victory.

How then can we learn about developing an attitude of peace from this miracle account? We need to understand fully that a major disturber of our peace is Satan himself. We cannot assume that Satan has no spiritual interest in keeping us in an anxious state or an attitude of unease. Satan is an enemy of peace, specifically our peace. Knowing and encountering Jesus as the omnipotent God is the first step toward entering the peace that God wishes us to have. Fellowship with this God who has conquered the great enemy of peace, Satan, is a wonderful privilege of those who seek the peace of God in their lives.

Jesus the Savior of the World
Encountering Jesus as the omnipotent, devil-defeating God is the first step

toward building an attitude of peace. The second step comes to us in Luke's account of the anointing of Jesus by a sinful woman. Each of the Gospels reports one anointing event. Matthew and Mark describe an anointing of Jesus that seems to reflect a different historical episode. There the anointing occurs in the home of Simon the Leper and the woman anoints the head of Jesus. John's anointing record describes what happened in the village of Bethany when Mary, presumably the sister of Martha and Lazarus, anointed the feet of Jesus and wiped his feet with her hair. John's account may or may not be the same event as recorded in Matthew and Mark. But we can be quite certain that the Luke 7 story of a luncheon in the home of Simon the Pharisee is distinct from any of the others. In this story we learn how that second great enemy of peace, sin, is handled by Jesus.

> One of the Pharisees asked Jesus to eat with him, and he went into the Pharisee's house and took his place at the table. And a woman in the city, who was a sinner, having learned that he was eating in the Pharisee's house, brought an alabaster jar of ointment. She stood behind him at his feet, weeping, and began to bathe his feet with her tears and to dry them with her hair. Then she continued kissing his feet and anointing them with the ointment. Now when the Pharisee who had invited him saw it, he said to himself, "If this man were a prophet, he would have known who and what kind of woman this is who is touching him—that she is a sinner.". . . Then turning toward the woman, he said to Simon, "Do you see this woman? I entered your house; you gave me no water for my feet, but she has bathed my feet with her tears and dried them with her hair. You gave me no kiss, but from the time I came in she has not stopped kissing my feet. You did not anoint my head with oil, but she has anointed my feet with ointment. Therefore, I tell you, her sins, which were many, have been forgiven; hence she has shown great love. But the one to whom little is forgiven, loves little." And he said to the woman, "Your faith has saved you; go in peace." (Lk 7:36-39; 44-47, 50)

We know of three luncheons Jesus had in the homes of Pharisees (Lk 7; 11; 14), none of which turned out to be tepid society affairs. Jesus did not hesitate to confront his hosts if he thought they needed it. In one case (Lk 11:37-52), after his host had been critical of the behavior, Jesus launched a set of woes at Pharisees in general. Even when the luncheon host was prominent (Lk 14:1), Jesus could be quite critical (Lk 14:12-14). As word of these events circulated, the number of luncheon invitations Jesus received from Pharisees probably declined rapidly!

In the Luke 7 account, Jesus shows no hesitancy in accepting the luncheon invitation from Simon the Pharisee. The luncheon was probably a large gathering, with other villagers joining those who reclined at the table or at least observing the event from the sidelines. Normally a sinful woman would not gain admission to the home of a Pharisee, but in the hustle and bustle of the day she likely entered along with many others to observe this noteworthy meeting between Simon and Jesus. The text says she had lived a sinful past. Most observers feel that this description most likely fits the life of a prostitute, although she may have been an adulteress. (Marshall, 1978).

As the story unfolds, we can reconstruct that her life had been changed by the teaching and ministry of Jesus before he ever entered the home of Simon for that lunch. Her past was sinful, but it appears that she had already repented (Lk 7:48). Nonetheless, her reputation was still that of a sinner, and the village—and especially Simon the Pharisee—had not yet adjusted their attitudes toward her (Lk 7:39).

For reasons we do not know, Simon overlooked some of his most important obligations as a host. He neglected to offer his important guest water to wash his feet (7:44), a greeting kiss (7:45) or oil to anoint his head. Simon may simply have been preoccupied with other matters.

If Simon was a typical Pharisee, and we have no reason to think he wasn't, he was proud of his conformity to all the laws of the Old Testament plus adherence to countless additional standards, all designed to keep him removed from breaking one of the commandments. A major command of the Old Testament was not to commit sexual sin with a woman, and a precaution against even getting close to a violation of that commandment was the Pharisees' rule not to touch a woman of any kind, let alone a woman whose past reputation was bad. So when Simon observed that Jesus was allowing the woman to touch him, Simon concluded that Jesus could not possibly be the true prophet he was claiming to be. In fact, Simon no doubt figured that Jesus was just living up to his reputation as a "friend of tax collectors and sinners" (Lk 7:34).

The repentant woman honored Jesus by doing exactly what Simon had failed to do. As she approached Jesus, she was so overwhelmed with emotions of gratitude that her tears spilled onto the feet of the reclining Jesus. Anxious to cover up for this embarrassment, she let down her hair to wipe his feet. Normally a woman did not let down her hair in public. Jesus did not take offense at her behavior but accepted it as a sign of reverence and repentance. In her gratitude she kissed his feet as well. Then she anointed them. This act of bestowing honor usually involved the head, not the feet, but this woman humbly used her perfume to anoint his feet. Again Jesus did not take offense but accepted these acts of kindness—the very washing, kiss and anointing that righteous Simon had neglected. Later in the account Jesus announced that her sins have been forgiven; then he dismissed her by saying some wonderful words: "Your faith has saved you; go in peace" (7:50).

This farewell blessing of peace is consistent with first-century practice as well as with the Old Testament. In Judges 18:6 we read that a priest dismissed the five spying Danites by saying, "Go in peace. Your journey has the LORD's approval" (NIV). Eli blessed Hannah after he heard the pleas of her heart by saying "Go in peace" (1 Sam 1:17). The two other occurrences of the blessing (2 Sam 15:9 and 1 Kings 22:17) add to the tradition that Jesus observes when he sends the forgiven woman forth with his blessing. We have seen how Jesus honored the importance of farewells and greetings. The verb form of the command *to go* indicates a state of permanency that Jesus was granting to this now peaceful woman. In the face of the second great enemy of a peaceful attitude toward life, sin, Jesus grants forgiveness, which opens the door to peace of mind. When we encounter Jesus as the Savior of the world, we too can revel in the forgiveness he has granted us that allows us to enter fully into an attitude of peace.

Jesus the Lord of Creation

The third great enemy of personal peace and of the attitude that Jesus bestowed on the repentant woman of Luke 7 is danger. Danger that is real is always a threat to calmness of heart and soul. Danger is traumatizing and can be psychologically harmful. The victory that Jesus offers over danger is not always to remove the danger but always to be with us during the danger. The disciples, however, benefited from a stupendous miracle one day on the Sea of Galilee. In their case, Jesus graciously removed the danger totally and granted them peace of mind in its stead.

> One day he got into a boat with his disciples, and he said to them, "Let us go across to the other side of the lake." So they put out, and while they were sailing he fell asleep. A windstorm swept down on the lake, and the boat was filling with water, and they were in danger. They went to him and woke him up, shouting, "Master, Master, we are perishing!" And he woke up and rebuked the wind and the raging waves; they ceased, and there was a calm. He said to them, "Where is your faith?" They were afraid and amazed, and said to one another, "Who then is this, that he commands even the winds and the water, and they obey him?" (Lk 8:22-25)

In this episode Jesus reveals himself as the Lord of Creation, who brings peace to his own in the face of danger. Luke and Matthew omit the exact command Jesus uttered to the raging waves and howling winds; but Mark tells us he said, "Peace! Be still!" (Mk 4:39). We have already seen that the biblical view of peace of mind includes quiet, and now we learn that it also includes calm. Peace, calmness, quiet and stillness all coalesce to form an attitude of mind that can miraculously sustain and guide us through times of danger.

Many of the disciples were skilled fishermen who had learned their trade on this very lake. The Sea of Galilee, 689 feet below sea level, is a small lake but is subject to quick and violent storms because of the steep ravines around its rim through which wind can gain great velocity. These experienced fishermen would not react with panic if the storm danger was not serious, nor would they quickly conclude that they were about to drown if such were not a real possibility (Lk 8:24). The storm was ferocious. Matthew uses a very strong word to describe the storm, and, since he himself was on the boat, his description takes on a striking poignancy. "Without warning, a furious storm came up on the lake, so that the waves swept over the boat" (Mt 8:24 NIV). Literally, Matthew writes of a great shaking (*seismos*) on the lake. This word for earthquake also appears in Matthew's description of the birth pangs of the end of the age (Mt 24:7), of what happened during the darkness at the scene of the crucifixion (Mt 27:54) and of the scene of the garden tomb (Mt 28:2).

Matthew tells us that the storm's strength reminded him of what it would be like if an earthquake had shaken the entire lake.

And where is Jesus during this dangerous storm? He is in the stern sleeping on a cushion (Mk 4:38). This is the only time in the Gospels where we read of Jesus sleeping, and it is in the most unlikely of conditions. How could Jesus sleep during this violent storm? Even extreme exhaustion, which he no doubt sustained at this time, would not explain his calm. But "he knew that he was as near to God by sea as ever he was by land" (Barclay, 1975, p.105). His pervasive attitude of peace in the face of danger was a prelude to the peace he wished to convey to his disciples.

When Jesus woke up and commanded "Peace!" a great calm descended on to the surface of the lake. The resulting peace was more than just the cessation of the storm. "It instead means there was a mysterious, supernatural calm that testified to the sovereign power of Jesus but that also symbolized the deep peace and security that belong to those who follow Jesus" (Hagner, 1993, p. 222). In Judaism only God had authority over the waves and the sea. Clearly, Jesus was God, the Lord of creation who could bring peace even in the face of grave danger. The disciples, like us, were learning more about who Jesus was. They were amazed at the peace that Jesus could bring to their situation, a lesson they never forgot. The disciples experienced that day the same peace described centuries earlier by David (Ps 65:5-8).

Jesus the Great Physician
Illness is a great disturber of the peace. Injury, accident, disease, illness, poor health and disability breed worry and concern. Peace can give way to panic when we do not know what is happening to us, when we fear chronic or disabling consequences, or when we anticipate a dreaded diagnosis that our condition is terminal. The peaceful attitude of mind that we might wish to foster is difficult to maintain when our health is in jeopardy and when outcomes are hidden from us. The biblical attitude of peace of mind comes to those who cower in the face of illness when we encounter Jesus as the Great Physician.

In Luke 8 we read one of several double stories: one account interrupted by another with the conclusion of the first event coming at the end of the passage. Luke begins to write about the sick daughter of Jairus, interrupts the story to describe the healing of the woman with a hemorrhage, then returns to the account of the resuscitation of Jairus's daughter (Lk 8:40-56). The interruption builds tension in the first story regarding the urgency of the little girl's illness.

> Now when Jesus returned, the crowd welcomed him, for they were all waiting for him. Just then there came a man named Jairus, a leader of the synagogue. He fell at Jesus' feet and begged him to come to his house, for he had an only daughter, about twelve years old, who was dying.
>
> As he went, the crowds pressed in on him. Now there was a woman who had been suffering from hemorrhages for twelve years; and though she had spent all she had on physicians, no one could cure her. She came up behind him and touched the fringe of his clothes, and immediately her hemorrhage stopped. Then Jesus asked, "Who touched me?" When all denied it, Peter said, "Master, the crowds surround you and press in on you." But Jesus said, "Someone touched me; for I noticed that power had gone out from me." When the woman saw that she could not remain hidden, she came trembling; and falling down before him, she declared in the presence of all the people why she had touched him, and how she had been immediately healed. He said to her, "Daughter, your faith has made you well; go in peace." (Lk 8:40-48)

The passage concludes with a beautiful account Jesus raising the only daughter of Jairus from the dead. Two women, one twelve years old and one ill for twelve years, both in great need of help from Jesus the Great Physician, one suddenly ill and one chronically ill, both marvelously healed by Jesus.

Jairus was an important official in his synagogue, a person responsible for leading the service and for recruiting persons to pray, preach and read the Scripture (Geldenhuys, 1966). He also supervised the work of service attendants such as the man who gave Jesus the Isaiah scroll in the Nazareth synagogue (Lk 4:17, 20). His name, which means "He will give light," is the equivalent of the Old Testament Jair (Num 32:41). When Jairus came to Jesus, he fell at the feet of the Master in reverence and respect (Lk 8:41), just as the woman who touched the cloak of Jesus later did (Lk 8:47).

Luke is a historian with an eye for detail. Luke loves to give his readers precise information. Here he tells us the daughter is twelve years old; in chapter two he tells us that after an eight-year marriage Anna remained a widow until she was eighty-four (2:36-37, 42); in 3:23 he gives us the age of Jesus at the beginning of his ministry (the only Gospel to give us this information); in 13:11 he records that the woman Jesus healed had been bent over for eighteen years. This attention to detail reflects not only his skill as a historian but his professional training as a physician.

We wonder why Luke also is so sensitive to the agony of parents. He mentions that Jairus has only one daughter (Lk 8:42), that the widow of Nain had only one son (Lk 7:12) and that the epileptic boy Jesus healed (Lk 9:38) was an only child. None of the other Gospel writers give us this detail in these three stories. Perhaps Luke's tenderness toward parents with ill or dying children had been kindled by tragedy in either his personal or professional life.

The woman's encounter with Jesus concluded when he told her, "Go in peace." All the restlessness, all the anxiety, all the worry of those twelve frustrating years now yielded to great peace of mind. This peace was *shalom* peace, an attitude toward life that represented the extent of the healing she received that day from Jesus. Tradition tells us in the *Acts of Pilate* and the *Gospel of Nicodemus* that her name was Bernice.

> It was believed that the woman was a gentile from Caesarea Philippi. Eusebius, the great church historian (A.D. 300), relates how it was said that the woman had at her own cost erected a statue commemorating her cure in her native city. It was said that the statue remained there until Julian, the Roman Emperor who tried to bring back the pagan gods, destroyed it, and erected his own in place of it, only to see his own statue blasted by a thunderbolt from God. (Barclay, 1975, p. 112-113)

Unfortunately, we have greatly circumscribed the truths and lessons this episode teaches us. We think that an encounter with Jesus as the Great Physician has to be in the context of a "miracle" performed by a faith healer. Or perhaps we limit our understanding of healing from God to those rare occurrences when tumors or cancers disappear to the astonishment of our doctors. But such limitations are wrong. All healing comes from God. He may choose to heal us in an unusual manner, he may choose to use the skill of physicians or surgeons, he may choose to use medications to accomplish his healing purposes, or he may heal through the natural course of the disease. Whenever a disease abates or a wound heals or a surgery repairs or an illness fades, it is a healing from the good hand of God. We need to acknowledge God's gracious deliverance from the scourge of the illness and to enter into the peace that God gives in its place—whether God heals or whether our illness remains.

Jesus the Resurrected Lord

The final enemy of a peaceful attitude is fear. Anxiety, worry and fear are all attitudes that keep the human psyche in turmoil. They are noisy, not peaceful. They are upsetting, not settling. And they are tumultuous, not calm. In Luke 24 we read an account of the disciples who were gathered together on the evening of the first day of the week after the crucifixion. The Luke 24 appearance of Jesus to the fearful disciples is probably the same appearance as the one recorded in John 20:19-20. John makes it clear that Thomas was not present during that first appearance of Jesus (Jn 20:24), so the "eleven" of Luke 24:33 is quite likely just a general term for the remaining group of disciples now that Judas was dead rather than an accurate attendance report (Plummer, 1906).

The resurrection of Jesus was reported by the women who visited the tomb, the angels at the tomb, the two disciples who met Jesus on the road to Emmaus, and Peter (an appearance about which we have no details). But only a personal appearance by Jesus would convince them that the resurrection reports were true. John tells us that on the very day of the resurrection, the disciples gathered together behind closed doors "for fear of the Jews" (Jn 20:19). The events of the past few days had been so disturbing and violent that the disciples did not know what to expect next. So they met in secret. With the great enemy of fear robbing them of peace, they were in need of an encounter with the resurrected Lord.

Luke's account of this important appearance begins when the two disciples, fresh from their Emmaus road encounter with Jesus, return to Jerusalem to find the other disciples.

> That same hour they got up and returned to Jerusalem; and they found the eleven and their companions gathered together. They were saying, "The Lord has risen indeed, and he has appeared to Simon!" Then they told what had happened on the road, and how he had been made known to them in the breaking of the bread.

While they were talking about this, Jesus himself stood among them and said to them, "Peace be with you." They were startled and terrified, and thought that they were seeing a ghost. He said to them, "Why are you frightened, and why do doubts arise in your hearts? Look at my hands and my feet; see that it is I myself. Touch me and see; for a ghost does not have flesh and bones as you see that I have." And when he had said this, he showed them his hands and his feet. While in their joy they were disbelieving and still wondering, he said to them, "Have you anything here to eat?" They gave him a piece of broiled fish, and he took it and ate in their presence.

Then he said to them, "These are my words that I spoke to you while I was still with you—that everything written about me in the law of Moses, the prophets, and the psalms must be fulfilled." (Lk 24:33-44)

John records that Jesus gave this greeting of peace not once but twice during that appearance, as well as on the following Sunday when he appeared to the entire band of disciples including Thomas (Jn 20: 19, 21, 26). The disciples did not immediately experience the peace with which Jesus had greeted them. In fact, they were terrorized by the appearance. Who was this person that looked like Jesus? How did he get into the locked room so easily? What was happening? Jesus understood their fear and gently waited for them to process his peace. Here the peace Jesus wanted to convey to them would have to work its way into their attitudinal lives slowly. Fear does not quickly vanish even in the face of the peace of Jesus. Peace of mind takes time to establish itself in fearful hearts.

We too serve and worship the resurrected Lord. To us he bestows this same peace, the perfect antidote to our fears. Encountering Jesus as the resurrected Lord will bring to our attitudinal lives the transforming peace of Jesus.

Conclusion

Encountering Jesus as the Omnipotent God, as the Savior of the World, as the Lord of Creation, as the Great Physician or as the Resurrected Lord is not an instant event that occurs superficially. Rather it is a lifelong process of growth and maturation. As we learn more of how to love the Lord who has loved us so much, peace of mind is the result.

10

Live in Acceptance

THE SECOND BASIC ATTITUDE TO WHICH JESUS CALLS US RELATED TO AGREEABLE-ness is living in acceptance. A major goal for the disciple of Jesus is to cultivate both peace and acceptance as ways of enriching our personality attitudes.

We live in an era of history when it is assumed that we can and should know ourselves. Such has not always been the case. The great philosopher David Hume (1711-1776) argued that a person cannot analyze the self with any accuracy and that introspection never leads to true knowledge of the self (Torrance, 1987). Immanuel Kant (1724-1804) wrote that the self can never be known as it actually is, only as it appears to be. These themes recurred in the theology of Rudolph Bultmann, the great German scholar. "It follows, therefore, that, just as there can be no 'knowledge' of God, there can also be no true 'knowledge' of the self as it really is—nor indeed of other selves" (Torrance, 1987, p. 489). Some scholars continue to feel that the self can never be known by unipolar means (one cannot know oneself) but only in relationship or by bipolar means. "True knowledge of the self is therefore irreducibly bipolar" (Torrance, 1987, p. 500). Any time the philosophical climate of the day maintains that the self cannot be accurately known, the contemporaneous psychological arena is not going to have much interest in self-acceptance, self-esteem or other forms of self-knowledge.

While a few philosophers in our day might argue that the self cannot be known, the vast majority in our philosophical climate have been convinced of the very opposite: the self can and should be known. And for most of the current century, our culture has had a persistent and widespread interest in learning about the self and in exploring how the self can be understood and esteemed. In this chapter we will present a case based on the teachings of Jesus, showing that he desires his disciples to live in acceptance, to accept themselves because Jesus first accepted them. Our exploration of this subject will also require that we face the current debate among Christians regarding self-esteem.

Jesus and the Self

In our earlier chapter on love, we explored extensively the interpersonal demand the gospel places on the followers of Jesus, namely that they love their neighbors and their enemies. Jesus built his teaching on the basic Old Testament command to love neighbors (Lev 19:18), adding the far more demanding standard of loving neighbors and enemies alike (Mt 5:43-48). In the midst of this teaching about the love for others that Jesus expects us to show, we also find material regarding how Jesus expects us to accept ourselves. Jesus first assumes that we will love ourselves, and then he animates this normal human attitude toward the self by giving us his friendship.

Acceptance Assumed

The Levitical commands to love our neighbors and the aliens around us contain one additional and important phrase that we have yet to explore. "Love your neighbor *as yourself*." The phrase occurs in both Leviticus 19:18 and Leviticus 19:34: "The alien who resides with you shall be to you as the citizen among you; you shall love the alien as yourself" (v. 34). In the Greek New Testament, this phrase *as yourself* (*hos eautou*) occurs seven additional times in connection with the command to love others. Jesus quoted Leviticus 19:18 in its entirety to the rich young ruler (Mt 19:19) and to the questioning lawyer (Mt 22:39, with parallels in Mk 12:31 and Lk 10:27). *As yourself* also occurs in the quotations of Leviticus 19:18 that occur in Romans 13:9, Galatians 5:14 and James 2:8. Clearly, God expects us to love others (neighbors and aliens) as we love ourselves. The command appears a total of nine times in Scripture, a remarkable repetition that the Spirit may have designed for the purpose of impressing these truths indelibly on our minds and hearts.

In each of these nine occurrences, we must understand two very obvious characteristics of the command to love others as ourselves. First, the emphasis is placed on the command to love others. Moses, Jesus, Paul and James are each concerned that those who follow the teachings of God understand their important obligation to love others. This command counters the natural and sinful predisposition of humans to love only themselves. God calls us out of ourselves and toward others. This love for neighbors, enemies and aliens also exists in the context of our love for God, which is to be without limits (see chapter seven).

Second, Jesus expects this love of others to extend as far as does our love of ourselves. How we love ourselves becomes the standard that we must meet when we love others. We can love them no less than we love ourselves. But Jesus does not command us to love ourselves; he merely assumes that we do. The emphasis is not on loving ourselves but on loving others, an assumption that Moses, Paul, Jesus and James take for granted. Grammatically, the verb used in the command to love others is the same verb that governs the assumed love of self; and this verb is the strongest verb for love (*agapao*) found in the New Testament.

What is the exact nature of this assumed love of self?

1. It is not selfishness. These texts make absolutely no sense if this self-love has anything whatsoever to do with self-centeredness or selfishness. "We are so apt to confuse self-love, genuine caring for ourselves, with selfishness and egotism. They are very, very different" (Kelsey, 1981, p. 48). Moses, Jesus, Paul and James could not be calling us to selfless love of others based on some sort of selfish love of the self.

2. This assumed love of the self is a non-sinful love that is an expected part of human functioning. These texts do not suggest that this normal love of self is an attitude or frame of mind that must be cultivated or developed. Rather, it comes naturally to the human person.

3. This assumed love of self is a feature of one's life that can be known and that can be used as a standard or measure against which one can love other people. These texts seem to imply that the person obeying this

command must evaluate and know self to some extent so as to be able to fulfill the expectations of the law of neighbor/enemy/alien love.

Some people react vigorously to any suggestion that *as yourself* implies self-love. But New Testament scholar James Moffatt wrote, years before the current self-esteem controversies, that self-love is obviously implied by these texts. "Love of self, in this high sense, means the realization of one's value to God. . . . In the teaching of Jesus love to oneself implies that one must never neglect one's capacities, nor fail to live up to the full measure of one's powers. . . . We dare not undervalue our personalities" (Moffatt, 1929, p. 97-98). This approach to these texts stands in a long tradition dating back to Augustine. The second great command was at the heart of Augustine's moral thinking; O'Donovan has calculated that Augustine quoted the second greatest commandment over 120 times throughout his theological work. *As yourself* is a measure or standard of love.

> Augustine also recognized as entirely coincident and coextensive with the love of God the principle of right self-love. The perfection of the one was the perfection of the other. There was no kind of right self-love which did not imply the love of God; there was no way in which God could be loved without the lover loving himself as well. (O'Donovan, 1980, p. 37)

The self-love that Jesus assumes here, "right self-love" according to Augustine, is related to two other New Testament concepts. Paul refers to normal self-care and self-regard that seems to describe the self-love assumed in the neighbor-love command. "For no one ever hates his own body, but he nourishes and tenderly cares for it, just as Christ does for the church" (Eph 5:29). Paul is stating that self-care is a normal human function. "In the biblical sense, then, the self-love of which Jesus speaks refers to the natural protection we give ourselves. We feed, defend, shelter, preserve, support, and care for ourselves. This is what Jesus assumes" (Hart, 1992, p. 63). This type of self-esteem is not sinful; in fact, it is necessary if we are to fulfill our love obligations to God and others (Anderson, 1995). Jonathan Edwards referred to this self-love as measured, proportional and limited self-regard (Brand, 1991).

The other New Testament concept to which the self-love of the neighbor love command is related is found in the Golden Rule. "In everything do to others as you would have them do to you; for this is the law and the prophets" (Mt 7:12). Jesus assumed that every person would have a clear and well-defined sense of how he or she would like to be treated by others. The rule makes no sense if Jesus believed that everyone should hate the self and desire harm and pain to be inflicted on the self. "The implication is that what we desire for ourselves is morally good; in preserving our 'self' or life we are conserving what is also of supreme value in the life of anyone else" (Moffatt, 1929, p. 101).

The New Testament teaches that the way we are to love ourselves (Mt 19:19), care for ourselves (Eph 5:29) and know ourselves (Mt 7:12) is to use sober judgment about who we are. "For by the grace given to me I say to everyone among you not to think of yourself more highly than you ought to think, but to think with sober judgment, each according to the measure of faith that God has assigned" (Rom 12:3). Thus the assumed self-care that Jesus spoke of is distinct from pride, an evaluation of self that exceeds what is more than warranted by reality.

> To think with "sober judgment" is to think accurately and truthfully, without yielding to unreasonable influences or unjustified extremes. Thus the scriptural teaching on this point is simpler than we might have expected: We should see ourselves as truthfully and accurately as possible. (Kinzer, 1980, p. 27)

By way of contrast, egotism is "the crass and crude attempt of self-esteem impoverished persons to 'prove that they're somebody!'" (Schuller, 1982, p. 16). Sober, accurate judgment about the self prevents the insecurity displayed by selfish persons (Mohler, 1975; Wilson, 1985). As Bernard of Clairvaux preached, only excessive love of the self is sinful (Bernard, 1895).

The texts we have examined demonstrate that Jesus does not call us to self-rejection, self-loathing or self-derogation. We are to simply and accurately accept ourselves.

Acceptance Animated

Jesus then takes these givens and adds to them an animating force: He calls his disciples friends and gives them his friendship. Thus his followers can enrich and enliven their self-acceptance with the rich and certain knowledge that they are the friends of God.

> This is my commandment, that you love one another as I have loved you. No one has greater love than this, to lay down one's life for one's friends. You are my friends if you do what I command you. I do not call you servants any longer, because the servant does not know what the master is doing; but I have called you friends, because I have made known to you everything that I have heard from my Father. (Jn 15:12-15)

Again we see that several themes are interconnected: love, identity of self and relationship to others. We learn of God's attitudes toward us—love and friendship. We learn that in light of that love and friendship we are to love one another and to bask in the knowledge that we are blessed to be included in the circle of the friends of God. We learn that this relationship we enjoy with God is made possible because of the intimacy with which Jesus has treated us: He has made known to us everything he learned from his father. And we learn that this relationship is dependent on our obedience to the commands of Jesus. These strands of teaching are all interconnected and mutually interdependent (Moffatt, 1929). We cannot separate one from the other. For our purposes here, however, it is vital that we understand how our privileged position as friends of the Savior impacts our understanding of who we are. We are not worthless, despicable persons. We are not to indulge in masochistic self-hate. How could we do that, given our status as friends of the King? In other words, we are to accept ourselves as God has accepted us. We are to esteem ourselves to the extent that God has esteemed us—no more, no less. To the normal, usual levels of human acceptance that we are to extend to ourselves, Jesus invites us to accept ourselves as his friends who belong to this accepted circle of persons because of obedience to the commands of Jesus. In this way Jesus calls us to live life with an attitude of acceptance. Living in acceptance consists of "a conscious decision to see ourselves through the eyes of the Divine Lover" (Kelsey, 1981, p. 58).

The acceptance that Jesus forwards to us, and the acceptance in which he wants us to live, is further established by the work of Jesus on the cross. The death of Christ on the cross satisfied the penalty for our sin. The death of Jesus calls down upon our lives great acceptance. The salvation we enjoy as believers brings to us reconciliation and justification (McGrath & McGrath, 1992). These are not just theological themes that have no practical consequence. They are life-changing transactions wrought by the Lord of the Universe toward those who love and obey him. Given these realities, we can do no less than live in the light of God's acceptance.

The acceptance that we receive from God prompts us to bask in our relationship with God and to cultivate loving relationships with others. Never is the goal of acceptance some type of private, self-contained enjoyment. It stimulates us in our relationship with God and others (1 Jn 4:10). To move from the status of an enemy of God (Rom 5:10) to that of a child of God (Jn 1:12) who is first a servant (Jn 15:15) and then a friend (Jn 15:15) literally transforms one's normal attitudes toward self from mere self-care and nurture to attitudes built upon the acceptance God grants toward us.

Summary
Before we look in detail at current self-esteem debates, we need to be sure of our biblical moorings regarding attitudes toward the self. The Bible instructs us how to think of ourselves. The believer is "a person who is not only a creature of God but also an object of God's redemptive love" (Hoekema, 1975, p. 105). Being an object of God's love is not something we have earned or achieved. It is not due to our performance, our accomplishments, our behavior, our attractiveness (Day, 1992; Wright, 1977). It is related only to who we are as created beings on whom God has set his love—apart from any worthiness based on our private effort. We have been created a little lower than the angels (Ps 8:5) at the culmination of creation (Gen 1—2). Humans have been given a dominion mandate to care for the glorious world God created with his fingers (Gen 1:28). Angels have been delegated to watch over those who inherit salvation (Heb 1:14). And we are much more valuable than lesser parts of creation, such as the plants and animals that receive gracious care and protection from God himself (Mt 6:26). Because we are created in the image of God, we possess great significance and value. "We are loved by God and deserving of the love of ourselves and others" (Narramore, 1978, p. 29).

The Great Self-Esteem Debate
A major feature on the twentieth-century landscape among evangelicals

has been the great self-esteem debate. No one is quite sure if anyone has ever been convinced of a new position as a result of this noisy debate; nonetheless, it has persisted with fairly predictable arguments now for over fifty years. Unfortunately, both sides have done their share of misrepresenting the other, both sides have claimed that their approach is the only true biblical approach, and both sides have done their best to claim victory. Why has the great self-esteem debate been such a difficult one for both sides to argue, and why has the issue generated a veritable firestorm of controversy? Perhaps because the stakes are high. The validity and usefulness of the mental health disciplines in the larger mission of the church seems to be at stake. If self-esteem proponents can make a biblical case, perhaps they can earn a more permanent role in the affairs of church ministry. If opponents of self-esteem prevail, then counseling and psychotherapy can be declared interlopers and can be summarily dismissed from forms of church ministry. In other words, the great self-esteem debate is an important battle in a larger war.

Proponents argue that positive self-esteem is different from conceit or egotism. For them, a healthy self-concept is mandated by plain common sense. God loves us and values us; so should we. Proponents argue against rampant individualism and self-centeredness and argue that a healthy self-concept is merely a necessary starting point from which the individual can move into love of God and others. Opponents argue that an emphasis on self-esteem is in direct conflict with the Bible's clear teaching regarding self-denial. We are not to think well of ourselves because we are worthy only as we are related to Jesus and that we have no worthiness in and of ourselves. Instead of working to help people think well of themselves, we need to be calling them to take up their cross, follow Jesus and deny themselves. Only then will we be faithful to the true nature of the gospel. We must die to self and allow the indwelling Savior to live his life through us in spite of who we are. We don't need self-esteem, we need God-esteem. As Ray Anderson sums up the debate:

> Is the core of the human self really so corrupt that it must be valued as worthless and replaced by a "Christ-self"? Or, is the self's deepest longing for fulfillment and value an intrinsic aspect of the image of God which has become disempowered and cast back upon itself in

a backlash of negative and self-defeating perceptions and actions? (Anderson, 1995, p. 100).

And so the arguments continue with little resolution in sight.

The Psychological Role of Esteem

Why do we need to talk about esteem? Is it important enough to justify all this fuss? How one esteems self is an important issue. We have all known capable individuals who hesitate to use their talents and skills because of lack of confidence. In extreme cases an entire life can be squandered by a person who cannot forward to the self a realistic and appropriate amount of self-esteem. We do not have to be therapists to see the tragedy in such a waste.

Or in another instance a person could fail to take reasonable risks in life because of a misattribution—a mistaken idea that he or she could not enroll in a college or apply for a promotion because "I'm short," "I'm from a rural area," "I'm not attractive" or some other irrelevancy. As friends, we would disagree with these people, would urge them to try anyway, and would express our disappointment if our friends continued to wallow in needless self-pity.

A much healthier approach to life is to work at developing within ourselves a realistic and accurate self-evaluation. While we can never understand ourselves fully or be completely free from all self-delusion, we should surely work at keeping these distortions to a minimum. Learning how to view oneself realistically is obviously better than constantly basing our opinions of ourselves solely on what other people think of us. Marcus Aurelius, the great Roman emperor, is thought to have said, "I have often wondered how it is that every man sets less value on his own opinion of himself than on the opinion of others. So much more respect have we to what our neighbors think of us than to what we think of ourselves." Life without a realistic self-appraisal and with a dependence on the opinions of others is difficult to live. Hence most social scientists in this century have urged people to develop healthy or realistic self-evaluations as the core of how we evaluate ourselves.

Research has shown that self-esteem is a complex configuration with several dimensions: identity (how the person views self), self-satisfaction (how the person accepts self) and behavior (how the person acts). In addition individuals tend to evaluate the self in several categories: the physical self, the moral-ethical self, the family self and the social self (Fleck, 1976). We also know that in the absence of a healthy level of self-esteem some people develop patterns of self-hatred or self-delusion. Self-hatred is a pathological condition in which people can pursue self-destructive behavior patterns (excessive smoking or alcohol consumption), engage in high-risk, death-defying activities, or become workaholics, always seeking to establish self-worth through achievement but never quite succeeding (Ashford, 1977). Self-deception can be yet another consequence of a lack of healthy and realistic self-esteem (Haught, 1980). The self-deluded are the last to realize how skewed are their perceptions, and occasionally the price of self-delusion is great. We do not realize how valuable and important an honest and realistic level of self-esteem can be until it is absent.

The Excesses of Both Sides

One reason the great self-esteem debate among twentieth-century evangelicals has been so intractable is that excess has appeared on both sides of the disagreement. Many secular and some Christian advocates of positive self-esteem have indulged in hyperbole and excess that have attracted predictable and justifiable criticism. And many Christian opponents of positive self-esteem as an important component of the Christian life have also attracted criticism because of their extreme teachings.

Excesses of the advocates. At times advocates of positive self-esteem claim more for the corrective and psychologically curative powers of a positive self-concept than the research supports. A great deal of research effort has explored the area of self-esteem, and a consistent and clear finding emerges: A positive level of self-esteem is related to many forms of achievement and human endeavor. Children who possess strong self-images are also likely to do well in school. Conversely, children with very poor self-concepts are often the most behaviorally disturbed and poorly achieving students in a classroom. But the research does not tell us which is the cause and which is the effect. That they are related is unquestioned; that self-esteem is the cause rather than an effect of achievement is far more difficult to establish with empirical research. Even though proponents have sometimes claimed more efficacy from a positive level of self-esteem than the data support, the strong relationship between high levels of self-esteem and many commendable characteristics of human personality still exists.

Although it may be difficult for critics of the self-esteem movement to believe it, proponents of positive self-esteem have consistently maintained a distinction between a healthy self-concept and narcissism. In Greek mythology, the story of Narcissus and Echo recounts the tragic role that extreme self-centeredness can play in human life. A blind seer had prophesied regarding the infant Narcissus that he would live a long life if he never came to know himself. Narcissus encountered Echo who provided a perfect reflection of his every word. Narcissus was enamored—the first piece of self-knowledge that would prevent him from enjoying a long life. Later Narcissus saw on the surface of a placid lake the image of the most beautiful person he had ever seen. As he drew near the image, the image drew near to him. As he spoke, so did the image. When he retreated so did the image. Narcissus was thrilled to find another "person" who so truly matched his own self. This self-love soon became self-knowledge, and Narcissus died within the hour, just as the blind seer had predicted (McDonald, 1991). We now label cases of extreme self-centeredness "narcissism." Narcissism is seen as developmentally appropriate for the infant but pathological for everyone else. Narcissism is not advocated or promoted by the modern mental health movement; instead it is treated.

In a more general sense, however, proponents of healthy levels of self-esteem can be justifiably criticized for sometimes promoting and advocating a self-referenced ethic. As mentioned above, many secular and some Christian proponents of positive self-esteem make the self the major reference point for personal ethics. What I want, what I think is right, what is good for me, is the norm. When the self thus becomes a pivot on which swing all moral decisions and value judgments, all other external codes for behavior take on a secondary role, and a nonbiblical ethic takes over. Or when people place undue emphasis on self-scrutiny, the resulting introspection can become regressive and damaging to normal relationships and obligations (Torrance, 1987). While mental health personnel maintain that they have succeeded in keeping narcissism distinct from positive self-regard, some critics such as Christopher Lasch (1979) and Paul Vitz

(1994) maintain that our current emphasis on helping people develop self-esteem is, in fact, a new narcissism. The modern self-esteem movement could never be criticized for creating selfishness. The human race apart from a biblical ethic has been consumed with selfishness for millennia; however, an untamed advocacy of positive self-esteem has certainly perpetuated this ancient human problem and given it a twentieth-century face.

Excesses of the opponents. The Christian counseling movement has made its greatest impact on the evangelical world in the last half of the twentieth century. When counselors began their work with Christian people referred by their pastors—believers who displayed symptoms of severe mood disorders or various anxiety syndromes—the counselors immediately began to notice that most of these people sustained a deeply ambivalent attitude toward the self. They had faithfully listened to decades of preaching that derogated the self on the basis of certain New Testament texts. They had learned that they were to crucify the self, to count the self as having no worth in and of itself, and to die to self. Self-denial was the path to discipleship, and self-denial meant putting self last and setting aside any and all self-interest. They were to cease living their own lives and let Christ do the living for them. They had learned these approaches to Christian living by paying heed to the teachings at deeper life conferences, revival meetings and discipleship seminars. The pietism of the mid-twentieth-century in American evangelicalism had stimulated powerful ambivalence in these people toward the self.

Essentially this approach to the "deeper" Christian life had created a generation of believers who did not know how to handle four different tasks.

1. They did not know how to incorporate biblical confidence into this scheme of dying to self. The apostle Paul wrote, "Yet I am not ashamed, because I know whom I have believed, and am convinced that he is able to guard what I have entrusted to him for that day" (2 Tim 1:12 NIV). Such bold confidence was hard to integrate into a scheme that seemed to call for boasting only in the Lord and for constant vigilance in having no assurance in the self.

2. Believers seemed handicapped in knowing how to handle their own achievements. If I am not supposed to live my own life but only let Jesus

live through me, how can I handle the promotion I just received? If I am not to strive on my own to achieve but only let Christ do the achieving, how do I handle compliments? This dilemma is characterized by a male soloist—we shall call him Sam—who contributes movingly to a worship service by singing a fitting vocal solo. At the conclusion of the service when worshipers attempt to give him a compliment, he replies, "Oh, no—it was all the Lord." The incongruity of that statement is profound. Everyone knows it was not the Lord singing; it was Sam who sang that song. Granted, the Lord gave Sam the voice and the talent, and the Lord enabled Sam to make such a stirring contribution to the service, but it was Sam singing the solo!

3. Believers seemed unable to distinguish among pride, humility, false humility and false pride. All of these concepts jumbled together, and all people could do was continue to seek to die to self and allow the Lord to live through them.

4. Finally, this evangelical approach to pietism bred considerable discontinuity between public presentation and private experience. Pragmatically, believers had to display confidence and self-assurance in their work lives and in many other spheres of daily living, but they had to give all the credit to God in their church contacts.

The basic reason for all these deficiencies in the application of sanctification teaching revolves around the fact that the dying-to-self and the Christ-in-you themes were presented as the full truth, while the New Testament presents them to us as some among many other principles that govern the living of the Christian life. A one-sided approach to sanctification, emphasizing only its self-denial components, is incomplete and will lead to practical difficulties.

The Christian counseling movement thus began at a time when excessive self-denial teaching had left an entire generation of believers dispirited and confused regarding how they were to view the self. Granted, some Christian counselors have overcorrected for this problem by going to the opposite extreme: advocating a view of the self that includes no self-denial at all. Thus the pendulum swings from one extreme to another, from teaching that sanctification is nothing but self-denial to teaching that no self-denial is needed. Reacting to the excesses of a previous generation with new excesses is a common problem for the church. We cannot explore the New Testament's broad scope of sanctification teaching within the space of this chapter. But we can examine the self-denial teachings of Jesus to determine how they relate to acceptance of self and how Jesus wants us to form attitudes toward the self.

Jesus and Self-Denial

The Synoptic Gospels record for us an important event when Jesus predicted his own death. Peter's abrupt reaction brought a rebuke from Jesus, who then proceeded to call his disciples to their cross-bearing vocation.

> From that time on, Jesus began to show his disciples that he must go to Jerusalem and undergo great suffering at the hands of the elders and chief priests and scribes, and be killed, and on the third day be raised. And Peter took him aside and began to rebuke him, saying, "God forbid it, Lord! This must never happen to you." But he turned and said to Peter, "Get behind me, Satan! You are a stumbling block to me; for you are setting your mind not on divine things but on human things." Then Jesus told his disciples, "If any want to become my followers, let them deny themselves and take up their cross and follow me." (Mt 16:21-25)

In this well-known passage, the self-denial teaching of Jesus consists of four major components (v. 24). Each of these components is matched by a feature of the experience and future of Jesus that is described in the preceding verses (vv. 21-23).

First, Jesus describes the desire to honor God. In the case of the disciples, to honor God would be to follow Jesus; in the case of Jesus, honoring God was displayed in his willingness to obey his Father even unto death. Jesus told his disciples that he *must* go to Jerusalem.

Second, Jesus gives the first condition that must be met if someone is to honor God: to deny (*arneomai*) self. In the case of Jesus, this self-denial consisted of putting aside his own will and purpose so that he could engage in the will and purpose of his Father. As Jesus later prayed in the Garden of Gethsemane, "My Father, if it is possible, let this cup pass from me; yet not what I want but what you want" (Mt 26:39).

Third, Jesus gives the second condition that must be met for honoring God: replacing the will of self that has now been set aside and taking up a cross. In the case of Jesus, this condition would be quite literal: he would take up his own cross (Jn 19:17) and carry it part way to the place of execution. As the residents of Jerusalem watched Jesus walk toward Golgotha on the day of his death, down the streets now called the Via Dolorosa (Lk 23:26-31), they knew that Jesus was a condemned man; the cross clearly linked him with death. In the case of the disciples, Jesus called them to become cross-bearers. They were to be prepared for their own deaths, they were to be associated with the death of Jesus, and they were to make the purpose and mission of Jesus their own.

Fourth, Jesus calls them to action: they are to follow him.

Self-denial then refers to vocation. For those who formerly were fishermen, they would now become cross-bearers. For those who formerly were tax collectors, they would now be cross-bearers. The passage goes on to imply that this new vocation would continue until the Son of Man would return (Mt 16:27). The passage thus becomes a prototype for all who want to follow Jesus, not just the few who traveled with him during his earthly life. We too are to leave our former vocation with all its purposes and intents and substitute for what we have surrendered a new vocation, that of a cross-bearer. The disciples of Jesus were to be known not for their importance, their greatness or for their rank in the kingdom. They were to be known as women and men prepared to die and willing to die while carrying out the business of the King.

To deny oneself means to reorder our priorities so that the priorities God wishes for us become our own. Denying self means loving Christ more than we love ourselves. Denying self does not mean that we are to punish ourselves or reject ourselves. Archibald Hart has summarized other mistaken notions as to the meaning of self-denial.

> You must deny yourself because it is sinful to do anything that gives you pleasure. Others must be allowed to take advantage of you, because being a Christian means you must let other people walk all over you. You must never think of yourself, because this is selfish. You must always take care of others first and put yourself last. You are not allowed to think for yourself. You must never have fun, only do your duty. Whenever possible, do something to humiliate yourself. You don't have any rights. Your self is

vulgar and should be hated. (Hart, 1992, p. 56)

The list of mistaken notions about self-denial is almost endless. Utter self-denial was rejected by most Christian theologians throughout history—thinkers such as Augustine and Jonathan Edwards—even though mystics have at times attempted to practice a total renunciation of self as the true meaning of the call of Jesus to self-denial (Post, 1987).

Several New Testament texts speak of hating our own lives (Lk 14:26), putting to death the actions of the body (Rom 8:13), crucifying the self (Rom 6:6) and knowing that no good thing dwells within (Rom 7:18). Yet other texts speak of delighting in the law of God with one's inmost self (Rom 7:22). A biblical approach to self-denial must be constructed carefully, giving attention to the broad scope of texts rather than a select few (Anderson, 1995). Brownback's position that we should have "no self-image at all" because of the self-denial principle of the New Testament is literally not possible to achieve (Brownback, 1982, p. 133).

Thus when twentieth-century evangelicals engage in their great self-esteem debate, the positions chosen by opponents or proponents of self-esteem all have historical precedents. Both those who advocate a healthy or positive level of self-esteem for the believer and those who feel that the self-esteem emphases of our century are heretical and dangerous represent positions taken by Christians throughout the history of the church. Proponents of self-esteem argue that consideration should be given to the self when obeying the commands to love God and to love others, whereas opponents of self-esteem are in the tradition of those who say that no consideration should be given to the self. The debate rages on, perhaps because both opposition to and advocacy of self-esteem are venerable and historic Christian approaches to the issue. If Christians have been unable to adopt a solitary and uniform position on how to regard the self over the previous twenty centuries, how can we expect them to solve the problem now? Honesty requires that we refrain from labeling our approach as *the biblical approach*; rather, we should advocate our personal position on this issue as *the approach that best reflects our Spirit-led, biblical convictions.*

Biblical Balance
In this chapter we have been looking at one of the basic attitudes Jesus

wishes his disciples to display. In addition to a basic attitude of agreeableness or lack thereof, Jesus calls us to an attitude of peace of mind and an attitude of basic acceptance of the self. An attitude of basic acceptance is related to but not totally equal with self-esteem. We are simply urged to view ourselves as God views us. We all display basic self-care toward ourselves, and to this basic attitude Jesus adds his promise to regard us as his friends when we obey his commands. To be regarded as a friend of God is as affirming and assuring to us as it was to Abraham, who was regarded as a friend of God (2 Chron 20:7; Is 41:8; Jas 2:23).

Scripture contains principles that enable us to keep this basic self-acceptance from becoming pride, self-centeredness or egotism. We are, first, to love God with all our capacity (Deut 6:4-5; Mt 22:37; Mk 12:30; Lk 10:27) and, second, to love our neighbor as much as and in the same way as we love ourselves.

> We cannot love God to any depth with an unknown self. He said that we should love him with all our hearts and souls and minds and might and thoughts and feelings. If I never have met all of me, how can I love with all of me? Before I can fulfill that commandment, I must know something of who I am and why I am and how I am—then I can knowingly give my gift to my Lord. (Cranor, 1979, p. 27)

These two commands, along with the assumed love of self, serve as a compact triad of obligations in which each serves as a standard for the others.

Truly obeying the greatest and second-greatest commandments of the Law and the Prophets will certainly prevent anyone from lapsing into God-displeasing narcissism. The New Testament urges us to know ourselves and to evaluate who we are with sober judgment (Rom 12:3). God expects us to engage in a certain amount of introspection (1 Cor 11:28). We are to conduct this self-examination so that we know ourselves honestly and truthfully (Hart, 1992). By doing it with sober judgment we will protect ourselves from the folly of pride or self-deceiving aggrandizement. Only when we know ourselves accurately can we commit ourselves totally to Christ (Rom 12:1-2) or use our spiritual gifts well (Rom 12:4-8). "Realistic thinking about our distinctiveness, then, is essential to a sound self-concept. When this is combined with the sort of exhilaration and humility we have talked about, it adds up to a healthy self-image" (Smith, 1984, p. 42). Extremes on the continuum of self-knowledge, either very negative self-appraisal or inflated egotism, are always inaccurate and displeasing to God (Joosse, 1987).

Conclusion

After all is said and done, after all the texts have been examined, after all the logic and reasoning have been exhausted, what is the importance of the great self-esteem debate and of the need for the followers of Jesus to truly accept themselves? All the theological discussion and biblical exegesis in the world cannot hide the fact that this issue is directly relevant for how people function in their daily lives. The issue has flesh and blood on it precisely for this reason. Perhaps a case study about one individual will illustrate how and why self-acceptance is far more than just an esoteric or academic debating topic.

> As for many of his contemporaries, the junior high years were the most stressful of Jimmy's entire life. The rapid adolescent changes occurring in his own life as well as in the lives of his classmates created a swirl of both excitement and worry. He and his friends were beginning to jostle for positions of social leadership and popularity, now increasingly based on factors that never had been too important during elementary school days. Those who were assertive, athletic, "popular," all seemed to have a different ranking in the pecking order than those who lacked these graces. He remembered well the humiliation of gym class. Overcrowding forced the coaches to form baseball teams of fifteen players on each side. Teams were picked by captains, the most desired players first, the least desirable last. Standing with toes on the line until nearly all others had been chosen was embarrassing enough, but being assigned to play second backup catcher was even worse.
>
> Jimmy had always been able to achieve well in school. His classroom work seemed to bring him a measure of acceptance that did not come from his ability to socialize or his athletic ability. Clumsy, encumbered with glasses from an early age, he cherished this one

notch that seemed to help him stay in the game: his ability to do well on tests and to learn. His church background had prepared him to regard the approval of others with a slightly less degree of importance than some of his non-churched friends attached to social acceptance. But the reality was still painful—he could keep up with peers in only one area of life; in all others he seemed to be inferior.

In addition to church life, family life was a second factor that attenuated the tremendous power of peer influence. Jimmy knew he was accepted by his parents, that they loved him unconditionally and that their love for him was like God's love for him. His life was stable and secure, surrounded at home and church by those who cared for him, mentored him and showed sincere interest in his welfare. Yet the subtle and slightly corrosive effects of inferiority nagged at his soul. Why could he not experience the same social facility as did some of his friends? Why could he not enjoy sports and other physical activities to the same degree as did some of his friends? Was he inferior? If not, why did these lacks in his life prove to be so unsettling?

Then as a young adult he was exposed to a Bible study group that was exploring the New Testament theological doctrine of "acceptance in the Beloved." Among the many titles bestowed on the believer, none is quite a fascinating as this one: the believer is *accepted in the Beloved.* Slowly the truth of that doctrine began to make some practical impact on Jim's life. If Jesus accepted him, then surely he could accept himself. If Jesus had loved him, if the Spirit had gifted him, if God had chosen him, why was there any need to feel inferior? Slowly the security of knowing that he was accepted in the Beloved began to enable him to accept himself and to diminish the painful sense of inferiority that had dogged his steps.

Later, when spiritual life conference speakers would urge their hearers to discount the self, to count the self as totally unworthy and unlovable, Jim could turn a deaf ear, because Jesus had already whispered into his ear a different message. Later when critics of self-esteem would assert that helping people accept themselves because Jesus had first accepted them was simply another way of leading them astray or teaching them a different gospel, he could look the other way because Jesus had already shown him a far different vision. His faith had grown stronger when he was better able to accept himself. And later, when people would tell him not to view himself with any worth, he could turn his heart from that harsh thought to the acceptance that Jesus had written on the table of his own heart.

So what is the significance of this case study? It is a true instance of the growth of healthy self-esteem in one individual by God's grace. And it is personally significant as well, because I am that individual.

Section Five
Neuroticism

Introduction

Jesus & Our Emotional Life

THE FINAL PERSONALITY FACTOR IN THE BIG FIVE PERSONALITY THEORY IS NEUROTI-cism. In some ways the choice of names for this factor is outdated and unfortunate. *Neurosis* is a word that originated in the work of Freud, and it has primarily had meaning associated with Freudian theory. For that reason among others, the term *neurosis* was dropped from the diagnostic manual of the American Psychiatric Association because it did not reflect theoretical approaches across a broad spectrum of clinicians. However, the word *neuroticism* has remained attached to this personality factor and is used only as a general term for human maladjustment rather than as a term reflective of Freudian theory. Although both Hans Eysenck and McCrae & Costa have consistently called this factor neuroticism, others suggest that the emotional content of the factor could be better summarized with the term *emotional stability* or *ego strength/emotional disorganization* (Digman & Inouye, 1986).

What does this factor measure? In sum, it measures human weakness and imperfection. The scale measures the emotional life of the individual from emotional stability (low scores) to general maladjustment (high scores) among the normal population. The scale appears to measure negative affectivity—the negative emotions of fear, sadness, embarrassment, anger, guilt and disgust (Costa & McCrae, 1992c). People whose lives are characterized by these emotions are often quite distressed and maladjusted when compared to low scorers on this factor. Not all persons who would score high on this factor are necessarily diagnosable with a psychiatric condition; however, they may be at a higher risk of psychopathology. Some people with a diagnosable psychiatric condition such as the Antisocial Personality Disorder may, in fact, obtain a low score on this factor.

Subfacets

The six subfacets of the neuroticism factor are named for the primary clusters of negative emotions that high scorers tend to display.

1. Anxiety. Individuals who score high on the neuroticism factor tend to be sensitive to general anxiety, worry and fear. They are tense and jittery and tend to think a great deal about what might go wrong.

2. Angry hostility. High scorers show a readiness to get angry. Whether the anger is ever expressed cannot be determined by a score on this factor. High scorers here are often also low scorers on the agreeableness factor: they are disagreeable and quick to get angry as opposed to those who are slow to anger and who are easygoing toward life.

3. Depression. These people are easily discouraged and often have feelings of sadness, hopelessness and guilt. Low scorers on this factor are not necessarily cheerful; to determine whether lightheartedness is present one would have to look at the extraversion factor.

4. Self-consciousness. These persons are sensitive to the emotions of embarrassment and shame and prone to feelings of inferiority. Low scorers here are not necessarily socially poised; they merely do not experience high levels of self-consciousness in social encounters.

5. Impulsiveness. High scorers typically have an inability to control wishes and urges. Low scorers are better able to tolerate frustration and resist temptations to indulge in desire.

6. Vulnerability. The self-concept of low scorers here is one of capability; the self-concept of high scorers is much more negative, since they feel dependent and stressed.

Jesus and Paul on Neuroticism

The conjectured scores of Jesus and Paul on these six subfacets (see table

10) show us that Paul was an average person emotionally with many of the same struggles we all encounter in our lives. His low score on vulnerability probably reflects the tremendous sense of call and confidence he had in the mission Jesus had set before him. He pursued the service of Jesus with as much confidence as he previously had pursued the persecution of believers. Paul was not a vulnerable man.

Neuroticism	Jesus	Paul
Anxiety	VERY LOW	AVERAGE
Angry Hostility	AVERAGE	AVERAGE
Depression	LOW	AVERAGE
Self-Consciousness	VERY LOW	AVERAGE
Impulsive	LOW	AVERAGE
Vulnerability	VERY LOW	LOW

Table 10. Jesus and Paul on neuroticism

Some people might prefer to see scores for Jesus all registering as "very low" on all the subfacets of the neuroticism factor. After all, Jesus was perfect, and any measure of human weakness should register as nonexistent! But we must distinguish in our mind the difference between weakness and sin. Jesus was sinless in that he committed no sins during his earthly life. That does not mean that he was immune from some human weaknesses and limitations. He was sad on occasion; he grew weary and tired, he was frustrated at times with the Pharisees and at other times with the disciples. His conjectured score on angry hostility is no doubt influenced by the large amount of material in the Gospels that records for us the encounters of Jesus with the religious leaders of his day. To them he displayed strong anger. But he did not sin while being angry.

Warfield (1912) has made the very interesting observation that Bible translations tend to subdue the intensity of description when they treat strong Greek words used to depict the anger of Jesus. For example, we read of the anger of Jesus regarding a leper in Mark 1:43 and concerning two blind men in Matthew 9:30. The NRSV translates these verbs as "sternly warning" and "sternly ordered"; the Greek word means "simply 'to be angry at,' or, since it commonly implies that the anger is great, to 'be enraged with,' or perhaps better still, since it usually intimates that the anger is expressed by audible signs, to 'rage against' " (Warfield, 1912, p. 55). Warfield cites many other examples of this tendency among Bible translators. Basically, we have trouble imagining that Jesus could be as angry as the text of the New Testament states. We want to put a patina on his anger, to soften it. The conjectured score we show for Jesus on angry hostility may then help us correct our warped view of Jesus and his anger.

Other Features of Neuroticism

Research indicates that high levels of neuroticism are associated with poorer physical health than low levels (Marshall et al., 1994). It is tempting for us to think that persons who score high on this factor have simply had more than their share of negative life experiences, so they display more negative affect that the rest of us because of the difficulties they have had in life.

Research shows that the opposite may be closer to the truth. While external events may have a role in shaping the personality of the human being, especially at the most malleable of developmental stages, people with high scores of neuroticism may attract more negative life events their way than do those whose basic personality configuration does not contain so much negativity. "The negative emotions of neurotics lead them to create more negative events for themselves, especially interpersonal negative events where others react in a punishing way to the neurotic's expression of negative affect" (Magnus et al., 1993, p. 1050).

Neuroticism also seems to be quite stable over time, suggesting that once negativity sets in to color a person's emotional life, it can take on the nature of character or of those parts of personality that remain constant (Watson & Clark, 1984).

Jesus had much to say about negative emotions in his sermons and teaching. We will not attempt to survey all that he taught about the weaknesses we all possess. Instead, we will look at two major teachings that form a basic set of skills we all need in dealing with the imperfections with which we all struggle: the interlocking dynamics of confession and forgiveness.

11

Offer &
Accept Confession

THE NEUROTICISM FACTOR DEALS WITH THE WEAKNESSES AND STRUGGLES OF LIFE
that characterize the emotional domain. The Bible deals extensively with
human weakness; this chapter could not possibly survey all of that
material. But we can explore two major themes in the teaching of Jesus
that do deal with a distinctively Christian approach to the resolution and
resolving of human weaknesses and sin: confession and forgiveness.

The follower of Jesus must be able to offer and accept confession and
to grant and receive forgiveness. Confession and forgiveness are closely
related topics, but we will artificially separate our consideration of them
into two different chapters.

Confession As Ministry
The church has two major vehicles available to help it accomplish its goal
of shaping the children of God into the image of Christ. The first and most
familiar is *spiritual formation* through worship, edification, instruction,
discipleship and other ministry forms. The ministry of the church thus
becomes a channel through which the Holy Spirit engages the believer in
the process of sanctification. The Holy Spirit fosters the believer's maturation through other channels as well, but the thrust of the Spirit's work
through the standard ministries of the institutional church is well summarized by the concept of spiritual formation.

The second major vehicle available for the maturing of God's people is *psychotherapy*. When psychotherapy is rightly conducted by Christian therapists working with believing clients, its goals will be similar to the goals of spiritual formation: the shaping of persons into the image of Christ. All too often Christian mental health professionals overlook this similarity in function. Yet the parallels between these two enterprises are too profound to ignore. Both seek to move people forward in growth and maturation. Both seek to accomplish this goal in a God-honoring manner. Both must depend on the energizing power of the Holy Spirit if any lasting goals are to be realized. Both must use Christ as a model of full personhood and the Bible as the guide for achieving it.

Leaders in these two fields, however, all too often do not envision their work as tandem or parallel. Christian mental health workers often implicitly work as if therapy with Christian clients is something radically different from what the church seeks to do with the very same people. Church leaders often view the counseling enterprise with a substantial amount of puzzlement. Rare is the community where church and clinic conceptualize their work with shared populations as complementary, interdependent and mutually helpful. Leaders of church and clinic alike have failed to seize the opportunity to forge a strong alliance of cooperation in working toward the same goals.

It is the thesis of this book that spiritual formation and Christian psychotherapy share the same goals, that both are ministry, that both are essential at this time in our current cultural context, and that when both enterprises are able to work more closely together, each will be the stronger for it. To explore this thesis, we will take one component of ministry, confession, and look at its expression (1) in the work of the church, both past and present, and (2) perhaps surprisingly, in psychotherapy. We will see that confession is a shared function of both enterprises and can become a bridge that will narrow the gap between church and clinic.

Many authors have noted that guilt, shame and anxiety form an emotional nexus between psychotherapy and spiritual formation (Belgum, 1963; Jung, 1933; Mowrer, 1976, 1989). The resolution of those emotional complexes, most broadly considered, is an important function of both enterprises. A more significant and fundamental connection between the two, however, exists in their shared use of confession as a vehicle to accomplish this change. Confession in the church is often ritualized and closely committed to sins of commission and omission. In psychotherapy we observe confession in a wider sense: the uncovering of secrets, the disclosure of painful memories, the admission of weakness and imperfection. Confession serves as the means by which emotional turmoil is uncovered and exposed to the healing touch of the Holy Spirit. Confession is also the prelude to any successful resolution of the painful effects of guilt, shame and anxiety.

Jesus and Confession

The Gospels use the Greek words for confession (*exomologeo* and *homologeo*) to denote three major forms of confession. In each case, these three meanings appear also in the remainder of Scripture; together they form a definition of confession that is broader than the more restricted meanings of the word that we normally utilize.

First, *confession* is used to indicate the giving of praise to God. In Matthew's Gospel (Mt 11:25, with a parallel passage in Lk 10:21) we read a prayer of Jesus that he uttered after pronouncing woes on the cities of Korazin, Bethsaida and Capernaum. The woes reflect some of the strongest language ever uttered by Jesus. He seems propelled into an attitude of praise when he prays, "I thank you, Father, Lord of heaven and earth, because you have hidden these things from the wise and the intelligent and revealed them to infants." This section of Matthew's Gospel concludes with the very famous invitation of Jesus, "Come to me, all you that are weary and are carrying heavy burdens, and I will give you rest" (Mt 11:28). The contrasting themes in the space of just ten verses speak to the powerful emotional tone of the woes, the prayer and the invitation of Jesus found here (Beck, 1993).

When Jesus prayed, "I thank you . . . " he was using the word for confession. "These words imply the acknowledging of God with eulogy, and honoring Him in what is here mentioned of Him" (Geldenhuys, 1966, p. 308). The use of the word *confession* here is in keeping with the practice of the Septuagint (Hagner, 1993) as he praises God and recounts how God's will is worked out both in the reception of the gospel as well in the rejection of it.

The second major use of the word *confession* occurs in connection with affirming that Jesus is Lord. When the priests and Levites came from Jerusalem to ask John the Baptist who he was, John writes, "He confessed and did not deny it, but confessed, 'I am not the Messiah'" (Jn 1:20). Eventually, the Jewish religious leaders of the day would excommunicate anyone who confessed that Jesus was the Messiah (Jn 12:42). This threat intimidated the parents of the man born blind so much that they deferred answering the question of Jesus regarding the restoration of the sight of their son (Jn 9:20-23). When Jesus sent out the Twelve with an elaborate set of missionary instructions, he used confession in this second sense. "Everyone therefore who acknowledges [confesses] me before others, I also will acknowledge before my Father in heaven" (Mt 10:32).

The third usage of the concept of confession in the Gospels is the sense with which we are most familiar: the confession of sins.

> Now John wore clothing of camel's hair with a leather belt around his waist, and his food was locusts and wild honey. Then the people of Jerusalem and all Judea were going out to him, and all the region along the Jordan, and they were baptized by him in the river Jordan, confessing their sins. (Mt 3:4-6)

Biblical Confession

Biblically, confession then is used in three major ways: the giving of praise to God, the acknowledgment of Jesus Christ as Savior and the acknowledgment before God of personal sin. These three expressions of confession are goals toward which spiritual formation seeks to move people. Likewise they are also three major goals of Christian psychotherapy.

1. Therapy seeks to bring clients to peace with others, self and the past so that rightful praise can again be given to God.

2. Therapy seeks to help people become fully aware of their humanness and the resulting need of the creature to be rightly related to the Creator.

3. Therapy seeks to promote an honesty about weakness, wrongs committed, needed actions neglected and unresolved issues so we can fully invoke the forgiveness of God.

The church has historically majored in the first two of these types of confession. Since the Reformation, the third has been primarily restricted among Protestants to private, individual confession before God. The modern Christian counseling movement has majored in this third component, the baring of one's soul before God in the presence of another human being. All too often Christian counseling has not given enough attention to the first two functions. We can safely say that both church and clinic have failed to give full due to all three aspects of confession, each doing some tasks better than others.

This shared process of helping shape the needed confessions of hurting people illustrates how Christian psychotherapy, like spiritual formation, is ministry, how confession is interpersonal with both vertical and horizontal dimensions, and how church and clinic share common tasks. With the hope that pastors and counselors can increasingly dialogue together and collaborate with each other, we will discuss these three aspects of confession in both church and clinic, giving the most extended treatment to the third.

Confession As Giving Praise to God

The first main use of the concept of confession that we will consider is related to the giving of praise to God. In modern speech we are likely to refer to this aspect as the giving of testimony or the proclamation of the works of God before others so that they can share in our grateful praise. In this sense we confess the good works of God as an affirmation of our awareness that all good gifts come from God and that blessed recipients of those good gifts owe the Giver words of praise.

Throughout the centuries these confessions have often been offered before God in written form. The most famous of these, the *Confessions* of Augustine (written in the fourth century), merely foreshadowed countless others. Augustine desired to confess in his heart to God and with his pen before many witnesses about the wonderful work of God in his life. Why would he wish to reveal his soul before others? "The human race is inquisitive about other people's lives, but negligent to correct their own" (Augustine, 1991, p. 180). He hoped that his shared story would serve as a stimulus to change.

A significant portion of Augustine's *Confessions* deals with his sinful past (including the famous theft of pears, his sexual adventure, and his involvements with a concubine and astrology). But a substantial contribution of the book emerges when we observe the remarkable way in which

Augustine described his inner world and how skillfully he self-disclosed. Von Harnack asked, "For what do the *Confessions* of Augustine contain? The portrait of a soul" (von Harnack, 1901, p. 136). According to von Harnack, Augustine was an incredible observer of human nature, at times morbid, over-strained and somewhat unhealthy, but when compared to contemporary self-disclosure in "an age of depraved taste and lying rhetoric," we are amazed at how superior was Augustine's self-description (1991, p. 180). This powerful ability to disclose the innermost self while giving written reason for others to praise God is precisely how this form of confession parallels the goals of modern psychotherapy. Of Augustine, Chessick said, "The writing of the *Confessions* was an act of self-therapy" (1987, p. 124).

In fact one can turn to the confessions of great Christians and, with just a little imagination, read them as if they were transcripts of psychotherapy sessions with the comments of the therapist excised. One example will suffice. Listen to Tolstoy as he wrote his confessions, and imagine a therapist's reflections (italicized words).

> I cannot think of those years without horror, loathing and heartache.
>
> *Your experiences must be painful to remember.*
>
> I killed men in war and challenged men to duels in order to kill them. I lost at cards, consumed the labor of the peasants, sentenced them to punishments, lived loosely, and deceived people.
>
> *Your regrets sound long and extensive.*
>
> Lying, robbery, adultery of all kinds, drunkenness, violence, murder—there was no crime I did not commit, and in spite of that people praised my conduct and my contemporaries considered and consider me to be a comparatively moral man.
>
> *You seem to be describing a major portion of your life.*
>
> So I lived for ten years. (Non-italicized segments, Tolstoy, 1882, 1974, p. 8)

As Tolstoy confesses from the innermost recesses of his life, he sounds very much like a modern-day client. Tolstoy's goal was the giving of praise to God. Yet all too often this form of confession is not readily acknowledged as an ingredient of Christian psychotherapy. When clients celebrate with their therapists the gains and accomplishments of their pilgrimage through the therapy process, do we help shape that celebration into a confession of the goodness of God to us all? Or do we merely affirm our clients' progress and maturation as a testimony to their good work and to our effective clinical interventions? Therapy that fails to have as one of its major goals the giving of praise to God risks becoming self-focused, self-serving and an affront to the God from whom all change and growth ultimately flow.

Confessing Christ As Lord and Savior

The second major form of confession is likewise a central focus of church life but is sometimes only mildly present in Christian psychotherapy. Although the word *confession* is still used in many circles with reference to the initial response a person makes to the gospel of Jesus Christ, we also commonly use the word *profession* to refer to this aspect of confession. In the ancient church a confession of Jesus as Savior was often a costly, life-changing event that could trigger persecution and danger. The most significant statement the martyrs could make would be their final response to the questions posed by the executioners: Do you hereby renounce your faith in Jesus Christ? Their affirmation and reiteration of their faith in Jesus Christ became known as their confession; hence martyrs are known as confessors (Bianchi, 1987).

In more recent church life the confession an individual makes of Jesus Christ as Savior and Lord may be a private or a public event. A private confession can be solitary, or it can be done in the presence of another person. If private, the new confessor is urged to make a public proclamation of that commitment, often based on the text of Romans 10:9: "If you confess with your mouth, 'Jesus is Lord,' and believe in your heart that God raised him from the dead, you will be saved" (NIV). The revivalistic movement in nineteenth-century American religion developed an altar call at the end of evangelistic services to facilitate this public confession of Christ as Savior and Lord. More recent evangelistic crusades have continued that emphasis.

The use of the word *confession* for one's initial response to the gospel is connected to the fact that faith is preceded by repentance. The gospel requires of its hearers an acknowledgment of personal sin and failure. This confession of personal need that accompanies conversion is, in part, an exteriorizing of unhappiness and misery that gives a sense of relief and joy (Clark, 1958).

The issue of evangelism in psychotherapy is a difficult tangle of ethics, attitudes and unresolved complexes. Critics of the psychotherapy movement in the church often express concern that Christian counseling seems to overlook a critical and basic need of its nonbelieving clients: the need these people have to come to terms with their own lost state and to believe in the Lord Jesus Christ. Only then, say the critics, can substantial and significant changes in the lives of clients have eternal consequences. With stark and perhaps crass directness, critics of Christian counseling argue that therapizing a sinner condemned to hell merely outfits a person for the coming condemnation.

Obviously those within the Christian counseling movement approach this issue differently. We are commanded in Scripture to love our neighbors by showing them acts of kindness and mercy irrespective of their spiritual state. A cup of cold water given in the name of Jesus may be the prelude to a subsequent and profound encounter with Jesus as Savior. God uses many means and persons to accomplish his task of drawing women and men toward himself. The Christian counselor may be just such an instrument. Or the therapist may providentially participate in a larger, more comprehensive plan designed to bring the client to a point of confession of faith.

A brief review here of these well-worn arguments will not settle the ongoing debate and discussion. But we who labor in God's vineyard as Christian counselors can well take to heart the reminder that we do have obligations to represent this aspect of confession fairly in our professional practice. We need to be aware of all the ethical implications of this issue. We need to be aware of the claims of the gospel on the lives of lost souls. And we need to be aware of the mandate of Jesus himself, who sent his workers out into the world with this demanding charge: "So be wise as serpents and innocent as doves" (Mt 10:16).

Confession As Acknowledgment of Personal Sin

The final aspect of confession we will consider is also the most familiar: the acknowledgment of personal sin before God and others. Repentance of sins is a major theme of the Bible in both testaments. John the Baptist, the prophesied forerunner of Jesus Christ, preached repentance. "John the baptizer appeared in the wilderness, proclaiming a baptism of repentance for the forgiveness of sins. And people from the whole Judean countryside and all the people of Jerusalem were going out to him, and were baptized by him in the river Jordan, confessing their sins " (Mk 1:4-5).

Soon thereafter Jesus himself began preaching the good news of the kingdom. "Repent, and believe in the good news" (Mk 1:15). The preaching of the early apostles likewise contained a central emphasis on the importance of repentance. Peter said,

> "Therefore let the entire house of Israel know with certainty that God has made him both Lord and Messiah, this Jesus whom you crucified."
> Now when they heard this, they were cut to the heart and said to Peter and to the other apostles, "Brothers, what should we do?" Peter said to them, "Repent, and be baptized every one of you in the name of Jesus Christ so that your sins may be forgiven." (Acts 2:36-38)

The early documents of the growing church urged readers, "Confess your sins to one another, and pray for one another, so that you may be healed" (Jas 5:16). Confessors can be assured that God will forgive. "If we confess our sins, he who is faithful and just will forgive us our sins and cleanse us from all unrighteousness" (1 Jn 1:9).

Public Confession in the Early Church

The precise practice of the early church with regard to confession is difficult to ascertain. What evidence is available points to the primary use of public confession. The public nature of confession was justified on the basis of the final judgment which, some claimed, would be a public exposure of everyone's sins (Rev 20:12). "The Didache shows us that this confession was public, in church, and that each believer was expected to confess his transgressions on Sunday, before breaking bread in the Eucharistic feast" (Lea, 1968, p. 174).

The demands of justice imposed by the church when someone confessed a sin were high. Often absolution, the assurance of forgiveness, was not given until the entire procedure of penance had been fulfilled by the confessing believer (Snoeck, 1964). For a time in the church all those who were doing penance—those who had confessed but who had not yet received the absolution—were enrolled in the order of penitents and were separated from the church community. Often the penance was public (Fazzalaro, 1950).

The rite of confession was sometimes accompanied by other acts of contrition such as prayer, fasting, prostration, dressing in sackcloth (Van Becelaere, 1955). At first a baptized believer could confess sin only one time after baptism (Donoghue & Shapiro, 1984). "Thus the main preoccupation of Hermas seems to be that the church has no place for the recidivist, the offender who continually falls back into sin and who presumes upon unlimited pardon" (Geddes & Thuriston, 1928, p. 58). Later the possibility of repeating this rite of confession spread throughout the church (Manuel, 1991).

At some point, however, the practice of public confession of sin before assembled worshipers fell into disuse. Several reasons for this change have been suggested (Elwin, 1883): (1) The church greatly expanded in its size and scope. The use of public confession became a practical obstacle with larger congregations. (2) Some of the sins confessed were scandalous in nature and thus posed pastoral problems relative to the varied maturation and age levels of congregants. (3) Some of the sins confessed made the person liable for prosecution by the laws of the state. Such an eventuality was especially difficult when the state was openly hostile toward even the existence of worshiping Christian communities. For these and other reasons the church began to move away from its use of public confession before others.

For the purposes of this chapter, however, we need to highlight several facts. (1) The early church felt a corporate obligation to include confession in its forms of worship. (2) They interpreted biblical texts to mean that confession was to be made before others as in the example of John the Baptist's followers. (3) They viewed the instruction of James to confess mutually as referring to all occasions, not just to times when physical healing was needed. The early church clearly attempted to implement the practice of public confession of sin before others.

Leo the Great, in the fifth century of the church, urged that churches move toward the privatization of confession. From the sixth century on, confession was totally private (Manuel, 1991). At the Fourth Lateran

Council (1215) the bishops decreed that all persons should confess privately to a priest at least once a year or face the risk of excommunication. This confession is called "auricular" because it is made into the ear of a priest.

The scholastic movement solidified this new configuration of dogma. Now the rite of confession became a sacrament consisting of three distinct acts by the penitent: contrition, confession and satisfaction. The satisfaction or penance performed by the penitent satisfied the temporal punishment required for that sin. On the basis of these three acts the priest could offer absolution, which, according to official Roman Catholic teaching, granted the sinner a remission of guilt and removal of the eternal punishment associated with that particular postbaptismal sin. Any residual guilt or punishment could later be purged in purgatory.

The confession could be heard only by a priest, who was empowered to offer absolution by virtue of the two powers of ordination and jurisdiction. The priest's ordination connected him to the unbroken chain of apostolic succession and to the power to forgive sins originally given by Jesus, according to Roman Catholic teaching, to the early apostles (Mt 16:19; 18:18; Jn 20:21-23).

> The church was careful to make the confession given to a priest inviolate. Inviolable secrecy (except by express permission of the penitent), even at the cost of life or honour, is enjoined on the priest, and on any one, interpreter or the like, who has in any manner become informed of the contents of a confession. (Van Becelaere, 1955, p. 714)

Public safety or the fulfillment of legal justice did not contravene this privacy. This confidentiality was theologically guaranteed by three seals: natural, divine and ecclesiastical (Melia, 1865).

The confessional as a separate piece of furniture in the church was introduced in 1576 by St. Charles Borromeo (1538-1584), Archbishop of Milan (Fazzalaro, 1950). This development then gave to the sacrament of penance, in addition to its strict confidentiality, another major feature consonant with modern psychotherapy: privacy in the presence of another human being.

Roman Catholic pastoral theology soon began to produce manuals to be used by the confessor (the priest hearing confessions). The manuals contained ever-increasing elaborations regarding how the priest was to conduct the sacrament. These manuals, especially in more recent times, contain material concerning scrupulosity, a condition of conscience known to psychotherapists as obsessional ideation, a problem not uncommon among evangelical believers (Beck, 1981). The manuals recognized this category of psychopathology as a condition that must be distinguished from mere tender conscience or normal guilt feelings (Snoeck, 1961). Twentieth-century manuals argue that confession by Catholics should be simple, humble, prudent, sincere, vocal, softly spoken, truthful, voluntary and frequent (Belton, 1949).

Protestant Protestations

The Reformation of the sixteenth century forever changed how its descendant churches would view the confessional and the sacrament of penance as outlined above. The reactions of the Reformers to the doctrine of obligatory confession as it had developed by their time were harsh and unrelenting. In fact, the spark that ignited the Protestant Reformation concerned abuses that had grown up around the sacrament of penance. The system of indulgences, with all its attendant graft and greed, struck the Reformers as a travesty on the biblical texts that outlined how believers should confess their sins.

The Reformers were adamant in their objection to the power to forgive that the Roman church had vested in its priests. The bulk of their attacks on the confessional dealt more with the word of absolution given by the priest than with the words of confession whispered by the penitent. The Reformers objected vociferously to the "power of the keys" that had accrued around the office of the Roman Catholic priest.

Yet in spite of Luther's hatred for the abuses of the confessional, he sought to maintain the practice of individual confession. Six types of confession are found in Lutheran theology: (1) secret confession in the heart, (2) general or public confession in the liturgy, (3) individual confession before an assembled congregation, (4) reconciliatory confession based on Matthew 5, (5) the mutual consolation of the brethren and (6) private, individual confession before another believer (Koehler, 1982).

This sixth type of confession reflects the remnants of the Roman doctrine once Luther had stripped it of what he felt were unjustified accretions.

Luther wrote:

> Private confession, which alone is practiced, though it cannot be proved from Scripture, is wholly commendable, useful and indeed necessary. "I would not have it cease, but rather I rejoice that it exists in the Church of Christ, for it is the one and only remedy for troubled consciences. . . . The one thing that I abhor is the employment of confession to further the despotism and the exactions of the pontiffs." (Bettenson, 1961, p. 282)

Luther practiced confession before another believer all through his life (Richter, 1966).

Nonetheless, the use of individual confession fell into disuse almost to the point of extinction in the Lutheran tradition. Pietism and Rationalism both worked against its continuing use. Auricular confession involves a personal encounter with pain and the humiliation of disclosure, further leading to its disuse (Stevenson, 1966). Also, the practice of individual confession declined because it became linked with church discipline (Koehler, 1982). Thus it no longer was characterized by absolute privacy and confidentiality. As a result, believers could not as freely use the rite of confession for their own spiritual growth and development.

Calvin likewise encouraged believers to make use of the James 5 provision for confession one to another. For Calvin, such confession was made to God, was voluntary and nonsacramental, was made to others after being made first to God, and was based wholly on the confession to a priest (McNeill, 1951). Regarding Lutheranism and the Reformed tradition,

> Both discard vigorously the medieval requirement of confession and affirm on scriptural grounds the sufficiency of unmediated confession to God by the penitent and of the private and secret confession to a trusted counselor, ordinarily the minister, but quite legitimately a layman. (McNeill, 1951, p. 216)

More Recent Ecclesiastical Usage of Confession

Roman Catholics continue to make use of the confessional. Vatican II affirmed and expanded the practice and made it a part of the rites of reconciliation (Manuel, 1991). A Roman Catholic analyst states, "I think it is also a fact that wherever the practice of confession has remained alive there has been less demand for psychoanalytic treatment" (Snoeck, 1964, p. vii). His statement suggests a therapeutic value in the regular use of confession.

Among Protestants, private confession before another believer is almost extinct. William James wrote, "We English-speaking Protestants, in the general self-reliance and unsociability of our nature, seem to find it enough if we take God alone into our confidence" (1958, p. 531). Protestantism has normally emphasized the forensic quality of God's forgiveness. The believer need only enter a plea before the Judge of all judges in order to experience true forgiveness. Contrition, absolution and the need to confess before another believer do not loom large as issues of concern (Bowman, 1969).

Some Protestant groups have made notable efforts to utilize various forms of confession to other people. At times the Reformed Church of Scotland, the Moravians and the Methodists have used mutual confession as part of their spiritual formation practices. The Oneida Movement in the United States made use of what they termed mutual criticism (Hurvitz, 1976). The Oxford Movement has emphasized that confession is a prerequisite to change.

E. B. Pusey, a leader in the nineteenth-century Oxford Movement, inspired people from all over Great Britain to come to him to confess. He and other leaders in the movement would respond not with a word of absolution but with another confession that "would probably be more exactly termed 'testimony' " (Bergren, 1975, p. 16).

Bonhoeffer recounts his experience in a community of vicars where all participants practiced confession one to another. Bonhoeffer asked why it is easier to confess to God than to a brother.

> We must ask ourselves whether we have not often been deceiving ourselves with our confession of sin to God, whether we have not been confessing our sins to ourselves and also granting ourselves absolution. . . . Self-forgiveness can never lead to a breach with sin. (Bonhoeffer, 1954, p. 116)

Private confession before another believer or a priest has always been possible, although underutilized, within the Anglican communion. John Stott argues that auricular confession is of value in extraordinary cases to help calm a conscience not otherwise calmed by normal, secret confession to God. Early leaders in the English church, Ridley, Latimer, Becon and Tyndale all seem to have approved of confession for this purpose (Stott, 1964).

Some authors argue that Protestants should return to some measure of private confession before another believer. Any renewed ecclesiastical use of confession would have to capitalize on its advantages while seeking to offset shortcomings of the system (Brink, 1985; Clewell, 1987; Gilmore, 1989).

Among the values of confession before another person are these: (1) The penitent can receive on a direct, interpersonal basis words of assurance and encouragement. (2) The penitent can resolve real guilt through confession before God but in the presence of a witness. (3) Confession before another person assaults the deadly secrecy that surrounds most of our unresolved issues. This secrecy, or covering, adds insult to injury and must be counter-balanced by at least some honesty before another human being. "When one man opens his heart to another, that in itself means help, it means being lifted out of inner loneliness, out of egocentricity, and out of a cramped state of mind" (Thurneysen, 1957, p. 42). Confession to God in the presence of another person becomes detrimental to good spiritual health if it is perfunctory or if it obscures God as the actual forgiver.

Confession of Sin in Psychotherapy

We now will turn to examine the place of confession of sin in Christian psychotherapy. Most therapists have experienced the confession of sin by clients during the course of counseling. The confessions do not emerge because the clients confuse the therapist with a priest, but because in the process of exploring the agonies of one's soul it sometimes becomes necessary and helpful to reveal inner secrets.

To expose oneself verbally or otherwise to God or another human being involves a radical lowering of one's defenses, and the act of penitent confession itself brings profound healing—reordering values and freeing energies that had been bound up by the process of trying to hide. (Harrison, 1988, p. 315).

Both Allport and Weatherhead refer to this aspect of confession as an aid in the integration process. When we confess our faults and sins to another, we can benefit by increased insight, by improved clarity regarding our personal assets and liabilities, and by further knowledge of our own values, all components of a healthy integration (Allport, 1950; Whitehead, 1952). Confession likewise helps prevent the shifting of blame and the formation of projection. Bergren says, "It is common knowledge that talking about painful and disturbing memories or experiences which have lain on our minds unburdens us of them and affords a sense of relief" (1975, p. 3).

When psychotherapy includes a frank and open discussion of sin before God, we respect the interpersonal quality of sin. Sin is defined as an offense to God. When we hide our guilt we cut ourselves off from the surrounding community. Hidden sins thus not only offend God but cut us off from others (Drakeford, 1964). If all of our confession is private before God only, we never deal with the wider offense we have contributed to the community. Sin has both horizontal and vertical dimensions; thus confession should likewise have two dimensions. "Both kinds of confession are necessary and both serve a theological and psychological purpose" (Gilmore, 1989, p. 94).

Carl Jung noted that all sin is accompanied by concealment or repression. These secrets cut a client off "from communion with his fellow beings" (1933, p. 36). Confession was, for Jung, the first stage of psychotherapy and the first stage of spiritual and psychological growth (Meadow, 1989; Todd, 1985). Mowrer likewise noted that people want to remain open with others and thus have a need to repair their interpersonal breaks (1976, 1989).

Including the confession of sin as a legitimate task of Christian psychotherapy also helps bring encouragement into the life of the believer. Nearly all clients suffer from demoralization. Outcome studies have repeatedly demonstrated that successful therapies offer clients encouragement and support (Frank, 1982). When a client is able to unburden a weighty soul to another human being and is heard, the result can be direct and personal support and affirmation. The hiding of secrets is hard on the soul. "There is no worse suffering than a guilty conscience and certainly none more harmful" (Tournier, 1960, p. 210).

> The widespread need for open avowal and acknowledgment and confession occasionally comes to light in the blooming of some new cult in which communication and disclosure are made a part of self-realization. Such cults are often evanescent because they depend too much on superficial solution, but they are popular because unconfessed guilt feelings are hard to bear. They must be confessed to someone! (Menninger, 1973, p. 197)

Confession is a way of sharing the load (Pruyser, 1968).

Confession in psychotherapy can also foster a healthy encounter with reality and personal responsibility (Mulholland, 1974; Pattison, 1989). William James wrote, "For him who confesses, shams are over and realities have begun; he has exteriorized his rottenness" (1958, p. 351). Psychotherapy began as the exploration of pathogenic secrets (Meares, 1980). Some of these secrets shape the self in twisted and unhealthy ways. Therapy for these distortions thus involves the revelation of the secrets that have been both hidden and influential.

If we broaden the definition of confession to include other kinds of uncovering, not just the revelation of secret sin, we can see even greater connections between confession as it has occurred in ecclesiastical settings and confession in psychotherapy (Reik, 1959). The very essence of the client's task is to reveal what has been hidden, unexpressed, cut off or disconnected from experience. The therapist's role often bears sharp similarity to that of the confessor (Worthen, 1974). Both listen to what has previously been undisclosed and to that which is shrouded in guilt and shame. "Confession is the traditional, theological word for what we have been discussing as pastoral psychotherapy" (Wise, 1983, p. 284).

A few decades ago the evangelical church was challenged to work harder at shedding masks of pretense, to engage in more transparency and to self-disclose (Palmberg & Scandrette, 1977). The movement paralleled a therapeutic movement that advocated the same goals (Jourard, 1964, 1971). Empirical studies suggest that uncovering and disclosure of the hidden have positive value on health (Pennebaker, Hughes, & O'Heeron, 1987). Each of these factors contributes to the larger picture that confession is vital to our spiritual and psychological health.

Conclusion

Protestants have for the most part expelled the confessional from church life. But in our effort to privatize our relationship with God so that we can avoid interacting in a confessional way with another human being, we have neglected an important vehicle for personal change. And, in spite of our vigilance to keep the confessional out of the church, it has in fact come back into the church—this time in the form of Christian counseling. Here again we have people uncovering the hidden in the presence of God and another human being, protected by powerful values of confidentiality, and removed from the tentacles of church discipline. Perhaps we have stronger ministries now with people because of this subtle intrusion. And perhaps our shared interest in confession will stimulate ever-increasing dialogue between pastors and therapists as we jointly engage in the same formation tasks with God's people.

Confession in all its biblical forms gives all the followers of Jesus an important tool we can use to deal with our weaknesses, our neuroses, our sins, our frailties. Along with the accompanying dynamic of forgiveness, we can thus maintain—even though we are frail humans subject to great imperfections—our solid and sure connection with God.

12

Seek &
Grant Forgiveness

IF THE NEUROTICISM FACTOR IN HUMAN PERSONALITY REPRESENTS HUMAN frailty and weakness, then forgiveness represents God's provision for that universal human condition. The essence of Christianity is that "God forgives sin through Jesus Christ" (Childs, 1990, p. 438). Forgiveness is a distinctive and defining part of Christianity.

Based on National Opinion Research Center surveys using the Rokeach Value Survey, forgiveness was the most distinctively Christian of all eighteen instrumental values (Gorsuch & Hao, 1993). God's forgiveness and the forgiveness that we give to and receive from others heals the bruises and scrapes that we incur and inflict in life. To consider a physical analogy, if our body never healed its black-and-blue bruises, its nicks and cuts and its aches and pains, the total accumulation of these common physical flaws would render us unsightly messes. When the body works as it should, these imperfections heal and disappear. Forgiveness, when it operates as it should in our lives, performs the same function for all the neuroticisms of our life (McMinn, 1996).

Confession and forgiveness form a dynamic pair. In actuality, one does not exist without the other. Separating them is somewhat artificial, but for the purposes of these two chapters, we need to understand each part of this dynamic pair in order to appreciate fully how marvelous these provisions of God for our neuroticisms truly are. Forgiveness is related to justice and mercy, topics we have previously discussed. Forgiveness is the bond that links justice to mercy (McCullough, Sandage, & Worthington, 1997), the bridge that enables us to go beyond justice to mercy (Walters, 1984).

A Fighter Pilot's Story

Frank Clark joined the army in 1943 as a hopeful eighteen-year-old who wanted desperately to become a fighter pilot. He had to settle for gunnery school instead. The B-17 to which he was assigned had a crew of ten, including eight gunners. His position in the ball turret at the bottom of the plane left him vulnerable and exposed. "Actually there weren't any very good positions on the plane. War does not discriminate. We were just like the people on the ground when the bombs dropped" (Clark, 1995, p. 42). The big lumbering B-17 participated with twenty-four other such planes in missions aimed at various targets in Germany: synthetic oil plants, marshaling yards, rail lines, refineries.

The excitement of the first few missions soon gave way to dread. "Thoughts of doom were present every day, I felt terrible—gloomy day after gloomy day—flying like a machine and not really caring if I returned or not. All the days blended into one another" (p. 46). In March 1945 a faceless colonel warned these young American bombardiers that dirty work was ahead. "You're going to be baby killers" (p. 46). Clark's crew experienced one harrowing ordeal after another as they progressed toward their mandated service allotment of thirty-five missions.

Clark's agony increased as he realized the tremendous civilian toll that must be occurring as he dropped bombs over military and sometimes nonmilitary targets. No one is closer to the death and destruction of a bomb than the gunner who is responsible for releasing it. Sometimes he literally had to physically push a bomb out if it became entangled in the plane's underbelly mechanism.

Missions to Kiel, Bremen, Leipzig and Freiham finally concluded his longed-for quota of thirty-five missions. The last mission was the worst ever for young Frank Clark. He survived, but his reentry into civilian life was awkward and tortured. He began to drink excessively. Doctors hospitalized him in psychiatric units during two unstable episodes. He never spoke to others about his experiences in the war, let alone his nagging regret about the civilian deaths that had occurred as bombs from his B-17 plunged into the earth.

> Early in the morning on May 16, 1987, half-asleep, I wrote an open apology to all the cities I had bombed. I wanted the people to know how I felt about what I had had to do during the war. Just writing the letter made me feel better, but it was not intended merely to unburden my conscience. I wanted it to get there on Memorial Day so that the Germans could understand what kind of people Americans are. I requested a response from someone, anyone, just so I'd know my letter had arrived. I never thought anything would come of it. (Clark, 1995, p. 52)

Frank Clark sent the letters addressed only to "Public Officials" in each city he had bombed. Soon letters began arriving from Germany, not only from city officials but from the general public who had read his extraordinary plea for forgiveness in the newspapers. His request for forgiveness—his thirty-sixth mission—obviously triggered thoughtful reflection among hundreds of Germans who, like Frank Clark, still had not dealt with the past.

> Still the letters kept coming. Some were highly emotional, loving, and heartfelt; others, equally heartfelt, were mean and accusing. But an odd thing had happened to me. The understanding letters, which far outnumbered the others, had brought me peace. Vicious letters that might once have sent me into deep depression now merely rolled over me. I realized for the first time the whole world didn't need to forgive me. I could finally forgive myself. (Clark, 1995, p. 60)

What Frank Clark experienced by seeking forgiveness is part of the forgiveness process Jesus taught about and part of God's provision for us to help us deal with the imperfections, evils and disappointments of life.

A Definitional Problem

The most familiar of concepts are often the most difficult to define, and forgiveness is no exception to that rule. The main definitional problems have to do not with the core of what forgiveness is but what its outer boundaries are. Does forgiveness include reconciliation of relationship? Is forgiveness dependent on the repentance of the other party? If so, how? If not, under what circumstances? We will address some of the issues of the outer boundaries of forgiveness later in this chapter. Now we will identify some of the core characteristics of forgiveness.

A comprehensive treatment of forgiveness should include its cognitive, affective and behavioral dimensions as well as address its volitional, motivational, spiritual, religious and interpersonal aspects (Gorsuch & Hao, 1993).

Forgiveness is a unified entity even though it has many components. In the recent past, many secular therapists seemed to feel that forgiveness was primarily a religious concept and should not receive much attention in the mental health field. Now, however, even secular theorists have taken renewed interest in forgiveness as a means of healing a damaged past and building a future that consists of love, justice and trust (Hargrave, 1994).

For secular therapists, forgiveness is most often portrayed as a problem-solving technique rather than a foundational approach to life which is the Christian's calling (McCullough & Worthington, 1994). Forgiving seeks to restore the interpersonal relationship by restoring communication, determining the exact wrong, pardoning the offense, releasing obligations and allowing trust to reappear (Veenstra, 1992). The offended party lets go of a record of wrongs, a need for revenge and associated negative feelings of bitterness and resentment (DiBlasio, 1992).

The word *forgiveness* can be used for individuals forgiving another individual or a group as well as for group forgiveness of another group, a much rarer form of forgiveness (Brakenhielm, 1993). Individual forgiveness is both an interpersonal transaction and an intrapsychic process (Benson, 1992). Forgiveness is both an act and an attitude (Patton, 1985). It springs from an internal motivation to repair and maintain a relationship that has been damaged by hurtful action (McCullough, Sandage & Worthington, 1997). Another way of looking at its motivational structure is to view forgiveness as a remotivation to renew what existed previously (Brakenhielm, 1993).

Forgiveness also involves replacing one's right to resentment, condemnation and subtle revenge with love toward the offender. It can be as difficult to ask for forgiveness as to forgive another who has committed a wrong against us (Enright, 1996). When someone is unforgiving, such an attitude is expressed in a toleration of revenge, an acceptability of rejoicing in the misfortune of the offender, an acceptability of wishing to respond in kind, a tolerance for harboring long-lasting grudges, and a tolerance for ruining the reputation of the offender (Mauger, Perry, Freeman, Grove, McBride, & Mckinney, 1992).

In general, the closer the relationship, the more difficult forgiveness may be when the connection is wounded or injured by offense and wrongs.

> We are abused by selfish persons more powerful than we, ignored by persons from whom we wish respect, condemned by perfectionistic parents or bosses, rebuffed by those we would love. This rejection leads to the most painful emotional suffering we experience. (Walters, 1984, p. 365)

Marital and parent-child relationships are among those that can cause the most severe of pain. These relationships are intense, with many invisible loyalties involved (Patton, 1985). We can easily have irrational expectations of a parent, spouse or child and be greatly defended against understanding that would ameliorate these intensities. Consequently, hurts are great, and forgiveness for those hurts can be very difficult to grant.

Forgiveness in the Bible

The Bible contains many accounts of the positive effects of forgiveness. One such event occurs when Joseph forgives his brothers of their crimes against him. In Genesis 45 we read that Joseph said to his brothers, "Do not be distressed, or angry with yourselves, because you sold me here; for God sent me before you to preserve life" (v. 5). Joseph forgave by releasing his brothers from the offense they had committed and by developing a wider and more comprehensive view of those events that had occurred years earlier.

Another positive example of forgiveness occurs in 1 Samuel 24 when David passes up a perfect opportunity to slay the pursuing King Saul. "See, my father, see the corner of your cloak in my hand; for by the fact that I cut off the corner of your cloak, and did not kill you, you may know for certain that there is no wrong or treason in my hands. I have not sinned against you, though you are hunting me to take my life" (v. 11).

In the New Testament the first martyr, Stephen, prays immediately before his death, "Lord, do not hold this sin against them" (Acts 7:60).

The Bible also gives examples of how a lack of forgiveness can ruin a person's life. Esau was consumed with hatred toward Jacob for the wrongs committed by Jacob against him (Gen 27:41-45). Jacob had to flee for his very life. Jonah could not forgive the people whom Jehovah had forgiven (Jon 4:1). Proverbs 19:11 says, "Those with good sense are slow to anger, and it is their glory to overlook an offense."

Forgiveness in the Teachings of Jesus

Our primary interest in this chapter is to examine the teachings of Jesus for material regarding forgiveness. Each of the four Gospels begins and ends with a prominent emphasis on forgiveness. The Holy Spirit seems to have enveloped these inspired documents with gracious parentheses regarding the gospel of forgiveness.

Matthew begins his account of the life of Jesus with the preaching of John the Baptist regarding the need for repentance in the kingdom of God (Mt 3) and ends with the Great Commission given to the church, which commands them to spread the good news of forgiveness offered through Jesus Christ to the uttermost parts of the earth (Mt 28). Mark also begins his account with descriptions of the baptism of repentance preached by John the Baptist (Mk 1:4) and ends with the disciples spreading the good news God's forgiveness everywhere (Mk 16:20). Luke records the prayer of Zechariah at the time of the birth of John the Baptist. He prayed, "And you, child, will be called the prophet of the Most High; for you will go before the Lord to prepare his ways, to a give knowledge of salvation to his people by the forgiveness of their sins" (Lk 1:76-77). Luke ends his gospel with an account of a postresurrection appearance of Jesus.

> Then he opened their minds to understand the scriptures, and he said to them, "Thus it is written, that the Messiah is to suffer and to rise from the dead on the third day, and that repentance and forgiveness of sins is to be proclaimed in his name to all nations, beginning from Jerusalem." (Lk 24:45-47)

The apostle John begins his account of the life of Jesus with a proclamation that those who believe (and receive forgiveness) can become the children of God (Jn 1:12). And he ends with an account of the forgiveness Jesus extended to Peter, who had just recently denied knowing him (Jn 21). Forgiveness characterizes the entire ministry of Jesus.

Christ's ministry is marked by a persistent breaking down of barriers, declaring that God's forgiveness is present for all. Indeed, Christ judges others in the righteousness of God precisely by embodying forgiveness as a way of life. In the midst of the brokenness of human community occasioned by the universal and ongoing disaster of both personal and structural sin, Christ draws others into communion with himself and with one another, and the sign of that communion is self-giving love (Jones, 1995, p. 120).

Table 11 illustrates how the theme of forgiveness pervades all phases of the teachings of Jesus. In each instance, his teachings illustrate a different facet of forgiveness, a series of topics to which we now turn.

Aspect of Jesus' Teaching	Passages Involved	Aspects of Forgiveness Depicted
Direct Teachings	Mt 6; Lk 17	Its Model
Parables	Mt 18; Lk 7	Its Difficulty
Behavior of Jesus	Lk 23; Jn 8; Jn 21	Its Costliness
Problem Passages	Mt 12:31; Mk 4	Its Problems
Opposition	Mt 9; Lk 7	Its Provocative Nature
Spiritual Formation	Mt 18	Its Centrality

Table 11. Forgiveness in the Gospels

The Two Dimensions of Forgiveness

When we look at the direct teachings of Jesus, we find two passages that give us information about the importance Jesus attached to the concept of forgiveness. In Matthew 6 (with a parallel passage in Lk 11) Jesus teaches his disciples to pray. It was the custom of rabbis to teach their disciples how to pray; John the Baptist had done that for his disciples (Geldenhuys, 1966).

In the middle of this model prayer we find the fifth petition, "And forgive us our debts, as we also have forgiven our debtors" (Mt 6:12). In

Matthew's theology, sin is a debt, a debt that brings us into obligation to God (Marshall, 1978). The debts are defined by verse 14 where they are named as trespasses or sins. Debtors could become slaves to their creditors, but God offers forgiveness without restitution to his followers who ask for it. We do not forgive others as a way of earning merit with God and thus obligating him to forgive us. We forgive others and ask for forgiveness from God as an expression of consistency and congruency. To Jesus it is inconceivable that someone would dare ask God for full and free forgiveness while remaining as an unforgiving person toward others. The forgiven forgive and the forgivers are forgiven.

These two dimensions of forgiveness fit together and, Jesus says, do not exist apart from one another. If we cannot forgive and release others, we will never fully know how God has done that for us (Patton, 1985). And if we have never accepted the boundless forgiveness God has offered us, we can never know that value of forgiving one another.

Appended to the Lord's Prayer in Matthew's Gospel are two additional verses. Although not a part of the prayer, they are added by Matthew, who apparently felt it important to add explanatory material regarding the fifth petition. "For if you forgive others their trespasses, your heavenly Father will also forgive you; but if you do not forgive others, neither will your Father forgive your trespasses" (Mt 6:14-15). "These verses are a forceful way of making the significant point that it is unthinkable—impossible— that we can enjoy God's forgiveness without in turn extending our forgiveness toward others" (Hagner, 1993, p. 152). The primary word in the New Testament for *forgive* is *aphesis,* to let go (Grider, 1984). We are to let go of the wrongs others have committed against us, just as the Father lets go of our sins when we ask for forgiveness (McNeile, 1961). In Luke's Gospel, Jesus adds yet another theme to his teaching on forgiveness.

> Be on your guard! If another disciple sins, you must rebuke the offender, and if there is repentance, you must forgive. And if the same person sins against you seven times a day, and turns back to you seven times and says, "I repent," you must forgive. (Lk 17:3-4)

In this passage Jesus is speaking about interpersonal forgiveness when someone repents. The process involves rebuking—warning in a serious fashion. "The saying implicitly forbids the nursing of grudges and criticism of the offender behind his back" (Marshall, 1978, p. 642). In the Luke passage, Jesus is prompting his disciples to magnanimity with regard to forgiveness. They are to be generous and without limit in forgiving.

These two teachings then give us two distinguishing marks of Christian forgiveness that sets it apart from the forgiving that those unrelated to God can or might do with one another.

First, our interpersonal forgiving is related to the forgiveness that God offers us. Because we have been forgiven, we are to become forgivers. Our forgiving is anchored in the very character of God. The apostle Paul makes this most explicit when he writes, "Put away from you all bitterness and wrath and anger and wrangling and slander, together with all malice, and be kind to one another, tenderhearted, forgiving one another, as God in Christ has forgiven you" (Eph 4:31-32). The Bible does not ignore the practical reality that interpersonal functioning is often very difficult for us fallen creatures. In light of this universal difficulty, Jesus calls us to aggressive, proactive action to keep our interpersonal relationships functioning smoothly.

In the place of what comes naturally to us (bitterness, wrath, anger, wrangling, slander, malice) we are to cultivate kindness and tenderheartedness, both made possible by continual forgiving just as God in Christ continually forgives us. *Lex taliones,* the repaying of like for like, is almost a human instinct (Weaver, 1994); Jesus calls us to replace that universal impulse with Godlike forgiveness. "I led them with cords of human kindness, with bands of love. I was to them like those who lift infants to their cheeks. I bent down to them and fed them" (Hos 11:4). Grace and gratitude form the context in which our forgiving is to occur: grace because of the favor God bestows on us by freely forgiving us and gratitude because that is the only acceptable response to such kindness (Childs, 1990).

Second, Jesus teaches that our forgiving should not have limits on it. "The Christian standard of forgiveness must immeasurably exceed the best the world can achieve" (Barclay, 1975, p. 216). All too often those whose frame of reference is totally secular or nonreligious will need great encouragement to start forgiving; for the unbeliever, a convincing case needs to be made in order to get the process started. The unforgiven are at a distinct disadvantage when it comes to learning how to make forgiving a way of life. There is a direct connection between accepting forgiveness and our capacity to forgive (Benson, 1992). In contrast, Jesus assumes we already know how to forgive, so he prompts us to keep on forgiving so that it is an embodied way of life (Jones, 1995).

A biblical view of forgiving also includes additional distinguishing marks. Jesus expects us to seek out forgiveness from those we have offended (McMinn, 1996). Jesus is not content that we forgive others; he wills that we pursue those who can and should forgive us. "So when you are offering your gift at the altar, if you remember that your brother or sister has something against you, leave your gift there before the altar and go; first be reconciled to your brother or sister, and then come and offer your gift" (Mt 5:23-24). In addition, Jesus assumed that all persons "are burdened with a need to be forgiven" (Alter, 1994, p. 2). When Jesus confronts the crowd of accusing men who have taken the woman in an act of adultery, he invites the sinless to throw the first stone, and there are none; every one of them skulks away. All humans stand in need of forgiveness.

Forgiveness is at the heart of who God is. When the Lord granted favor on the people of Israel and agreed to write his commands on a second set of stone tablets, he revealed himself in a new and fuller way when he proclaimed,

> The LORD, the LORD,
> a God merciful and gracious,
> slow to anger,
> and abounding in steadfast love and faithfulness,
> keeping steadfast love for the thousandth generation,
> forgiving iniquity and transgression and sin,
> yet by no means clearing the guilty,
> but visiting the iniquity of the parents
> upon the children
> and the children's children,
> to the third and the fourth generation. (Ex 34:6-7)

Human transgression wreaks deadly havoc, but the Lord's gracious forgiveness is always available. The forgiving father in the parable of the prodigal Son forgives foolishness, wastefulness and abandonment, just as God forgives all sins. "Bless the LORD, O my soul, and do not forget all his benefits—who forgives all your iniquity, who heals all your diseases" (Ps 103:2-3). "Let the wicked forsake their way, and the unrighteous their thoughts; let them return to the LORD, that he may have mercy on them, and to our God, for he will abundantly pardon" (Is 55:7). "To forgive is to dance to the beat of God's forgiving heart" (Smedes, 1983, p. 26).

Forgiveness Is Communal

Biblical forgiveness consists of yet another unique feature not found in secular emphases. It is to be communal in nature, not just individual. The secular world often urges people toward forgiveness because it is something healthy that you do for yourself (Simon & Simon, 1990). While partially true, this emphasis only reveals the depth of individualism and narcissism to which our culture has come. Individualism has marginalized forgiveness, which is by definition a communal transaction. Even the church has succumbed to the temptation to make forgiveness primarily a private transaction between the individual and God. True forgiveness, however, is both intrapersonal and interpersonal (Jones, 1995).

Only when the interpersonal and communal aspects of forgiveness are experienced will the forgiven person and the forgiving person truly understand the dynamics of God-ordained forgiveness. The forgiveness that Jesus gives us "calls believers to live *penitent* lives that seek to reconstruct human relationships in the service of holiness of heart and life" (Jones, 1995, p. 121).

As a believer, I am to forgive not because it makes me feel better, because it benefits me as much as anyone else, or because I will live a more tranquil life once I forgive. I am to forgive because God has forgiven me. We forgive so as to thwart Satan, who wills that the community of God be fractured and disrupted (2 Cor 2:10-11; Weaver, 1994). In this community God intends love of neighbor to be the dominant ethic, and love of neighbor includes a willingness to forgive and a desire to seek forgiveness. Love replaces the bearing of grudges, which is forbidden to the people of God (Gladson, 1992). The Holy Spirit energizes this forgiving function in the community of God (Jn 20:21-23).

The Parables of Jesus

The next source of information from the life of Jesus regarding forgiveness is his parables. In Luke 7 we have recorded the parable of the two debtors, and in Matthew 18 we find the parable of the unforgiving servant. Together these parables speak to the difficulty of forgiveness. Had the topic of forgiveness been easy or simple, Jesus no doubt would not have spent the time he did discussing the subject. Forgiveness can be very difficult, just as its opposite, bitterness, can be. We can describe forgiveness as an "impossible possibility" (Patton, 1985, p. 11).

The parable of the two debtors speaks powerfully to the ease of maintaining an unforgiving heart and the difficulty of following a forgiving lifestyle.

> [Jesus said,] "A certain creditor had two debtors; one owed five hundred denarii, and the other fifty. When they could not pay, he canceled the debts for both of them. Now which of them will love him more?" Simon answered, "I suppose the one for whom he canceled the greater debt." And Jesus said to him, "You have judged rightly." (Lk 7:41-43)

The creditor forgave each debtor freely and fully, just as God does for all sinners. The context helps us know that the debtor with the smaller of the obligations was likened to Simon the Pharisee, who had invited Jesus to dine with him. As we have seen previously, Simon reacted to the outpouring of repentance demonstrated by the sinful woman who anointed the feet of Jesus and bathed his feet with her tears. Though the woman had been forgiven by Jesus of great sin, similar to the debtor who owed 500 denarii in the parable, Simon apparently felt she was still a sinner who deserved repudiation and isolation from the community. Instead Jesus was welcoming to her, an attitude foreign to the Pharisee.

The parable reveals why Jesus received gladly the worship and adoration of the previously sinful woman: she had been forgiven more and therefore loved more. We can see the difficulty of forgiveness in the attitude of Simon. Those of us who have been generously forgiven by our loving heavenly Father, whether our sins were greater or lesser, can easily remain in our own judgmental and unforgiving attitudes. It is hard for us to embody the forgiveness God has granted us.

The second parable establishes a similar point. A forgiven servant displayed grossly unforgiving attitudes and behavior toward a debtor of his own. When the master discovered how the ingrate had behaved, he was furious.

> Then his lord summoned him and said to him, "You wicked slave! I forgave you all that debt because you pleaded with me. Should you not have had mercy on your fellow slave, as I had mercy on you?" And in anger his lord handed him over to be tortured until he would pay his entire debt. So my heavenly Father will also do to every one of you, if you do not forgive your brother or sister from your heart. (Mt 18: 32-35)

These are among the most severe and stern warnings that Jesus ever uttered. The forgiven servant demonstrated no awareness of the implications of being forgiven. The debt forgiven for the first servant was massive, an amount "neither inconceivable nor within the bounds of their experience" (Blomberg, 1990, p. 242). The debt of the second servant who was not forgiven by the first servant compared to the first servant's debt at a ratio on 1:6,000! For Jesus, it is not optional for the forgiven to be forgiving. The parable of the unforgiving servant warns what will happen if we fail to make forgiveness a way of life for ourselves (Jones, 1995). As difficult as it may be, what God expects of us is clear: we must forgive one another. God calls us to do the difficult.

Many people who have been tragically wronged by someone close to them will honestly feel that is simply is too difficult to forgive. A carefully tuned ear to the pained and tortured stories these people tell should prompt us to be understanding and slow to demand of them some type of superficial compliance with the Christian standard of forgiveness. The body of Christ needs to encourage one another to pursue forgiveness, to be motivated to forgive, to be made willing to forgive even though the actual process may take a protracted amount of time. "There are some issues which simply cannot be addressed by trying harder" (Patton, 1985, p. 12). In these instances, we need the power of the Holy Spirit and patience to see our goal accomplished.

If forgiving can be difficult, so is its opposite: bitterness. Bitterness has a seductive quality to it because I can retain power over the offending person by not forgiving him or her. The allure of power over another is a strong human temptation (Simon & Simon, 1990). "When we define ourselves by the people who have hurt us, or the people who hate us, we remain in bondage to those people until we are able to forgive them" (Libby, 1992, p. 6). Not only do we bind ourselves to our offenders—they control our lives.

"One of the most serious consequences of lacking forgiveness is that we become bonded to those we need to forgive, and indebted to those who need to forgive us, which in effect gives others control over our lives" (Benson, 1992, p. 77). Bitterness kills the spirit. It is a "cyclical, repetitive, tightly closed circle of self-centered pain" (Augsburger, 1988, p. 17).

We must remember that the Golden Rule precludes wallowing in bitterness with no motivation to work toward forgiveness. One research project found that older therapists were much more likely to urge their clients to forgive than younger therapists (DiBlasio, 1992). Perhaps it takes us all time and maturation to realize the wisdom of God's teaching on this subject. When we are younger we may flirt with ineffective alternatives to God's way of forgiveness, only to discover later in life the great value of God's way in this matter.

Many factors contribute to the difficulty of forgiveness. We have already mentioned the severity of the hurt and wounding that can complicate the forgiving process. A lack of acknowledgment by the offender or the fact that the original hurt was intentional can make the process exceedingly hard (Rosenak & Hagner, 1992). Spiritual and emotional maturity must be in place as well as a certain level of moral development before persons can take the painful forgiving step (McCullough & Worthington, 1994). At times certain kinds of psychopathology interfere with forgiving. All of these factors contribute to its difficulty.

The Personal Example of Jesus

Jesus lived a life characterized by forgiveness. The life of forgiveness he led demonstrates the costliness of forgiveness. Countless examples of his behavior are recorded in the Gospels, none more striking than the account of the woman taken in adultery (Jn 7:53—8:11). When Jesus confronted her accusers and challenged anyone among them who was without sin to cast the first stone, he was exposing their unforgiven state. These were men who, like all their fellow humans, were imperfect and who were in need of mercy not justice. The unforgiven (the accusers) were unforgiving. One by one they left the scene, beginning with the oldest. When they had all departed, Jesus said to the woman, "Neither do I condemn you. Go your way, and from now on do not sin again" (Jn 8:11). His forgiveness touched the life of one who normally would not have received forgiveness from her culture, and he granted it without condoning, excusing or encouraging more sin.

Another great example occurs in John 21 after the resurrection. Jesus and Peter, two men who had build a close and important relationship together, experienced a massive disruption of their connection when Peter publicly denied that he even knew Jesus. He denied Jesus three times to several people (Jn 18:15-27). How would their fractured relationship be restored? When the women went to the tomb early on the first day of the week, a young man dressed in white was sitting inside. He announced the resurrection of Jesus the Nazarene and said, "But go, tell his disciples and Peter" (Mk 16:7). The angel was not suggesting that Peter was no longer a disciple but that he, especially, needed the message of the resurrection.

Peter was one of two disciples who ran to the empty tomb to witness in person the fact of the resurrection. "Stooping and looking in, he saw the linen cloths by themselves; then he went home, amazed at what had happened" (Lk 24:12). Jesus appeared to the disciples on a number of occasions, and John records in familiar detail an extended conversation that the resurrected Lord had with Peter. When it was over, Peter had personally experienced the wonder of being forgiven by the Lord he had so publicly denied just a few days earlier.

We can see the costliness of the forgiving lifestyle of Jesus most clearly in one of the "seven last words" of Jesus on the cross. We know that forgiveness is needed by those who have imposed on others disappointment, rejection, abandonment, ridicule, humiliation, betrayal, deception and abuse (Simon & Simon, 1990). No one has experienced all of these interpersonal injuries as deeply and as extensively as did Jesus. Yet he did not wallow in his victimized state. Instead, he prayed, "Father, forgive them; for they do not know what they are doing" (Lk 23:34). Forgiveness is costly, and Jesus paid the costliest of prices so that forgiveness could be extended to all of earth's people.

We may also experience some of the costliness of forgiveness, although our encounter with its costliness will likely pale in comparison to what Jesus paid. Forgiveness is often the final phase of a long process of healing that occurs in the lives of the severely wounded. Corrie Ten Boom traveled the world preaching the good news of forgiveness as it related to her loss of her sister and her concentration camp experiences. But when it came time to walk up to one of the guards who had tormented them and extend a hand of forgiveness, Corrie realized just how costly forgiveness can be. With God's help she forgave him fully, but it was costly.

Sometimes the costliness of forgiveness is felt in the re-experiencing of hurt that may accompany forgiving. When the forgiveness process works as God intended it to work, however, that hurt is re-experienced in a new, less painful way as forgiveness is extended to the offender (Benson, 1992). True forgiveness includes affirming the worth and value of the offender, even though the offender's wrongdoing has brought into question the offended person's own worth and value (Brakenhielm, 1993). Hence forgiveness is costly. Pope John Paul II's historic prison visit with Mehmet Ali Agca, his attempted assassin, was a graphic and profoundly moving example of Christian forgiveness. The Pope gave up any and all rights he might have for resentment, animosity, anger and desire for revenge when he forgave the man who had attempted to kill him.

Yet the costs of forgiveness are far outweighed by its benefits. Secular research has established some important facts about forgiveness.

> You can forgive *without* compromising your moral integrity. Your painful memories of being hurt by others can be changed more easily than you might think. You can improve your ability to forgive by improving your ability to empathize with others. You can increase the likelihood of being forgiven by someone *you have hurt* by providing an adequate and sincere apology. Caring *too much* about what others think of you will inhibit you from seeking forgiveness when you hurt others. You can improve your ability to forgive others in as little as one hour. Resentment and hostility can affect your physical health. You can improve your physical health, mental health and relationships by maintaining a forgiving lifestyle. (McCullough, Sandage, & Worthington, 1997, p. 18)

We know from Scripture that the spiritual benefits of forgiving are endless. The practice of forgiving restores and maintains our relationship with God (Mk 11:25). It removes a hindrance that would otherwise interfere with our receiving forgiveness from God (Mt 6:12), and it proves our intent to model our lives after God himself (Mt 6:12-15). In summary,

> Forgiving is the only way to heal the wounds of a past we cannot change and cannot forget. Forgiving changes a bitter memory into a grateful memory, a cowardly memory in to a courageous memory, an enslaved memory into a free memory. Forgiving restores a self-respect that someone killed. And, more than anything else, forgiving gives birth to hope for the future after our past illusions have been shattered. (Smedes, 1996, p. 176)

Problem Passages

Two passages in Mark's Gospel regarding forgiveness have been very difficult to understand. Early in the public ministry of Jesus his disciples asked him about the meaning and purpose of parables. Jesus said that parables were to enlighten some and to remain obscure to others in order that "they may indeed look, but not perceive, and may indeed listen, but not understand; so that they may not turn again and be forgiven" (Mk 4:12). Taking this saying of Jesus totally by itself might lead one to believe that forgiveness is available to only certain people in some arbitrary or cruel fashion. Yet the balance of teaching in the Gospels and throughout the entire Bible is that forgiveness is available to all—and availed only by those who seek it. Forgiveness never comes from God to the person who does not ask for it.

The second problem passage regarding forgiveness occurs in Matthew 12:31: "Therefore I tell you, people will be forgiven for every sin and blasphemy, but blasphemy against the Spirit will not be forgiven." We do not have space in this short treatment of forgiveness to explore the difficulties of this saying of Jesus. We can only summarize by saying that the best explanation of the precise nature of this unforgivable sin consists of unbelief and rejection of the gospel. As in the previous problem passage, God always wishes all people to come to repentance (2 Pet 3:9), although some will not. For them, no forgiveness is available.

Three major problems emerge in almost any discussion regarding forgiveness: pseudoforgiveness, equating forgiveness with what it is not, and misunderstanding its stage or process nature.

Pseudoforgiveness

Christian leaders, pastors, counselors and therapists can risk a grave danger when they push a wounded person toward forgiveness before the Holy Spirit has completed the necessary internal spiritual preparation that can make the forgiveness process genuine and effective.

We can describe premature or forced forgiveness as pseudoforgiveness; it is ultimately destructive to all parties involved. Pseudoforgiveness is forgiving with strings attached, spoken or unspoken. Such forgiveness is cheap, selective and unbiblical. Undue haste toward forgiving may indicate a lack of respect for the offender and may result in pseudoforgiveness.

Research has uncovered at least four types of forgiveness: general, intrinsic, role-expected and expedient (McCullough & Worthington, 1994). In the first two types, the forgiver experiences an internal attitudinal change; in the latter two types, no internal attitude change occurs.

If we forgive only because it is expected of us or because it is expedient, our forgiving is actually pseudoforgiveness. False forgiveness lacks a will to forgive and, in effect, minimizes or trivializes the offense and the offender. Genuine forgiveness both seeks forgiveness from those we have offended and offers forgiveness to those who have offended us. It does not "abandon the importance of reparation for the former or justice for the latter, but it does transform the context in which they are to be understood and embodied" (Jones, 1995, p. 127). True forgiveness is often a slow, laborious and painful process rather than a flippant, cognitive formula that we recite because we know we should.

Misunderstandings

Forgiveness is not these things:

☐ an undoing of the wrong or an obliteration of a past event

☐ a promise to trust the offender unconditionally in the future

☐ an excusing or denial of the reality and severity of the offense

☐ reconciliation with the offender (a desired outcome that may or may not accompany forgiveness)

☐ a condoning of the offense, claiming that something doesn't matter when it does

☐ a pardon for the offense, something only an official can provide
☐ absolution of the offender, absolving any responsibility (a matter for God himself to adjudicate)
☐ forgetting

Too many Christian teachers have tried to maintain that if you remember an offense you have not truly forgiven it. Such a misunderstanding stems from taking literally what is meant to be metaphorical. When Scripture says that God forgives and remembers our sins no more, it is asserting metaphorically that God forgives completely and fully rather than literally teaching that God absolutely forgets, something he could not do since it is contrary to his nature. These and other misunderstandings obscure true forgiveness as modeled for us by Jesus in the examples above.

Forgiveness Is a Process

Often the process nature of forgiveness is overlooked. But we trivialize true, biblical forgiveness when we treat it as a perfunctory or quick-and-simple solution to life's hurts. "Just forgive and forget" can sometimes be the immediate response of an uncaring Christian upon hearing the painful and complicated account of an abuse victim. Yes, forgiveness is the ultimate answer God intends for the tragic offenses we sustain in life. But genuine, God-honoring forgiveness is never the same as some superficial, quick cure-all for all the pains and hurts of life. In fact, we can argue that traditional pastoral counseling has all too often espoused a quick form of forgiveness as the bandage to put on all painful residues of the past. Christian counselors, by way of contrast, have advocated forgiveness as a process that might indeed be a long one. This difference in approach may help explain the animosity and opposition to Christian counseling that exists in some pastoral circles (Beck, 1997; Enright, Eastin, Golden, Sarinopoulos, & Freedman, 1992).

Many authors have articulated a stage sequence for the forgiving process (McCullough & Worthington, 1994; Rosenak & Harnden, 1992; Smedes, 1996; Walters, 1983, 1984). In each case, these stage models are careful to identify the preliminary steps through which people need to go to ensure that the forgiveness attempted is genuine and not spurious.

First, the offense must be identified clearly, as well as the attending negative emotions (hurt, anger, desire for revenge) that have built up around it. What is the offense? What is it not?

Second, we must receive God's forgiveness. Only the truly forgiven are able to forgive well.

Third, we must rediscover the humanity of the offender and come to realize that we are probably more similar to the offender in our own fallenness than we are different from him or her (Patton, 1985).

Fourth, we must forgive. The actual forgiveness may involve contact with the offender, reconciliation with the offender or receiving an apology from the offender. However, the forgiveness act may not involve any of these features. The essence of the forgiveness is a letting go of the need for revenge and of the need for any further restitution.

Finally, the forgiving person must incorporate into awareness a new, re-framed perspective on what happened so that the positive emotions such as love can again appear in time toward the offender. These revised feelings may also eventually include acts of kindness (Ex 23:5; Rom 12:19-21; 1 Pet 3:9). All of these steps in the process of forgiveness need to be bathed in prayer so that the Holy Spirit can energize and enable us to accomplish this impossible possibility.

Opposition to Forgiveness

Nothing aggravated the enemies of Jesus more than his declaration of forgiveness toward sinners. A major reason for this fierce and sharp opposition originated in their awareness that the full forgiveness of sins is a prerogative of God himself. When Jesus extended forgiveness toward sinners, he was truly forgiving their sin, as only God can do, as well as forgiving (or letting go) of all personal offense these wrongdoings had caused him, as we humans are called to do. For example, when Jesus received the worship and adoration of the sinful woman who came to the house of Simon the Pharisee, Simon was not only opposed to the general attitude of forgiveness Jesus displayed toward the woman—he and his fellow Pharisees were opposed to the actual forgiveness Jesus extended to her (Lk 7:36-50). When Jesus healed the paralytic the Pharisees and other enemies of Jesus reacted vigorously (Mt 9:2-8). God's forgiveness is provocative in nature, and human forgiveness can likewise be fraught with opposition.

The chief form of opposition to human interpersonal forgiveness occurs when the offender refuses to acknowledge the offense, to offer an apology or to otherwise participate in the process. Bilateral interpersonal transactions in which the offender and the offended both participate are obviously easier and more complete. But often we are called upon to extend forgiveness toward the unapologetic or unacknowledging offender. Certain accounts in the Gospels seem to indicate that repentance does not seem to be required for God's forgiveness (Alter, 1994). Or perhaps repentance is always required, but it is sometimes not mentioned in the biblical accounts. We do know that repentance sometimes follows forgiveness.

> I will sprinkle clean water upon you, and you shall be clean from all your uncleannesses, and from all your idols I will cleanse you. A new heart I will give you, and a new spirit I will put within you; and I will remove from your body the heart of stone and give you a heart of flesh. I will put my spirit within you, and make you follow my statutes and be careful to observe my ordinances. . . . Then you shall remember your evil ways, and your dealings that were not good; and you shall loathe yourselves for your iniquities and your abominable deeds." (Ezek 36:25-27, 31)

Yet the Bible also clearly reveals that forgiveness from God cannot occur where there is no repentance or where there is great resistance (Is 22:12-14; Lam 3:42). In each and every case, "The grace of God prepares the way for both repentance and forgiveness in the Old Testament; it is their juxtaposition, rather than their sequential order that is important" (Gladson, 1992, p. 129).

The presence or absence of repentance has practical ramifications for worship planners who seek to engage worshipers in corporate confession of sin. Is such a request for forgiveness genuine? (Nitschke, 1994). Forgiving the unapologetic is difficult because the offender has not requested it; it is hard and unfair; the offender may repeat the offense. Yet at times we must forgive the unapologetic. In spite of these ambiguities, we do know from Scripture that loving our neighbors includes forgiving them; if we are to truly love our enemies as Jesus has commanded us, we will be engaged in loving and forgiving the unapologetic. Otherwise these persons would not be our enemies! A loving and forgiving attitude toward our enemies is exemplified by Jesus, who participated in table fellowship with tax collectors (such as Zacchaeus), sinners (such as the sinful woman of Lk 7) and Pharisees (such as Simon in Lk 7) alike.

Spiritual Formation

Yet another lesson we can learn from the Gospels regarding Jesus and forgiveness is how central the teaching of forgiveness is to the process of spiritual formation. A major strand of activity that pervades the four Gospels is the set of events that describe the spiritual formation of the disciples by Jesus. All twelve of the apostles were involved in this process, none more so than Peter. "Then Peter came and said to him, 'Lord, if another member of the church sins against me, how often should I forgive? As many as seven times?' Jesus said to him, 'Not seven times, but, I tell you, seventy-seven times' " (Mt 18:21-22).

The rabbis often taught that one should forgive up to three times, so Peter no doubt thought he was being generous when he suggested seven times (Keener, 1993). We cannot tell from the form of the Greek in this passage if Jesus answered seventy plus seven or seventy times seven. In either case, Jesus was obviously calling for unlimited forgiveness. Because God's forgiveness is inexhaustible, the forgiveness we are to model after his must also be extravagant (Hagner, 1995).

Because forgiveness is so central to the spiritual formation of individuals, we are surprised to learn that spiritual directors rank forgiveness as a spiritual discipline to be used in counseling lower than do Christian psychotherapists (Moon, Willis, Bailey and Kwasny, 1993). By way of contrast, the importance of forgiveness in the development of God's people is seen in Luther's teaching that there is one sacrament (God displaying mercy toward us through Jesus Christ) that is shown in three ways: baptism, the preaching of forgiveness and the Lord's Supper (Nichols, 1968). The blood of the Lord's Supper is poured out for the remission of sin (Mt 26:27-28; Weaver, 1994). All of these elements contribute to the development of true disciples of Jesus.

Conclusion

"In Rev. John Plummer's nightmare, the picture flashed huge, in black and white, as children screamed" (Gearan, 1997). The picture has become one of the most famous photographs of the entire Vietnam conflict: a photo of a young, naked girl running from a village that had just been napalmed by American aircraft. Plummer had organized the air strike against that village after being assured that no civilians inhabited it. He felt personally responsible for the tragic burns inflicted on this young girl as well as for the other civilian damage that the air strike caused. His life, like that of the World War II bombardier we earlier described, was wracked by unassuaged guilt manifest in divorce and drinking.

After Plummer entered the ministry he longed for an opportunity to apologize to the young girl. Meanwhile, Phan Thi Kim Phuc had grown up and had become a Christian. As she toured the United States speaking of her experiences, she would state that "if she met the pilot of the plane she would tell him that she forgives him and that, though they cannot change the past, she would hope they both could work together to build the future" (A picture of forgiveness, 1997, p. 183).

One day, with the help of friends these two erstwhile enemies met, embraced and reconciled. Another powerful example of how Jesus can bring to bear the grace of forgiveness on the most tortured and fractured of human relationships.

Forgiveness as demonstrated and taught by Jesus gives us what the prophets of old described: a sense of cleanness (Ps 51:2, 7), a sense of guilt remitted (Is 44:22) and a sense of healing and release (Mal 4:2) (Harvey & Benner, 1996). What greater grace can God bestow upon us to deal with the neuroticisms of our lives?

References

Achtemeier, E. R. (1962). Mercy. In *Interpreter's dictionary of the Bible*. (Vol. 3, pp. 352-354). Nashville: Abingdon.

Allport, D., & Odbert, H. S. (1936). Trait-names: A psycho-lexical study. *Psychological Monographs: General and Applied, 47* (1), 1-171.

Allport, G. W. (1950). *The individual and his religion: A psychological interpretation*. New York: Macmilian.

Alter, M. G. (1994). *Resurrection psychology: An understanding of human personality based on the life and teachings of Jesus*. Chicago: Loyola University Press.

Anderson, R. S. (1995). *Self-care: A theology of personal empowerment and spiritual healing*. Wheaton, IL: BridgePoint.

Arndt, W. F., & Gingrich, F. W. (1952). *A Greek-English lexicon of the New Testament and other early Christian literature* (4th ed.). Chicago: University of Chicago Press.

Ashford, R. (1977). *Loving ourselves*. Philadelphia: Fortress.

Augsburger, D. (1988). *The freedom of forgiveness*. Chicago: Moody Press.

Augustine. (1991). *Confessions* (H. Chadwick, Trans.). Oxford: Oxford University Press.

Barclay, W. (1975). *The Gospel of Luke* (Rev. ed.). Philadelphia: Westminster Press.

Barrett, C. K. (1978). *The Gospel according to St. John* (2nd ed.). Philadelphia: Westminster Press.

Beck, J. R. (1981). Treatment of spiritual doubt among obsessing evangelicals. *Journal of Psychology and Theology, 9*, 224-231.

Beck, J. R. (1988). Peace, freedom and security studies: A personal reflection. *ESA Parley, 5* (1), 2.

Beck, J. R. (1993). *The healing words of Jesus*. Grand Rapids, MI: Baker Book House.

Beck, J. R. (1997). Value tensions between evangelical Christians and Christian counseling. *Counseling and Values, 41* (2), 107-116.

Belgum, D. (1963). *Guilt: Where religion and psychology meet*. Minneapolis: Augsburg.

Belton, F. G. (1949). *A manual for confessors*. London: A. R. Mowbray.

Benjamin, L. T., Hopkins, J. R., & Nation, J. R. (1994). *Psychology* (3rd ed.). New York: Macmillan College Publishing.

Benson, C. K. (1992). Forgiveness and the psychotherapeutic process. *Journal of Psychology and Christianity, 11* (1), 76-81.

Bergeman, C. S., Chipuer, H. M., Plomin, R., Pedersen, N. L., McClearn, G. E., Nesselroade, J. R., Costa, P. T., & McCrae, R. R. (1993). Genetic and environmental effects on openness to experience, agreeableness and conscientiousness: An adoption/twin study. *Journal of Personality, 61* (2), 159-179.

Bergren, E. (1975). *The psychology of confession*. Leiden: E. J. Brill.

Bernard of Clairvaux. (1895). *Song of Solomon*. Minneapolis: Klock & Klock Christian Publishers.

Bettenson, H. (1961). *Documents of the early church.* New York: Oxford University Press.

Bianchi, U. (1987). Confession of sins. In M. Eliade (Ed.), *The encyclopedia of religion* (Vol. 4, pp. 1-7). New York: Macmillan.

Blackstone, P. (1991). *Things they never told me in therapy.* Kingston, WA: Port Gamble.

Block, J. (1995). A contrarian view of the five-factor approach to personality description. *Psychological Bulletin, 117,* 187-215.

Blomberg, C. L. (1990). *Interpreting the parables.* Downers Grove, IL: InterVarsity Press.

Bok, S. (1978). *Lying: Moral choice in public and private life.* New York: Pantheon.

Bonhoeffer, D. (1954). *Life together.* New York: Harper & Brothers.

Borkenau, P. (1992). Implicit personality theory and the five-factor model. *Journal of Personality, 60* (2), 295-321.

Bowman, G. W. (1969). *The dynamics of confession.* Richmond, VA: John Knox.

Brainerd, C. (1990). Hope and despair. In R. J. Hunter, Ed., *Dictionary of pastoral care and counseling* (pp. 532-535). Nashville: Abingdon.

Brakenhielm, C. R. (1993). *Forgiveness.* Minneapolis: Fortress.

Brand, D. D. (1991). *Profile of the last Puritan: Jonathan Edwards, self-love and the dawn of the beatific.* Atlanta: Scholars Press.

Brehm, S. S., & Kassin, S. M. (1996). *Social psychology* (3rd ed.). Geneva, IL: Houghton Mifflin.

Briggs, S. R. (1989). The optimal level of measurement for personality constructs. In D. M. Buss & N. Cantor (Eds.), *Personality psychology: Recent trends and emerging directions* (pp. 246-260). New York: Springer-Verlag.

Briggs, S. R. (1992). Assessing the five-factor model of personality description. *Journal of Personality, 60* (2), 253-293.

Brink, T. L. (1985). The role of religion in later life: A case of consolation and forgiveness. *Journal of Psychology and Christianity, 4* (2), 22-25.

Brody, N. (1988). *Personality: In search of individuality.* San Diego: Academic.

Brownback, P. (1982). *The danger of self-love.* Chicago: Moody Press.

Bruland, E. B., & Mott, S. C. (1983). *A passion for Jesus: A passion for justice.* Valley Forge, PA: Judson Press.

Brunner, E. (1956). *Faith, hope and love.* Philadelphia: Westminster Press.

Buchanan, D. (1985). *The counseling of Jesus.* Downers Grove, IL: InterVarsity Press.

Buschel, F. (1965). Mercy. In G. Kittel (Ed.), *Theological dictionary of the New Testament* (Vol. 3). Grand Rapids, MI: Eerdmans.

Buss, A. H. (1989). Personality as traits. *American Psychologist, 44* (11), 1378-1388.

Buss, A. H., & Plomin, R. (1984). *Temperament: Early developing personality traits.* Hillsdale, NJ: Lawrence Erlbaum.

Caplan, L. (1994, June 6). "Gouging" the honor system. *Newsweek, 123,* 33.

Caprara, G. V., Barbaranelli, C., Borgogni, L., & Perugini, M. (1993). The "Big Five Questionnaire": A new questionnaire to assess the five factor model. *Personality and Individual Differences, 15* (3), 281-288.

Caprara, G. V., & Perugini, M. (1994). Personality described by adjectives: The generalizability of the Big Five to the Italian lexical context. *European Journal of Personality, 8,* 357-369.

Carlson, D. E. (1976). Jesus' style of relating: The search for a biblical view of counseling. *Journal of Psychology and Theology, 4* (3), 181-192.

Carter, C. W., & Thompson, R. D. (1990). *The biblical ethics of love.* New York: Peter Lang.

Carter, S. L. (1996a). The insufficiency of honesty. *The Atlantic Monthly, 277,* 74-76.

Carter, S. L. (1996b). *Integrity.* New York: BasicBooks.

Casler, L. (1973). Toward a re-evaluation of love. In M. E. Curtin (Ed.), *Symposium on love* (pp. 1-36). New York: Behavioral Publications.

Chauchard, P. (1968). *Our need of love.* New York: P. J. Kennedy & Sons.

Chessick, R. (1987). *Great ideas in psychotherapy.* Northvale, NJ: Jason Aronson.

Childs, B. H. (1990). Forgiveness. In R. Hunter (Ed.), *Dictionary of pastoral care and counseling,* pp. 438-440. Nashville: Abingdon.

Christal, R. E. (1992). Author's note on "Recurrent factors based on trait ratings." *Journal of Personality, 60* (2), 221-224.

Clark, F. (1995). The 36th mission. *American Heritage, 46* (3), 40-60.

Clark, W. H. (1958). *The psychology of religion: An introduction to religious experience and behavior.* New York: Macmillan.

Clewell, R. D. (1987). Moral dimensions in treating combat veterans with Posttraumatic Stress Disorder. *Bulletin of the Menninger Clinic, 51* (1), 114-130.

Cloninger, S. C. (1996). *Personality: Description, dynamics and development.* New York: W. H. Freeman.

Coalter, M. J., Mulder, J. M., & Weeks, L. B. (1990). *The confessional mosaic: Presbyterians and twentieth-century theology.* Louisville, KY: Westminster/John Knox.

Coan, R. W. (1974). *The optimal personality: An empirical and theoretical analysis.* New York: Columbia University Press.

Coan, R. W. (1977). *Hero, artist, sage or saint?* New York: Columbia University Press.

Conway, B. (1992). *Christ's commandment: "Love one another as I have loved you."* New Berlin, WI: Grace.

Corsini, R. J., & Marsella, A. J. (1983). *Personality theories, research and assessment.* Itasca, IL: F. E. Peacock.

Costa, P. T. (1991). Clinical use of the five-factor model: An introduction. *Journal of Personality, 57* (3), 393-398.

Costa, P. T., & McCrae, R. R. (1992a). Four ways five factors are basic. *Personality and Individual Differences, 13* (6), 653-665.

Costa, P. T., & McCrae, R. R. (1992b). Normal personality assessment in clinical practice: The NEO Personality Inventory. *Psychological Assessment, 4* (1), 5-13.

Costa, P. T., & McCrae, R. R. (1992c). *Revised NEO Personality Inventory and NEO Five-Factor Inventory: Professional manual.* Odessa, FL: Psychological Assessment Resources.

Cox, H. (1969). *The feast of fools: A theological essay on festivity and fantasy.* Cambridge, MA: Harvard University Press.

Cramer, R. L. (1959). *The psychology of Jesus and mental health.* Grand Rapids, MI: Zondervan.

Cranor, P. (1979). *How am I supposed to love myself?* Minneapolis: Bethany Fellowship.

Cullmann, O. (1953). *Early Christian worship.* Chicago: Henry Regnery.

Dallas Times Herald (1978, February 17).

Davies, H. (1993). *Bread of life and cup of joy: Newer ecumenical perspectives on the Eucharist.* Grand Rapids, MI: Eerdmans.

Davis, C. (1984). Joy. In W. A. Elwell (Ed.), *Evangelical dictionary of theology.* Grand Rapids, MI: Baker Book House.

Day, L. G. (1992). *By design and in God's image: Self-esteem from a Judeo-Christian world view.* Portland, OR: Mt. Tabor.

DeBlassie, P. (1985). *Inner calm: A Christian answer to modern stress.* Ligouri, MO: Ligouri.

De Jong, J. (1974). *A new commandment: The unity of love of neighbor and love of God in recent theology.* Hales Corner, WI: Priests of the Sacred Heart.

Delitzsch, F. (1965). *Biblical commentary on the prophecies of Isaiah.* Grand Rapids, MI:

Eerdmans.

DiBlasio, F. A. (1992). Forgiveness in psychotherapy: Comparison of older and younger therapists. *Journal of Psychology and Christianity, 11* (2), 181-187.

Digman, J. M. (1996). The curious history of the five-factor model. In J. S. Wiggins (Ed.), *The five-factor model of personality: Theoretical perspectives* (pp. 1-20). New York: Guilford.

Digman, J. M., & Inouye, J. (1986). Further specification of the five robust factors of personality. *Journal of Personality and Social Psychology, 50* (1), 116-123.

Dods, M. (1901). *The Gospel of St. John.* New York: A. C. Armstrong & Son.

Donoghue, Q., & Shapiro, L. (1984). *Bless me, father, for I have sinned: Catholics speak out about confession.* New York: Primus.

Drakeford, J. W. (1964). *Psychology in search of a soul.* Nashville: Broadman.

Egan, E., & Egan, K. (Eds.). (1994). *Suffering into joy: What Mother Teresa teaches about true joy.* Ann Arbor, MI: Servant.

Elwin, W. (1883). *Confession and absolution in the Bible.* London: J. T. Hayes.

Engler, B. (1985). *Personality theories: An introduction* (2nd ed.). Boston: Houghton Mifflin.

Engstrom, T. W. (1990). *Personal integrity.* Wheaton, IL: Harold Shaw.

Enright, R. D. (1996). Counseling within the forgiveness triad: On forgiving, receiving forgiveness and self-forgiveness. *Counseling and Values, 40* (2), 107-126.

Enright, R. D., Eastin, D. L., Golden, S., Sarinopoulos, I., & Freedman, S. (1992). Interpersonal forgiveness within the helping professions: An attempt to resolve differences of opinion. *Counseling and Values, 36,* 84-103.

Evans, C. A. (1990). *Luke.* Peabody, MA: Hendrickson.

Fazzalaro, F. J. (1950). *The place for the hearing of confessions: A historical synopsis and a commentary.* Washington, DC: Catholic University of America Press.

Fishbein, L. (1993, December 1). Point of view. *The Chronicle of Higher Education 40,* A52.

Fiske, D. W. (1949). Consistency of the factorial structures of personality ratings from different sources. *Journal of Abnormal and Social Psychology, 44,* 329-344.

Fleck, J. R. (1976). A review of the Tennessee Self Concept Scale. In C. W. Ellison (Ed.), *Self esteem* (pp. 131-134). Grand Rapids, MI: CAPS.

Flynn, L. B. (1980). *The gift of joy.* Wheaton, IL: Victor.

Frank, J. D. (1982). Therapeutic components shared by all psychotherapies. In J. H. Harvey & M. M. Parks (Eds.), *Psychotherapy research and behavior change* (pp. 5-37). Washington, DC: American Psychological Association.

Friedman, M., & Rosenman, R. H. (1974). *Type A behavior and your heart.* New York: Alfred A. Knopf.

Funder, D. C. (1997). *The personality puzzle.* New York: W. W. Norton.

Gallardo, J. (1983). *The way of biblical justice.* Scottsdale, PA: Herald.

Gearan, A. (1997, April 20). Photo haunts Vietnam veteran. *Denver Post.*

Geddes, L., & Thuriston, H. (1928). *The Catholic Church and confession.* New York: Macmillan.

Geldenhuys, N. (1966). *Commentary on the Gospel of Luke.* Grand Rapids, MI: Eerdmans.

Gilmore, J. V. (1989). O. Hobart Mowrer: A psychological and theological critique. In L. Aden & D. G. Benner (Eds.), *Counseling and the human predicament: A study of sin, guilt and forgiveness* (pp. 85-98). Grand Rapids, MI: Baker Book House.

Gladson, J. A. (1992). Higher than the heavens: Forgiveness in the Old Testament. *Journal of Psychology and Christianity, 11* (2), 125-135.

Glick, D., & Turque, B. (1993, September 27). Sailing through troubled seas. *Newsweek, 122,* 44.

Goldberg, L. R. (1981). Language and individual differences: The search for universals in personality lexicons. In L. Wheeler (Ed.), *Personality and Social Psychology* (Vol. 2, pp. 141-165). Beverly Hills, CA: Sage.

Goldberg, L. R. (1992). The development of markers for the big-five factor structure. *Psychological Assessment, 4* (1), 26-42.

Goldberg, L. R. (1995). What the hell took so long? Donald W. Fiske and the big five factor structure. In P. E. Shrout & S. T. Fiske, *Personality research, methods and theory: A festschrift honoring Donald W. Fishe* (pp. 29-43). Hillsdale, NJ: Lawrence Erlbaum Associates.

Golphin, V. F. A. (1995, April 24). Taking a seat for justice. *Christianity Today, 39,* 10-11.

Gorsuch, R. L., & Hao, J. Y. (1993). Forgiveness: An exploratory factor analysis and its relationship to other variables. *Review of Religious Research, 34* (4), 333-347.

Greenfield, S. M. (1973). Love: Some reflections by a social anthropologist. In M. E. Curtin (Ed.), *Symposium on love* (pp. 37-52). New York: Behavioral Publications.

Grider, J. K. (1984). Forgiveness. In W. A. Elwell (Ed.), *Evangelical dictionary of theology* (p. 421). Grand Rapids, MI: Baker Book House.

Gundry, R. H. (1982). *Matthew: A commentary on his literary and theological art.* Grand Rapids, MI: Eerdmans.

Hagner, D. A. (1993). *Matthew 1—13.* Word biblical commentary 33A. Dallas: Word.

Hagner, D. A. (1995). *Matthew 14—28.* Word biblical commentary 33B. Dallas: Word.

Hallett, G. L. (1989). *Christian neighbor-love: An assessment of six rival visions.* Washington, DC: Georgetown University Press.

Hansen, G. W. (1997, February 3). The emotions of Jesus. *Christianity Today,* pp. 42-46.

Hargrave, T. D. (1994). *Families and forgiveness: Healing wounds in the intergenerational family.* New York: Brunner/Mazel.

Harris, R. L. (1980). *Theological wordbook of the Old Testament* (Vol. 1). Chicago: Moody Press.

Harrison, S. M. (1988). Sanctification and therapy: The model of Dante Alighieri. *Journal of Psychology and Theology, 16* (4), 313-317.

Hart, A. D. (1992). *Me, myself and I: How far should we go in our search for self-fulfillment?* Ann Arbor, MI: Servant.

Harvey, R. W. & Benner, D. G. (1996). *Choosing the gift of forgiveness: How to overcome hurts and brokenness.* Grand Rapids, MI: Baker Book House.

Haught, J. F. (1980). *Religion and self-acceptance: A study of the relationship between belief in God and the desire to know.* Washington, DC: University Press of America.

Henry, P. (1988). Getting involved in politics. In K. Hayes & R. Sider (Eds.), *JustLife 88* (pp. 12-13). Philadelphia: JustLife Education Fund.

Hess, J. D. (1978). *Integrity: Let your yea be yea.* Scottsdale, PA: Herald.

Hinthorn, A. (1996). *Quietly resting.* Kansas City, MO: Beacon Hill.

Hodges, A. G. (1986). *Jesus: An interview across time.* Birmingham, AL: Village House.

Hoekema, A. A. (1975). *The Christian looks at himself.* Grand Rapids, MI: Eerdmans.

Hogan, R., DeSoto, C. B., & Solano, C. (1977). Traits, tests and personality research. *American Psychologist, 32,* 255-264.

Holland, J., & Henriot, P. (1983). *Social analysis: Linking faith and justice.* Maryknoll, NY: Orbis.

Hoskyns, E. C. (1947). *The Fourth Gospel.* London: Faber and Faber.

Hull, B. (1987). *Anxious for nothing.* Old Tappan, NJ: Fleming H. Revell.

Hurvitz, N. (1976). The origins of the peer self-help psychotherapy group movement. *Journal of Applied Behavioral Science, 12* (3), 283-294.

Integrity under pressure: An interview with Mark O. Hatfield. (1988). *Leadership, 9,* 128-132.

James, W. (1958). *The varieties of religious experience.* New York: Mentor.

Jang, K. L., Livesley, W. J., & Vernon, P. A. (1996). Heritability of the big five personality dimensions and their facets: A twin study. *Journal of Personality, 64* (3), 577-591.

Jensen, J. (1984). *Isaiah 1—39.* Wilmington, DE: Michael Glazier.

Jerome. (1992). Protecting your integrity. *Leadership, 13,* 58-62.

Jeune, C. (1983). Justice, freedom and social transformation. In T. Sine (Ed.), *The church in response to human need* (pp. 331-342). Monrovia, CA: MARC.

John, O. P. (1989). Toward a taxonomy of personality descriptors. In D. M. Buss & N. Cantor (Eds.), *Personality psychology: Recent trends and emerging directions* (pp. 261- 271). New York: Springer-Verlag.

John, O. P. (1990). The "Big Five" factor taxonomy: Dimensions of personality in the natural language and in questionnaires. In L. A. Pervin (Ed.), *Handbook of personality: Theory and research* (pp. 66-100). New York: Guilford.

Johnson, J. A., & Ostendorf, F. (1993). Clarification of the five-factor model with the Abridged Big Five Dimensional Circumplex. *Journal of Personality and Social Psychology, 65* (3), 563-576.

Johnson, R., & Gallegos, A. (1995). Hunger for justice. *Sojourners, 24* (2), 14-15.

Jones, L. G. (1995). *Embodying forgiveness: A theological analysis.* Grand Rapids, MI: Eerdmans.

Joosse, W. (1987). The Christian's self-image: Issues and implications. *Occasional Papers from Calvin College, 5* (1), 1-51.

Jourard, S. M. (1964). *The transparent self: Self-disclosure and well-being.* Princeton, NJ: D. Van Nostrand.

Jourard, S. (1971). *Self-disclosure: An experimental analysis of the transparent self.* New York: Wiley & Interscience.

Jung, C. G. (1933). *Modern man in search of a soul.* London: Routledge & Kegan Paul.

Kaiser, O. (1972). *Isaiah 1—12.* Philadelphia: Westminster Press.

Karmel, L. J. (1973). The case for love. In M. E. Curtin (Ed.), *Symposium on love* (pp. 69-76). New York: Behavioral Publications.

Karris, R. J. (1986). Luke 23:47 and the Lucan view of Jesus' death. *Journal of Biblical Literature, 105* (1), 65-74.

Kauffman, D. T. (Comp.) (1962). *The treasury of religious verse.* Westwood, NJ: Fleming H. Revell.

Keener, C. S. (1993). *The IVP Bible background commentary: New Testament.* Downers Grove, IL: InterVarsity Press.

Kelsey, M. T. (1981). *Caring: How can we love one another?* New York: Paulist.

Kelsey, M. T. (1982). *Christo-psychology.* New York: Crossroad.

Kerlinger, F. N. (1973). *Foundations of behavioral research* (2nd ed.). New York: Holt, Rinehart and Winston.

Kibler, W. L. (1992, November 11). Cheating. *The Chronicle of Higher Education, 39,* B1-B2.

Kinzer, M. (1980). *The self-image of a Christian: Humility and self-esteem.* Ann Arbor, MI: Servant.

Kirkpatrick, W. D. (1994). Christian hope. *Southwestern Journal of Theology, 36,* 33-43.

Koehler, W. J. (1982). *Counseling and confession: The role of confession and absolution in pastoral counseling.* St. Louis: Concordia Publishing House.

Kottler, J. A., & Blau, D. S. (1989). *The imperfect therapist: Learning from failure in therapeutic practice.* San Francisco: Jossey-Bass.

Lasch, C. (1979). *The culture of narcissism: American life in an age of diminishing expectations.* New York: W. W. Norton.

Lea, H. C. (1968). *A history of auricular confession and indulgences in the Latin church,* Vol. 1: *Confession and absolution.* New York: Greenwood.

Lebacqz, K. (1986). *Six theories of justice: Perspectives from philosophical and theological ethics.* Minneapolis: Augsburg.

Lerner, M. J. (1980). *The belief in a just world: A fundamental delusion.* New York: Plenum.

Lewis, C. S. (1955). *Surprised by joy: The shape of my early life.* New York: Harcourt Brace Jovanovich.

Libby, B. (1992). *The forgiveness book.* Cambridge, MA: Cowley.

Liebman, J. L. (1946). *Peace of mind.* New York: Simon & Schuster.

Lightfoot, R. H. (1957). *St. John's Gospel.* Oxford: Clarendon.

Loehlin, J. C. (1992). *Genes and environment in personality development.* Newbury Park, NJ: Sage.

Macdonald, A. B. (1935). *Christian worship in the primitive church.* Edinburgh: T & T Clark.

MacDonald, D. A., Anderson, P. E., Tsagarakis, C. I., & Holland, C. J. (1994). Examination of the relationship between the Myers-Briggs Type Indicator and the NEO Personality Inventory. *Psychological Reports, 74,* 339-344.

Macgregor, G. H. C. (1929). *The gospel of John.* New York: Doubleday.

Magnus, K, Diener, E., Fujita, F., & Pavot, W. (1993). Extraversion and neuroticism as predictors of objective life events: A longitudinal analysis. *Journal of Personality and Social Psychology, 65* (5), 1046-1053.

Mahoney, M. J. (1991). *Human change processes: The scientific foundations of psychotherapy.* New York: BasicBooks.

Manuel, G. M. (1991). Group process and the Catholic rites of reconciliation. *Journal of Religion and Health, 30* (2), 119-129.

Marshall, G. N., Wortman, C. B., Vickers, R. R., Kusulas, J. W., & Hervig, L. K. (1994). The five-factor model of personality as a framework for personality-health research. *Journal of Personality, 67* (2), 278-286.

Marshall, I. H. (1978). *The Gospel of Luke.* Grand Rapids, MI: Eerdmans.

Mattingly, T. (1997, May 14). Breaking the silence on Sudan. Syndicated column.

Mauger, P. A., Perry, J. E., Freeman, T., Grove, D. C., McBride, A. G., & Mckinney, K. E. (1992). The measurement of forgiveness: Preliminary research. *Journal of Psychology and Christianity, 11* (2), 170-180.

May, R. (1969). *Love and will.* New York: W. W. Norton.

McCaslin, S. (1994). Her path is the path of justice. *Daughters of Sarah, 20* (3), 1.

McCrae, R. R. (1989). Why I advocate the five-factor model: Joint factor analyses of the NEO-PI with other instruments. In D. M. Buss & N. Cantor (Eds.), *Personality psychology: Recent trends and emerging directions* (pp. 237-245). New York: Springer-Verlag.

McCrae, R. R. (1991). The five-factor model and its assessment in clinical settings. *Journal of Personality Assessment, 57* (3), 399-414.

McCrae, R. R. (1992). Editor's introduction to Tupes and Christal. *Journal of Personality, 60* (2), 217-219.

McCrae, R. R. (1993). Openness to experience as a basic dimension of personality. *Imagination, Cognition and Personality, 13* (1), 39-53.

McCrae, R. R., & Costa, P. T. (1985). Comparison of EPI and psychoticism scales with measures of the five-factor model of personality. *Personality and Individual Differences, 6* (5), 587-597.

McCrae, R. R., & Costa, P. T. (1987). Validation of the five-factor model of personality across instruments and observers. *Journal of Personality and Social Psychology, 52* (1), 81-90.

McCrae, R. R., & Costa, P. T. (1989a). More reasons to adopt the five-factor model. *American Psychologist, 44,* 451-452.

McCrae, R. R., & Costa, P. T. (1989b). Reinterpreting the Myers-Briggs Type Indicator from the perspective of the five-factor model of personality. *Journal of Personality, 57* (1), 7-40.

McCrae, R. R., & Costa, P. T. (1990). *Personality in adulthood.* New York: Guilford.

McCrae, R. R., & Costa, P. T. (1991). Adding *Liebe und Arbeit*: The full five factor model and well-being. *Personality and Social Psychology Bulletin, 17,* 227-232.

McCrae, R. R., & Costa, P. T. (1996). Toward a new generation of personality theories: Theoretical contexts for the five-factor model. In J. Wiggins (Ed.), *The five-factor model of personality: Theoretical perspectives* (pp. 51-87). New York: Guilford.

McCrae, R. R., & Costa, P. T. (1997). Personality trait structure as a human universal. *American Psychologist, 52* (5), 509-516.

McCullough, M. E., Sandage, S. J., & Worthington, E. L. (1997). *To forgive is human: How to put your past in the past.* Downers Grove, IL: InterVarsity Press.

McCullough, M. E., & Worthington, E. L. (1994). Encouraging clients to forgive people who have hurt them: Review, critique and research prospectus. *Journal of Psychology and Theology, 22* (1), 3-20.

McDonald, C. D. (1991). Clarifying several nuances of narcissism and their implications for pastoral care. *The Journal of Pastoral Care, 45* (2), 149-156.

McGrath, J., & McGrath, A. (1992). *The dilemma of self-esteem: The cross and Christian confidence.* Wheaton, IL: Crossway.

McMinn, M. R. (1996). *Psychology, theology and spirituality.* Wheaton, IL: Tyndale House.

McNeile, A. H. (1961). *The Gospel according to St. Matthew.* London: Macmillan.

McNeill, J. T. (1951). *A history of the cure of souls.* New York: Harper & Brothers.

Meadow, M. J. (1989). Four stages of spiritual experience: A comparison of Ignatian exercises and Jungian psychotherapy. *Pastoral Psychology, 37* (3), 172-191.

Meares, R. (1980). The secret. In T. J. Cottle & P. Whitten (Eds.), *Psychotherapy: Current perspectives,* pp. 283-293. New York: New Viewpoints.

Melia, R. (1865). *A treatise on auricular confession.* Dublin: James Duffy.

Menninger, K. (1973). *Whatever became of sin?* New York: Hawthorn.

Michael, C. P., & Norrisey, M. C. (1981). *Arise: A Christian psychology of love.* Charlottesville, VA: Open Door.

Miller, C. (1975). *That elusive thing called joy.* Grand Rapids, MI: Zondervan.

Moffatt, J. (1929). *Love in the New Testament.* London: Hodder & Stoughton.

Mohler, J. A. (1975). *Dimensions of love: East and west.* Garden City, NY: Doubleday.

Mohline, D., & Mohline, J. (1997). *Emotional wholeness: Connecting with the emotions of Jesus.* Shippensburg, PA: Destiny Image.

Moon, G. W., Willis, D. E., Bailey, J. W., & Kwasny, J. C. (1993). Self-reported use of Christian spiritual guidance techniques by Christian psychotherapists, pastoral counselors and spiritual directors. *Journal of Psychology and Christianity, 12,* (1) 24-37.

Morrice, W. G. (1984). *Joy in the New Testament.* Grand Rapids, MI: Eerdmans.

Moule, C. F. D. (1963). *The meaning of hope.* Philadelphia: Fortress.

Mowrer. O. H. (1976). Changing conceptions of "neurosis" and the small-group movement. *Education, 97* (1), 24-62.

Mowrer, O. H. (1989). Psychopathology and the problem of guilt, confession and expiation. In L. Aden & D. G. Benner (Eds.), *Counseling and the human predicament: A study of sin,* guilt and forgiveness (pp. 76-84). Grand Rapids, MI: Baker Book House.

Mulholland, K. D. (1974). Integrity therapy: A theological study of key concepts. In R. K. Bower (Ed.), Biblical and psychological perspectives for Christian counselors (pp. 3-84). South Pasadena, CA: Publishers Services.

Murphy, J. (1988). Mercy and legal justice. In J. Murphy & J. Hampton (Eds.), Forgiveness and mercy (pp. 162-186). Cambridge: Cambridge University Press.

Murphy, J. G. (1979). Retribution, justice and therapy: Essays in the philosophy of law. Boston: D. Reidel.

Narramore, S. B. (1978). You're someone special. Grand Rapids, MI: Zondervan.

Nash, R. H. (1983). Social justice and the Christian church. Milford, MI: Mott Media.

Nelson, J. A. (1980). Hunger for justice: The politics of food and faith. Maryknoll, NY: Orbis.

Nichols, J. H. (1968). Corporate worship in the Reformed tradition. Philadelphia: Westminster Press.

Nitschke, B. A. (1994). Confession and forgiveness: The continuing agenda. Worship, 68, 353-368.

Norman, W. T. (1963). Toward an adequate taxonomy of personality attributes: Replicated factor structure in peer nomination personality ratings. Journal of Abnormal and Social Psychology, 66, 574-583.

O'Donovan, O. (1980). The problem of self-love in St. Augustine, New Haven, CT: Yale University Press.

Olson, M. (1994). Jesus' list. The Other Side, 30 (2), 6-7.

Ortberg, J. (1997, May 19). Do they know us by our love? Christianity Today, p. 25.

Palmberg, L., & Scandrette, O. (1977). Self-disclosure in biblical perspective. Journal of Psychology and Theology, 5 (3), 209-219.

Parsons, M. (1991). Hope. In J. D. Douglas (Ed.), The 20th century encyclopedia of religious knowledge (p. 407). Grand Rapids, MI: Baker Book House.

Passini, F. T., & Norman, W. T. (1966). A universal conception of personality structure? Journal of Personality and Social Psychology, 4 (1), 44-49.

Pattison, E. M. (1989). Punitive and reconciliation models of forgiveness. In L. Aden & D. G. Benner (Eds.), Counseling and the human predicament: A study of sin, guilt and forgiveness (pp. 162-176). Grand Rapids, MI: Baker Book House.

Patton, J. (1985). Is human forgiveness possible? A pastoral perspective. Nashville: Abingdon.

Pavot, W., Diener, E., & Fujita, F. (1990). Extraversion and happiness. Personality and Individual Differences, 11 (12), 1299-1306.

Pennebaker, J. W., Hughes, D. F., & O'Heeron, R. C. (1987). The psychophysiology of confession: Linking inhibitory and psychosomatic processes. Journal of Personality and Social Psychology, 52 (4), 781-793.

Perkins, J. (1982). With justice for all. Ventura, CA: Regal.

Pervin, L. A. (1989). Personality: Theory and research (5th ed.). New York: John Wiley & Sons.

Phillips, T. R., & Okholm, D. L. (Eds.). (1996). The nature of confession: Evangelicals and postliberals in conversation. Downers Grove, IL: InterVarsity Press.

A picture of forgiveness. (1997, February 19). The Christian Century, pp. 182-184.

Piedmont, R. L., Williams, J. E. G., & Ciarrocchi, J. W. (1997). Personality correlates of one's image of Jesus: A historiographic analysis using the five-factor model of personality. Journal of Psychology and Theology, 25 (3), 364-373.

Plummer, A. (1906). A critical and exegetical commentary on the Gospel according to St. Luke. New York: Charles Scribner's Sons.

Post, S. G. (1987). *Christian love and self-denial.* Lanham, MD: University Press of America.

Primus, W. (1996). The future of welfare reform: Issues of justice and love. *Discernment, 4* (3), 2-5.

Pruyser, R. W. (1968). *A dynamic psychology of religion.* New York: Harper & Row.

Pulver, A., Allik, J., Pulkinen, L., & Hamalainen, M. (1995). A Big Five personality inventory in two non-Indo European languages. *European Journal of Personality, 9,* 109-124.

Rall, H. F. (1955). Justice. In J. Orr (Ed.), *The international standard Bible encyclopedia* (Vol. 3, pp. 1781-1782). Grand Rapids, MI: Eerdmans.

Rankin, W. W. (1994). *Cracking the monolith: The struggle for the soul of America.* New York: Crossroad.

Reik, T. (1959). *The compulsion to confess.* New York: Harper & Row.

Reynolds, B. (1994). Dante, poet of joy. *Theology, 97* (778), 265-275.

Rhoades, D. (1990). Social justice issues in pastoral care. In R. Hunter (Ed.), *Dictionary of pastoral care* (pp. 1189-1190). Nashville: Abingdon.

Richter, S. (1966). *Metanoia: Christian penance and confession.* New York: Sheed and Ward.

Rodman, R. R. (1986). *Keeping hope alive: On becoming a psychotherapist.* New York: Harper & Row.

Rogers, A. (1996, November 11). For $6,000, you get a pencil with the answer included. *Newsweek, 128,* 69.

Rosado, C. (1995, November 13). God's affirmative justice: Affirmative action should not be based on what is fair. *Christianity Today, 39,* 34-35.

Rosenak, C. M., & Harnden, G. M. (1992). Forgiveness in the psychotherapeutic process: Clinical applications. *Journal of Psychology and Christianity, 11* (2), 188-197.

Rumberger, D. J., & Rogers, M. L. (1982). Pastoral openness to interaction with a private Christian counseling service. *Journal of Psychology and Theology, 10* (4), 337-345.

Samra, C. (1985). *The joyful Christ: The healing power of humor.* San Francisco: Harper & Row.

Saucier, G., & Goldberg, L. R. (1996). The language of personality: Lexical perspectives on the five-factor model. In J. Wiggins (Ed.), *The five-factor model of personality: Theoretical perspectives* (pp. 21-50). New York: Guilford.

Sawyer, J. F. A. (1984). *Isaiah* (Vol. 1). Philadelphia: Westminster Press.

Schaff, P. (1885). *The oldest church manual called the Teaching of the Twelve Apostles.* Edinburgh: T & T Clark.

Schuller, R. H. (1982). *Self esteem: The new reformation.* Waco, TX: Word.

Schultz, D., & Schultz, S. E. (1994). *Theories of personality* (5th ed.). Pacific Grove, CA: Brooks/Cole.

Schweitzer, A. (1948). *The psychiatric study of Jesus.* Boston: Beacon.

Sell, A. P. K. (1990). *Aspects of Christian integrity.* Louisville, KY: Westminster/John Knox.

Sider, R. (Ed.) (1980). *Cry justice: The Bible speaks on hunger and poverty.* Downers Grove, IL: InterVarsity Press.

Simon, S. B., & Simon, S. (1990). *Forgiveness: How to make peace with your past and get on with your life.* New York: Warner.

Skoglund, E. (1986). *Safety zones: Finding refuge in times of turmoil.* Waco, TX: Word.

Slotki, I. W. (1949). *Isaiah.* London: Soncino.

Smedes, L. B. (1983, January 7). Forgiveness: The power to change the past. *Christianity Today,* pp. 22-26.

Smedes, L. B. (1996). *The art of forgiving: When you need to forgive and don't know how.* Nashville: Moorings.

Smith, M. B. (1984). *One of a kind: A biblical view of self-acceptance.* Downers Grove, IL: InterVarsity Press.

Snoeck, A. (1961). *Confession and pastoral psychology.* Westminster, MD: Newman.

Snoeck, A. (1964). *Confession and psychoanalysis.* Westminster, MD: Westminster Press.

Sobrino, J. (1994). *The principle of mercy: Taking the crucified people from the cross.* Maryknoll, NY: Orbis.

Solomon, C. R. (1977). *Counseling with the mind of Christ: The dynamics of spirituotherapy.* Old Tappan, NJ: Fleming H. Revell.

Sorokin, P. A. (1972). Love: Its aspects, dimensions, transformation and power. In H. A. Otto (Ed.), *Love today: A new exploration* (pp. 251-267). New York: Association Press.

Stand for truth (1989). New York: South Africa Coordinating Committee.

Stanley, C. (1993). *A touch of his peace.* Grand Rapids, MI: Zondervan.

Stevenson, B. (1966). Confession and psychotherapy. *Journal of Pastoral Care, 20* (2), 10-15.

Storey, P. (1997). A different kind of justice: Truth and reconciliation in South Africa. *The Christian Century, 114* (25), 788-793.

Storms, C. S. (1991). *To love mercy: Becoming a person of compassion, acceptance and forgiveness* Colorado Springs, CO. NavPress.

Stotland, E. (1969). *The psychology of hope.* San Francisco: Jossey-Bass.

Stott, J. R. W. (1964). *Confess your sins: The way of reconciliation.* Philadelphia: Westminster Press.

Sue, D., Sue, D., & Sue, S. (1997). *Understanding abnormal behavior* (5th ed.). Boston: Houghton Mifflin.

Swindoll, C. R. (1991). *Laugh again.* Dallas: Word.

Thurman, C. (1993). *If Christ were your counselor.* Nashville: Thomas Nelson.

Thurneysen, E. (1957). *Evangelical confession.* Richmond, VA: John Knox.

Todd, E. (1985). The value of confession and forgiveness according to Jung. *Journal of Religion and Health, 24* (1), 39-48.

Tolstoy, L. (1882, 1974). *A confession; The gospel in brief; What I believe.* London: Oxford University Press.

Torrance, A. J. (1987). The self-relation, narcissism and the gospel of grace. *Scottish Journal of Theology, 40,* 481-510.

Tournier, P. (1960). *A doctor's casebook in the light of the Bible.* San Francisco: Harper & Row.

Travis, S. H. (1980). *Christian hope and the future.* Downers Grove, IL: InterVarsity Press.

Trueblood, D. E. (1964). *The humor of Christ.* San Francisco: Harper & Row.

Tulipan, A. B. (1986). Fee policy as an extension of the therapist's style and orientation. In D. W. Krueger (Ed.), *The last taboo: Money as symbol and reality in psychotherapy and psychoanalysis* (pp. 79-87). New York: Brunner/Mazel.

Tupes, E. C., & Christal, R. E. (1992). Recurrent personality factors based on trait ratings. *Journal of Personality, 60* (2), 223-251.

Tutu, D. M. (1983). *Hope and suffering.* Grand Rapids, MI: Eerdmans.

Tyrell, B. J. (1982). *Christotherapy II: The fasting and feasting heart.* New York: Paulist.

Van Becelaere, E. L. (1955). Penance. In J. Hastings (Ed.), *Encyclopedia of religion and ethics* (Vol. 9, pp. 711-715). New York: Charles Scribner's Sons.

Veenstra, G. (1992). Psychological concepts of forgiveness. *Journal of Psychology and Christianity, 11* (2), 160-169.

Vitz, P. (1994). Psychology as religion: The cult of self-worship (2nd ed.). Grand Rapids, MI: Eerdmans.

von Harnack, A. (1901). *Monasticism and the confessions of St. Augustine.* London: Williams

& Norgate.

Wallis, J. (1992). Keeping faith, doing justice, building community. *Sojourners, 21,* 12-23.

Wallis, J. (1994). The power of hope. *Sojourners, 23,* 14-19.

Walters, R. P. (1983). *Forgive and be free: Healing wounds of past and present.* Grand Rapids, MI: Zondervan.

Walters, R. P. (1984). Forgiving: An essential element in effective living. *Studies in Formative Spirituality, 5* (3), 365-374.

Warfield, B. B. (1912). On the emotional life of our Lord. In *Biblical and theological studies* (pp. 35-90). New York: Charles Scribner's Sons.

Watson, D., & Clark, L. A. (1984). Negative affectivity: The disposition to experience aversive emotional states. *Psychological Bulletins, 96,* 465-490.

Weaver, D. J. (1994). On imitating God and outwitting Satan: Biblical perspectives on forgiveness and the community of faith. *Mennonite Quarterly Review, 68,* 151-169.

Wegner, P. D. (1992). *An examination of kingship and Messianic expectation in Isaiah 1-35.* Lewiston, NY: Edwin Mellen.

Welch, E., & Powlison, D. (in press). "Every common bush afire with God": The Scripture's constitutive role for counseling.

Westcott, B. F. (1954). *The Gospel according to St. John.* Grand Rapids, MI: Eerdmans.

White, J. (1979). *Honesty, morality and conscience.* Colorado Springs, CO: NavPress.

Whitehead, L. (1952). *Psychology, religion and healing.* New York: Abingdon.

Widyapranawa, S. H. (1990). *The Lord is Savior: Faith in national crisis.* Grand Rapids, MI: Eerdmans.

Wiggins, J. (Ed.). (1996). *The five-factor model of personality: Theoretical perspectives.* New York: Guilford.

Wilson, E. D. (1985). *The discovered self: The search for self-acceptance.* Downers Grove, IL: InterVarsity Press.

Wirt, S. E. (1994). *The book of joy: A treasury of delights in God.* New York: McCracken.

Wise, C. A. (1983). *Pastoral psychotherapy: Theory and practice.* New York: Jason Aronson.

Witherspoon, A. (1995). This pen for hire. *Harper's, 290,* 49-57.

Wolterstorff, N. (1986). Why care about justice? *Reformed Journal, 36* (8), 9-14.

Worthen, V. (1974). Psychotherapy and Catholic confession. *Journal of Religion and Health, 13* (4), 275-284.

Wright, H. N. (1977). *Improving your self image.* Eugene, OR: Harvest House.

Yang, K., & Bond, M. H. (1990). Exploring implicit personality theories with indigenous or imported constructs: The Chinese case. *Journal of Personality and Social Psychology, 58* (6), 1087-1095.

Young, E. J. (1965). *The book of Isaiah.* Grand Rapids, MI: Eerdmans.

Zorilla, H. (1988). *The good news of justice: Share the gospel; live justly.* Scottsdale, PA: Herald.

Zuckerman, M., Kuhlman, D. M., Joireman, J., Teta, P., & Kraft, M. (1993). A comparison of three structural models for personality: The big three, the big five and the alternative five. *Journal of Personality and Social Psychology, 65* (4), 757-768.